POINTS OF VIEW

H. G. WELLS

POINTS OF VIEW

from Kipling to Graham Greene

ANDRÉ MAUROIS

Foreword by Georges Lemaitre

FREDERICK UNGAR PUBLISHING CO.
NEW YORK

Foreword

MORE THAN thirty years ago André Maurois presented a comprehensive panorama of modern English literature in his book *Magiciens et Logiciens,* which was then translated as *Prophets and Poets.* Maurois has always been considered an outstanding expert on all things English, and his personal insight into literary problems was so sharp and so shrewd that, to this very day, his original work has lost nothing of its full critical and informative value. Maurois did not attempt a continuous story of the various literary trends that developed in England since the turn of the century. He offered instead a succession of brief monographs—from Kipling to Aldous Huxley, and including such towering figures as H. G. Wells, G. B. Shaw, Joseph Conrad, and D. H. Lawrence— illustrating the most crucial aspects of the soul-searching responses that Britain gave to the numerous crises and challenges of that agitated phase of her history. These monographs bring out with unusual incisiveness and clarity the specific contributions that each of the authors studied made to the spiritual life of an England in the throes of the great modern agony.

At the end of his life, with a new edition of his book under consideration, Maurois decided to complete his old work by adding to it two significant essays on Virginia Woolf and Graham Greene. He was well acquainted with Virginia Woolf. Having been himself in close contact, during the early nineteen twenties, with the famous Bloomsbury group, he had met her there quite frequently. His deep, sympa-

thetic understanding of her tragic personality permeates every page of his essay. Thanks to his
evocative skill, he makes the reader share fully in her
aspirations, her achievements, and her woes.

In the case of Graham Greene, there was, seemingly, a great moral gap between Maurois and the
subject of his study. Maurois was an agnostic and,
even in the midst of the worst storms that shook his
own existence, he always maintained a stable emotional
equilibrium and a perfect mental equanimity. Graham
Greene is an ardent Catholic convert and he is obviously tormented, perhaps even morbidly obsessed,
with the haunting notions of Evil and Sin. In that respect, his works are very close—in spirit at least, and
apart from their usually exotic setting—to the twisted
and glum novels of the French Catholic writer François Mauriac. Yet, thanks to his remarkable breadth of
view, André Maurois, who was, by the way, one of
Mauriac's close personal friends, has succeeded amazingly well in probing Graham Greene's pervading
moral distress and in penetrating the hidden recesses
of his profound religious anguish.

It must be said that, during the last years of his
career, Maurois, who in his youth had sometimes been
reproached with tending to oversimplification and
even superficiality, gained tremendously in psychological intuitive insight. Thus, at the age of eighty, he
produced a biography of Balzac which is very generally considered a masterpiece. The two essays on
Virginia Woolf and Graham Greene are probably
the last two works that Maurois wrote before his

death. Although they are composed on a much more modest scale than the monumental *Balzac*, they partake of the same vein of creative thought. Advanced age, far from weakening Maurois' ability to grasp and interpret traits of character different from his own, seems to have increased his aptitude to peer into the depths of the human mind and to unravel the tangled skein of its most confused intricacies.

Thus his two last essays both enrich and conclude brilliantly the series of studies, based originally on lectures to his French audience, that he had consecrated many years before to those representative writers who were the glory of England during the best part of the last half-century. But none of those writers can be considered as more typical of his epoch than the others. Each one of them saw contemporary reality from a definite and often very special angle. The total sum of their works gives an impressive idea of the prodigious wealth of English thought during that period. Yet, at the same time, their very diversity precludes the possibility of reducing that richness to a factitious unity. It can be seen now, more clearly than three decades ago, that the views of the great modern English authors do not converge toward an agreement on the essentials of life. They remain widely separated, even scattered, points of view. That situation fully justifies the change of title of this enlarged volume to the present *Points of View*.

GEORGES LEMAITRE

CONTENTS

ILLUSTRATIONS

ACKNOWLEDGMENTS

Thanks are due to the following authors and publishers for permission to use the material reprinted in this book:

Curtis Brown: D. H. Lawrence, selections from *Collected Poems*.

Dodd, Mead & Company: H. G. Wells, extracts from *The New Machiavelli*. G. K. Chesterton, extracts from *The Man Who Was Thursday, Heretics, Orthodoxy*.

Doubleday, Doran & Company: Joseph Conrad, extracts from *Typhoon*, copyright 1902, 1930; *A Personal Record*, copyright 1912; *The Nigger of the Narcissus*, copyright 1897, 1914; "The Shadow Line" from *Sea Tales*, copyright 1902, 1930; *The Mirror of the Sea*, copyright 1906, 1934; *Youth*, copyright 1903, 1925; *Lord Jim*, copyright 1899, 1927. Aldous Huxley, extracts from *Point Counter Point*, copyright 1928; *Brave New World*, copyright 1932; *Essays Old and New*, copyright 1927. G. Jean-Aubry, extracts from *Joseph Conrad, Life and Letters*, copyright 1926, 1927.

Harcourt, Brace & Company: Lytton Strachey, extracts from *Books and Characters, Eminent Victorians, Elizabeth and Essex, Queen Victoria*.

Henry Holt & Company, Inc.: H. G. Wells, extract from *The Time Machine*.

Rudyard Kipling (and Doubleday, Doran & Company): extracts from *Stalky & Company*, copyright 1899, 1927; "The Man Who Would Be King," from *Under the Deodars*; *The Light That Failed*, copyright 1897, 1925; "The Lesson," from *The Five Nations*, copyright 1903, 1931; "The Sons of Martha" and "The Female of the Species," from *The Years Between*, copyright 1914, 1919; "Tommy," "Pagett M.P.," "Tomlinson," and "A General Summary" from *Departmental Ditties and Barrack Room Ballads*, copyright 1892, 1920; "Hymn Before Action," "Mary, Pity Women," and "England's Answer," from *The Seven Seas*, copyright 1893, 1921; *The Jungle Books* and "The Law of the Jungle," from

ACKNOWLEDGMENTS

The Jungle Books, copyright 1893, 1921; "The Story of the Gadsbys," from *Soldiers Three*, copyright 1897, 1925; *Plain Tales from the Hills*, copyright 1899, 1927; "A Conference of the Powers," from *Many Inventions*, copyright 1891, 1919; *Kim*, copyright 1900, 1901; *Puck of Pook's Hill*, copyright 1906, 1934; "The Beginnings," from *A Diversity of Creatures*, copyright 1910, 1917; "The Brushwood Boy," from *The Day's Work*, copyright 1895, 1923.

Alfred A. Knopf, the sole American publishers of all Katherine Mansfield's writings, extracts from her *Letters*, *Journal*, *Stories*. D. H. Lawrence, extract from *The Man Who Died*.

The Macmillan Company: H. G. Wells, extracts from *An Experiment in Autobiography*, *The Shape of Things to Come*. G. K. Chesterton, extracts from *Browning*.

Martin Secker (and G. P. Putnam's Sons): G. K. Chesterton, extracts from *Magic*.

George Bernard Shaw: extracts from *Man and Superman*, *The Man of Destiny*, *Mrs Warren's Profession*, *Arms and the Man*, *Candida*, *The Doctor's Dilemma*, *Saint Joan*, *Back to Methuselah* (Dodd, Mead & Company).

The Viking Press: D. H. Lawrence, extracts from *Fantasia of the Unconscious*, *Sons and Lovers*, *Women in Love*, *The Letters of D. H. Lawrence*, *Poems*.

For the new essays:

Harcourt, Brace & World: Virginia Woolf, extracts from *To the Lighthouse*, *Mrs. Dalloway*, *The Waves*, and *A Writer's Diary*, and photograph of the author.

The Viking Press: Graham Greene, extracts from *The End of the Affair*, *The Heart of the Matter*, *The Power and the Glory*, *The Quiet American*, and photograph by Islay Lyons of the author.

POINTS OF VIEW

Introduction

MY INTENTION in these pages which formed a series of lectures designed for, and delivered to, a French audience, is to examine certain English writers who, since the opening of the century, have played an important part in the spiritual moulding of one or two generations of human beings. The influence of a great mind often transcends temporal frontiers. The minds of young Englishmen have been shaped by Voltaire, by Flaubert, by Anatole France, by Marcel Proust, by Bergson; in France, Kipling and Wells, D. H. Lawrence and Aldous Huxley, have each their own disciples.

To be more precise, I do not propose here to survey contemporary English literature. We live so near to our epoch, and so closely does it envelop us, that we can hardly discern its outstanding lives. My choice of authors is confined to those who have offered to their contemporaries not only aesthetic enjoyment, but also a philosophy. And even there the choice is wide. Amongst the English writers who flourished between 1900 and 1914, the doctrine of "art for art's sake" was not much in favour. Kipling, Wells, Shaw, Galsworthy and Chesterton, even in their imaginative work, were all advocates of a doctrine.

This was natural enough during years of uneasiness; and before approaching the first of our chosen figures, Rudyard Kipling, we should perhaps examine briefly how England stood in these opening years of the twentieth century. In England as in France, it may be said, the nineteenth century had been a century of withered hopes. It had begun with the industrial revolution, which, especially in England, engendered high hopes of material progress and of happiness to be attained through comfort. As it turned out, the industrial revolution gave rise to vast misery, by the overcrowding of towns and by making the processes of the distribution of wealth at once more complex and more impersonal. It was not long before Charles Dickens and, in some of his books, Benjamin Disraeli, were expressing the painful surprise of writers confronted by the failure of industrial civilization.

A romantic view of business was succeeded, as the century advanced, by a romantic view of science. Important discoveries, in their turn, gave birth to immeasurable hopes. Orthodox beliefs were upset by Darwin's theory of natural selection, and the syntheses of chemistry encouraged the belief that Man could soon dominate, or even transcend, Nature. In France, certain aspects of this optimist philosophy were represented by Renan and Berthelot. The closing years of the century, in Darwin's own country, saw a breach in the Darwinian walls. Writers like Samuel Butler and Bernard Shaw were no longer Darwinians, but neo-Lamarckians. Humanity was learning that science may give men more power, but not more happiness. After industrial romanticism, scientific romanticism lay stricken.

INTRODUCTION

There remained a political romanticism. Throughout the nineteenth century, Liberal doctrinaires urged that social justice would be ensured by a widening of the suffrage. Between 1830 and 1870, it has been said, the general attitude of the ablest minds and loftiest characters was one of hope, which expected a vast increase in human happiness from the establishment of "free" institutions. According to the Liberal party, which, apart from a few Conservative intervals, dominated English political life, the destruction of privilege would make progress a certainty. During the second half of the century Gladstone was the leader of that party, the prophet of that faith.

Gladstone died in 1898. But Gladstonian Liberalism had been dying since 1885, and the disillusion of the masses was far advanced. Universal suffrage did not create human happiness any more than science did. Social problems had revealed complexities far more profound than had been seen by the Reformers of the eighteen-thirties. To many liberal-minded men the defeat of France by Prussia in 1870 seemed to mark at once the defeat of the French Revolution and that of the political doctrine which it had engendered. As Chesterton has said, in that one year, 1871, Englishmen saw the death of France and of Charles Dickens. And now, after the dream of science and the dream of industry, the dream of politics faded in the harsh revelation of mankind's plight.

By the end of the eighties the death of political idealism was leaving an empty dwelling-place, a mournful silence. It was not, in England, a religious epoch. General disillusion favoured a pessimistic scepticism, a proud detachment. If man, after all, could not dominate the universe, then let him seek refuge in art. It was the time of Oscar Wilde and Aubrey Beardsley, the time of the "decadent" aesthetes, the time when artists sought to shun the sentimental convention of progress, and to pursue the cult of art isolated from life.

This was the so-called *fin-de-siècle* attitude. But that aesthetic attitude, that scorn for life, that exaltation of art as something detached from reality, is inhuman and cannot last. It postulates that both the artist and his audience, if they are to be able to forget real life and admit only art, must both enjoy in that real life a degree of security that will free them from the struggle. The rich and prosperous England of that *fin de siècle* was able, momentarily, to enjoy that illusion; but the England of the early nineteen-hundreds could not preserve it. In 1885 the solidity of the Empire seemed unshakable; between 1900 and 1910 thoughtful Englishmen were perturbed by the South African War, by German armaments, by the shrinking of foreign trade, by increasing poverty amongst the masses. And in the face of such disquieting facts the aestheticism of a Wilde was a weak bulwark, too vulnerable a refuge. Already the younger men were seeking new creeds.

In the following epoch they were to have the choice of several. Kipling would show that salvation lay in respect for the oldest of all human values—order, discipline, and courage—and held out the ruling of an Empire to the youth of England as the noblest task their life could give, and as the nursery of the heroic virtues. In opposition to the realist and pessimistic imperialism of Kipling, Bernard Shaw and H. G. Wells offered the rising generation a rejuvenated political idealism, which to Shaw meant Fabian Socialism, and to Wells a more complex doctrine, a kind of aristocratic and intellectual fascism. G. K. Chesterton, hostile to both of these groups, urged that, in the very ardour of their search for a new faith, all these writers, whom he styled "heretics," were gravely at fault in forgetting the older faith which alone could save them. In his view, true progress would be found, not in the artificial creation of new and abstract institutions, but in a return towards the essentially human institutions and beliefs of the Middle Ages.

In this conflict of ideas, the War intervened, a cataclysm of still immeasurable consequences, which produced, as it were, a deep geological fault in the ideas of mankind. Doctrines and beliefs were shattered. A new generation of writers emerged, so numerous and interesting that we must be content with only a few representative names. Lytton Strachey, biographer and historian, scrutinized the august figures of the Victorian age with humorous, almost Voltairean realism, and became the master of a young generation who were wrenched apart from preceding generations by the shock of the upheavals of war, a generation abhorring vagueness, epigrammatic, bitterly realist. Aldous Huxley stands as a representative of that acute, somewhat abstract, intelligence; in opposition thereto, D. H. Lawrence represented an agonized and imperfect, but powerful, effort to restore the body and the instincts to their place in the human universe;

INTRODUCTION

and in Katherine Mansfield can be found a pure and
feminine mysticism, which is perhaps the only realiza-
tion of the miraculous synthesis of the intelligence
and the senses.

I
RUDYARD KIPLING

Rudyard Kipling

I

LIFE AND WORKS

SOONER or later, a novelist of outstanding talent will always find adepts; but the authors who appeal to great numbers of people outside their own country are very few. Amongst French writers, it is only Balzac, Victor Hugo, the elder Dumas, and possibly Anatole France, who have to some extent reached these wider strata of readers in the English-speaking countries. And conversely, amongst the English writers who are widely read in France outside the circles of professional literary men or enthusiastic lovers of literature, we could point to Shakespeare, Swift (but only with *Gulliver's Travels*), Defoe (only with *Robinson Crusoe*), Charles Dickens, and certainly Rudyard Kipling. Between 1900 and 1920, Kipling appealed to the rising generations in France as few French writers were able to do. His mannerisms ("but that is another story . . .") became French mannerisms. His legends inspired the games and moulded the ideas of French children. We shall try to trace the causes of this compelling power, the foremost of which must have been Kipling's revelation of heroism and a new, contemporary sense of mystery.

It is curious to observe how Kipling's fame, as it grew and spread over the whole world, found a considerable body of opponents in England itself. What had happened? Three things. First came the usual reaction of the critics against the public, when the public has adopted their first favourable judgements with excessive unanimity. A second was something more subtle, a kind of shrinking modesty which the Kiplingesque heroes were bound to develop on seeing the machinery of their virtues thus taken to pieces. It is a peculiarity of the Kipling hero not to know that he is either a brave man or a wise man. He is silent, especially concerning his own actions. In reading Kipling, who unveiled him to others, and doubtless also to himself, he may have felt faintly vexed. And thirdly, there was the fact that in England Kipling's work was for a time associated with a political doctrine, and party spirit is often unable to distinguish between genius and incidentals. When the passage of time has stripped his work clear of associations, it will be seen that Kipling was not only the greatest English writer of our generation, but the only modern writer who has created enduring myths.

The father of Rudyard Kipling was a very talented artist, John Lockwood Kipling. His mother, Alice Macdonald, was the daughter of a clergyman, and her three sisters all became the wives of eminent men: two of them married painters, Sir Edward Burne-Jones and Sir Edward Poynter, while the third married Alfred Baldwin, a manufacturer, and became the mother of Stanley Baldwin, destined to be leader of the Conservative Party and Prime Minister.

John Lockwood Kipling was appointed to a post at the school of art in Bombay, and there his son Rudyard was born in 1865. He was brought up in India until the age of five; and like the children of most Anglo-Indian families, he was looked after by one of those *ayahs* whom he has portrayed so well. Even before he could speak English, he was familiar with that Hindustani jargon which, as he has said, serves as a kind of key-language for the countless idioms that are spoken between the Himalaya and Cape Comorin. As a child, Kipling thought and dreamed in Hindustani. It is easy to imagine him as one of those Anglo-Indian children in his own books, chattering with the native Indians, taking their generous presents, listening entranced to their stories, and more learned in the deep, hidden character of India than many a member of the Legislative Council.

The boy was delicate, and his parents decided not to rear him in the East. At the age of five he was sent to Portsmouth and entrusted to the care of a retired Naval officer. When he was eleven, he entered the United Services College, at Westward Ho, Devon, of which he gave a picture at once exact and romantic in *Stalky and Co*. In a poem which prefaces this book, Kipling recalls the lessons imparted by the English public schools: that character is more important than knowledge; that a man should carry through his daily work with as little thinking or argument as possible; in fact, that he must play for the team and obey the leader.

> There we met with famous men
>   Set in office o'er us;
> And they beat on us with rods—
>   Faithfully with many rods—
> Daily beat us on with rods,
>   For the love they bore us.

> *And* we all praise famous men—
>   Ancients of the College;
> For they taught us common sense—
>   Tried to teach us common sense—
> Truth and God's Own Common Sense,
>   Which is more than knowledge!

By the age of seventeen Kipling had received from these Famous Men the passwords which a young Englishman should know before entering on active life. He then returned to India, where his father had become curator of the Lahore museum. A description of this museum, known to the natives as the Wonder House, forms the opening to *Kim*. And now, to earn his living, Rudyard Kipling becomes an assistant-editor of the *Civil and Military Gazette*. He was to learn, as Dickens learned, that a novelist can find a magnificent apprenticeship by watching the stream of men and events pouring through a newspaper office.

In *The Man Who Would Be King* he wrote: "A newspaper office seems to attract every conceivable

sort of person, to the prejudice of discipline. Zenana-
mission ladies arrive, and beg that the Editor will instantly abandon all his duties to describe a Christian
prize-giving in a back-slum of a perfectly inac-
cesssible village; Colonels who have been overpassed
for command sit down and sketch the outline of a
series of ten, twelve or twenty-four leading articles
on Seniority *versus* selection; Missionaries wish to
know why they have not been permitted to escape
from their regular vehicles of abuse and swear at a
brother-missionary under special patronage of the edi-
torial We; stranded theatrical companies troop up to
explain that they cannot pay for their advertisements,
but on their return from New Zealand or Tahiti will
do so with interest; inventors of patent punkah-pull-
ing machines, carriage couplings, and unbreakable
swords and axle-trees, call with specifications in their
pockets and hours at their disposal; tea-companies
enter and elaborate their prospectuses with the office
pens; secretaries of ball-committees clamour to have
the glories of their last dance more fully described;
strange ladies rush in and say, 'I want a hundred
lady's cards printed *at once*, please,' which is mani-
festly part of an editor's duty; and every dissolute ruffian that ever tramped the Grand Trunk Road makes
it his business to ask for employment as a proof-
reader. And, all the time, the telephone-bell is ringing madly, and Kings are being killed on the continent, and Empires are saying, 'You're another,' and
Mister Gladstone is calling down brimstone upon
the British Dominions, and the little black copy-boys

are whining, '*kaa-pi chayha-yeh*' (copy wanted) like tired bees, and most of the paper is as blank as Modred's shield."

Occasionally the young editor published verses in his own paper, humorous and often caustic poems on Anglo-Indian life. Those readers of the *Civil and Military Gazette* who had any literary taste must instantly have detected genius, for no poet—even the young Byron or the young Hugo, who so instantaneously mastered their form—ever made a more astonishing start. Kipling's earliest poems contain all his humour, all his harsh, powerful philosophy. In 1886, when he was twenty-one, he collected them into a volume which was published at Lahore under the title of *Departmental Ditties*.

He then joined the staff of a more important paper, *The Pioneer*, at Allahabad, and during the next couple of years he issued through a local publisher *Plain Tales from the Hills*, and several other stories, such as *Soldiers Three* and *The Story of the Gadsbys*. These masterpieces had appeared before Kipling was twenty-three years old, and the prose-writer was starting with no less assurance than the poet.

What did he want to do, or to be? He could hardly yet know that himself. His first stories were reminiscent of an exotic Maupassant, and he was describing the little world of Simla, the hill-station where the Anglo-Indians send their wives and children in summer to protect them from the ravages of the hot weather. Into this society of husbandless wives come unmarried men, themselves sent to the hills for rest or convalescence, as well as a number of high officials always ready to reward a lady's favours with useful patronage for her husband. All of which was described by the young Kipling with no mercy, no reserves. But already, in *The Story of the Gadsbys* and *Soldiers Three*, it could be seen that he did not view these emotional moods and administrative intrigues as the essentials of life. He was fundamentally concerned with the virtues taught by the Famous Men of his school-days at Westward Ho, and the inevitable clash in every man's life between these virtues and the world-as-it-is.

When the small, grey, paper-covered books began to reach London, there was a gasp of amazement. Strange as it may seem, there was no such thing as a literature of the British Empire. "At first, of course," writes Robert Graves in *Scrutinies*, "he was looked on with the greatest suspicion and even detestation by the Anglo-Indians of the Mutiny tradition. *Departmental Ditties*, with its references to corsets and pink dominoes and squeezing the waists of other people's wives, was disgusting, *Plain Tales from the Hills* was intolerable; adultery was taken as a matter of course; their Simla might be Paris. But because Simla was so exotic, farther removed even than Paris, *Plain Tales from the Hills* had a great success in London." And there was also, in the background of these stories, a sense of imperial fraternity which touched the English, and which before long—life once more imitating art—induced the Anglo-Indian to add a cubit to his stature so as to be more like his own portrait.

The success was instantaneous and overwhelming. A London publisher reissued the books, and the critics hailed a prodigy. It was an almost dangerous triumph. In *The Light that Failed* Kipling shows the temptation before a young artist who has succeeded only too well, and doubtless he then gave himself the same advice that he makes an older admirer give to his hero: "Unless you take precious good care you will fall under the damnation of the check-book, and that's worse than death.) You will get drunk—you're half drunk already—on easily acquired money. For that money and your own infernal vanity you are willing to deliberately turn out bad work. You'll do quite enough bad work without knowing it. . . ."

But this young genius was able to keep his head clear and steady in the hour of triumph, and he could certainly not be reproached with having ever written about things of which he was ignorant. About this time he travelled widely, and during a visit to America he married Caroline Balestier, daughter of an American publisher. They had two children, and when they were small, whilst he was living in a small American town, he wrote *The Jungle Book*, which appeared in 1894. By the age of thirty he had published most of his Indian stories, except the finest of them all, *Kim*, which did not appear until 1901.

His French translator and interpreter, Robert d'Humières, has given us a glimpse of Kipling at

the time of his return to England, when he had settled at Rottingdean, then a small village not far from
Brighton. "The poet," he wrote, "does not look
much more than thirty. It is his eyes in particular
which hold one's attention; behind the unchanging
glass lenses, they gleam full of sympathy and merri-
ment, eager to reflect life in all its aspects. His body
has unusual agility, and lacks the somewhat con-
stricted gestures of the ordinary Englishman. . . ."
And Robert d'Humières also noted the way in which
conversation was punctuated by his youthful laughter. Kipling told him of his favourite French writers
—Rabelais and Maupassant—and Kipling said: "Do
you know Loti? I admire him greatly. Is he a good
officer? I mean, professionally." That was a very
characteristic question. Then Kipling admitted to
Robert d'Humières that he did not like the novel
of sentiment. "Probably it is a result of my Eastern
upbringing, but, in novels, I don't like women away
from their homes. They are charming in real life,
but in literature we've seen too much of them. And
there are so many other subjects. . . ."

Literary success had been magnified tenfold by
political success. In prefacing a French translation
of Kipling in 1900, André Chevrillon showed how
the English were rediscovering in his poems both a
national and a religious ideal. "In his songs and ballads, which are now being repeated in Army bar-
racks, in His Majesty's Ships, on Colonial plantations,
Kipling has invoked the God who gives England
her astonishing cohesion. In the same poem which

celebrated the sea and its burden of British ships, the Englishman with his five meals a day, the banks with limitless credit, all the resources of the Empire, he turned back to hail the heart and core of Empire—Westminster, 'wehre the Abbey makes us *we*.'"

Wells also has noted in one of his books the importance which the Kipling influence then had for young men: "In the middle nineties this spectacled and moustached little figure with its heavy chin, its wild shouts of boyish enthusiasm for effective force, its lyric delight in the sounds and colours, in the very odours of the Empire . . . became almost a national symbol. He got hold of us wonderfully, he filled us with tinkling and haunting quotations . . . he coloured the very idiom of our conversation. . . . What did he give me exactly? He helped to broaden my geographical sense immensely, and he provided phrases for just that desire for discipline and devotion and organized effort the Socialism of our time failed to express."

About 1900, then, Kipling was the mouthpiece of the Empire. And just then came the South African War, the outcome of imperialist ideas. But the long-drawn-out difficulties of that war, and the disappointments it caused to the English people, were to lead to a revulsion of spirit. That reaction had far-reaching political consequences, as it ultimately caused the flood-tide of Liberalism in 1906. It also left a lasting and undeserved shadow on Kipling's literary fame. For many years, liberal critics were prevented by political passion from recognizing that

RUDYARD KIPLING, FROM A CHALK DRAWING BY SIR WILLIAM
ROTHENSTEIN

the genius in Kipling is something quite independent of political ideas.

Take as an example of this anti-Kipling reaction, a passage from Richard Le Gallienne's study: "A nation could hardly go on existing if it did not believe itself the finest nation on earth. . . . But a nation may feel that without falling into the old Jewish error of concluding that it is the chosen people of the universe. . . . Does Mr Kipling literally believe that there is a Lord God of Hosts whom we please by our commercial conquests . . . ? Conquests do not result from the exercise of the Christian virtues, but from their direct opposite. . . ." Of course, there has never been a Christian nation and never will be. A really Christian nation could not exist five minutes. In this matter of English conquests another poet, William Watson, has challenged the *Recessional* with unanswerable wit:

> Best by remembering God, say some,
>   We keep our high imperial lot.
> Fortune, I think, has mainly come,
>   When we forgot—when we forgot.

When Kipling retired to the English countryside after years of life abroad, in India, America and South Africa, many of his admirers thought that he would give up writing. He had found his subjects on the highway of Kim. Would he now live on his memories? Would he discover subjects to match his powers in the Sussex farmers? It was doubtful. *Puck of Pook's Hill* came in 1906 as an enchanting surprise. Here was Kipling transplanted, but renewed, and still Kipling. And all this without leaving his garden! The children of the book were his. The little stream that "for centuries had cut deep into the soft valley soil" was the brook which flows at the foot of his meadows. The mill and the feudal castle were his neighbours. Great subjects are always the simple ones. This land, so old in civilization, had seen the original peasantry, and the legionaries of Rome, and the Norman barons. Kipling had brought them all to life for his children.

Since the War, in the course of which he lost his son, Kipling has lived far from the hurly-burly of towns, in that beautiful garden of Bateman's. One finds him there now every bit as much alive as he was described by his visitors years ago. Under those thick eyebrows the eyes remain as keen as ever, and his tone is youthful and alert. I know of no conversation which gives more intensely than Kipling's the sense of genius, that is to say, of spontaneous and constant inventiveness.

For a good many years the younger men in England seemed to stand aloof from Kipling's work. But that caused him little concern, for he believes that every generation must have its own ways of feeling, its own chance of living. And just as he accepted with serenity a partial eclipse of his renown, so he seems indifferent to its renewed glamour. For the most fastidious critics, having preened themselves on their originality in making reserves about Kipling's work, have come in the end to discover that only one

original judgement was left for them to pass about it—
to be able to admire it unreservedly. To this they
have resigned themselves. The gesture, it has been
said, is superfluous: the elephant halts for a moment
by the roadside and the beetle raises an encouraging
hand! For my own part, I have never ceased to regard Kipling as the greatest writer of our time, and
one of the greatest of any time; and I should like to
attempt an analysis of the deeper reasons for that
admiration.

II

THE HEROIC VIEW OF LIFE

ROBERT GRAVES has spoken of Kipling as the literary
aspect of the British Empire. But the phrase hardly
suffices to explain the intensity of feeling which Kipling's work gave to so many young Frenchmen at
the time when the first translations were published.
Kim, Stalky and Co., and *The Jungle Book* were then
our favourite books. In the letters of Riviere and
Alain Fournier I find echoes of my own enthusiasm,
which I shared with my fellow schoolboys at Rouen.
How little we thought of British imperialism, as
we read *City of Sleep*, or *The Bridge Builders*! What
we sought in Kipling, apart from the admirable
stories, was first and foremost *an heroic conception
of life*.

That conception was neither exclusively British,

nor exclusively imperial. Kipling has shown that it was one and the same for the Roman official on the Welsh Marches and for the British officer isolated in the Himalaya, or for the French officer isolated in the Atlas. Again, it was neither exclusively military, nor colonial. Whatever the milieu he described, Kipling discerned amongst men a constant and necessary hierarchy, the framework of an heroic society which takes shape whenever a human group has a difficult task to accomplish.

At the summit are the heroes, who dominate its elements of idleness, envy, fear, ambition and desire, or at least drive these passions under a cloak of silence, and so obviate that disorder which, unless the heroes take matters in hand, will reduce any society to a state of impotence. When the heroes are exhausted and order is virtually restored, it is the turn of the great administrators. These "great sahibs" are strong, cautious, and silent. They use few words among themselves in their concerns, a native sage is made to remark, and fewer still when they talk about them to an outsider. By skill and self-control the statesmen, for a certain time, maintain the societies created by the heroes. Then the self-seekers and talkers, encouraged by the apparent solidity of the established order, come to the forefront, and then begins the reign of the politicians and exploiters, destroyers of any society, and the cycle starts again.

Kipling has depicted those three classes of men. With the men of action, the pioneering heroes, he was familiar at an early age, in India: "God be thanked, whatever comes after, I have lived and toiled with men. . . ." The man of action is omni-present in Kipling's work, whether he is building bridges or fighting famine, a Gurkhas' officer or a cotton-planter. His character is of the simplest. Neither love nor family counts for him so long as his day's work is not accomplished. He trusts no-body to take his place, unless it be other men of action, younger perhaps, but like himself, whom he treats as sons, as can be seen from the fact that he chooses the hardest tasks for them. But none others would he honour by subjecting them to the cease-less toil which he imposes on himself.

The man of action matches himself against the fierce resistance of the forces of nature. To think out a bridge and design it—this is comparatively easy: a man is alone with his drawing-paper. But when he is building a bridge, he must reckon with chains that give, pulleys that snap, workmen who mutiny, not to mention the anger of the river and the ever-present wrath of the gods. For the gods hold in horror the victories of men, as the Greeks well knew. The hero accepts these strokes of fate with perfect equa-nimity. And to this Kipling gave full expression in the four closely packed stanzas of his famous poem, *If*.

When a people is truly a people of *men*, then it can learn its lessons from ill fortune, and even a defeat will become a weapon for the winning of victories to come. And so, after the grave blow to England's pride which she sustained in the Boer

War, Kipling advised his country to turn that pain into a stimulus for fresh effort.

It was our fault, and our very great fault and now we
    must turn it to use.
We have forty million reasons for failure, but not a
    single excuse.
So the more we work and the less we talk the better re-
    sults we shall get—
We have had an Imperial lesson; it may make us an
    empire yet!

The hero gives his service neither for fame nor for coin, but for the honour of serving. "Scott counted eight years' service in the Irrigation Department, and drew eight hundred rupees a month, on the understanding that if he served the State faithfully for another twenty-two years he could retire on a pension of some four hundred rupees a month." Nearly always when the hero has worked devotedly in some post for several years, he learns that he is about to be transferred on the very eve of final success, that another will reap where he has sown; and here too is a good opportunity for moral discipline.

This heroic society, in the Roman legion or the Anglo-Indian regiment, amongst administrators or engineers, has always been built on a model which is practically unique. At the head is the Chief, who conceives, commands and controls—the real chief, for Kipling has no fondness or indulgence for the man who has the function without the virtues. He enjoys showing us, in *Tod's Amendment*, the ignorance of certain legal members and how a child can instruct them. In *Puck of Pook's Hill* he delights to show Maximus, the all-powerful general, soon perhaps to be a Roman Emperor, being quietly threatened by a centurion. And he is merciless towards the apoplectic colonel who pays attention to the wives of his junior officers. But it is because he appreciates the worth of the real chief that Kipling is so stern to the unworthy.

Beside the chief, the subaltern. The subaltern does heroic deeds, but changes the subject of conversation if anyone ventures to mention it. Some day he will be the chief's successor, but he never thinks of that day and would be outraged if anyone else raised the question: "Then the adjutant was promoted, and Cottar rejoiced with him, for he admired the adjutant greatly, and marvelled who might be big enough to fill his place; so that he nearly collapsed when the mantle fell on his own shoulders, and the colonel said a few sweet things that made him blush."

In the next grade one finds, in the Army, the non-commissioned officer, or in the engineering shops, the foreman. He too, in his way, is a chief. Kipling has great respect for the N.C.O. When England wants to make a man of Pharaoh, she sends him Sergeant Whatisname:

> It is not a Duke nor Earl, nor yet a *Vis*count—
> It was not a big brass General that came;
> But a man in khaki kit who could handle men a bit.

If the chief rules by his heroic virtues, the N.C.O.

imposes his authority by his respect for discipline and by his amazing efficiency.

And in the last grade of the race of heroes (last, that is, in order, not in worth or importance), come the good soldier and the good workman. It is about them that Kipling wrote one of his finest poems, *The Sons of Martha*:

The Sons of Mary seldom bother, for they have inherited
  that good part;
But the Sons of Martha favour their Mother of the
  careful soul and the troubled heart.
And because she lost her temper once, and because she
  was rude to the Lord her Guest,
Her Sons must wait upon Mary's Sons, world without
  end, reprieve, or rest.

It is their care in all the ages to take the buffet and
  cushion the shock.
It is their care that the gear engages; it is their care that
  the switches lock.
It is their care that the wheels run truly; it is their
  care to embark and entrain,
Tally, transport, and deliver duly the Sons of Mary by
  land and main.

They say to the mountains, "Be ye removèd." They say
  to the lesser floods "Be dry."
Under their rods are the rocks reprovèd—they are not
  afraid of that which is high.
Then do the hill-tops shake to the summit—then is the
  bed of the deep laid bare,
That the Sons of Mary may overcome it, pleasantly
  sleeping and unaware. . . .

RUDYARD KIPLING

When the Sons of Martha are in the Army, they are called Tommy Atkins:

O it's Tommy this, an' Tommy that, an' "Tommy, go
    away";
But its "Thank you, Mister Atkins," when the band
    begins to play—
The band begins to play, my boys, the band begins to
    play,
O it's "Thank you, Mister Atkins," when the band be-
    gins to play.

III

GOOD AND EVIL

AND now, in Kipling's work as in every ordered system, we must range the Powers of Evil against these Powers of Good. If the Man Who Acts is the god of light, Ormuzd, the Man Who Talks is Ahriman, the god of darkness. And when the Man Who Talks claims control over the Man Who Acts, Kipling becomes fiercely satiric. One feels his joy when Pagett, M.P., who has spoken of the Indian heat as a solar myth, himself experiences sandstorms and liver-attacks, and weeps as he talks of home:

We reached a hundred and twenty once in the Court
    at noon,
(I've mentioned Pagett was portly) Pagett went off
    in a swoon.

[21]

That was an end of the business. Pagett the perjured
    fled
With a practical, working knowledge of "Solar Myths"
    in his head.

And I laughed as I drove from the station, but the mirth
    died out on my lips
As I thought of the fools like Pagett who write of their
    "Eastern Trips,"
And the sneers of the travelled idiots who duly mis-
    govern the land,
And I prayed to the Lord to deliver another one into
    my hand.

This theme is again taken up in *The Story of the
Little Foxes*. Here we are told how certain men of
action, engaged in ruling a certain province, engage
in their beloved sport of fox-hunting, and in so doing
achieve a human and intimate knowledge of the
natives of the Nile valley, as well as supervising
the dams and irrigation canals and ensuring their
maintenance. Whereupon, enter the Man Of Words.
He is naturally incapable of understanding these ir-
regular methods of administration, interferes to correct the scandal, invoking the great principles of
humanity, and very properly becomes the general
laughing-stock.

The political concepts of Kipling are ascetic and
aristocratic. The hive prospers so long as the bees
toil, obey the law, and feed the queen. It is doomed
if the young bees begin to argue, or listen to the
parasites who talk about "loving their toiling com-

rades." The law of the hive lays it down that pillars of wax must be built to prevent the death's-head moth from entering, but the advanced thinkers about the young bees make light of such fears: " 'That's nonsense,' a downy, day-old bee answered. 'In the first place, I never heard of a Death's Header coming into a hive. People don't *do* such things. . . . If you trust a Death's Head, he will trust you. Pillar-building shows lack of confidence. Our dear sister in grey says so.'

" 'Yes. Pillars are un-English and provocative, and a waste of wax that is needed for higher and more practical ends,' said the Wax-moth from an empty store-cell. . . . 'If I can only teach a—a little toleration—a little ordinary kindness here towards that absurd old bogey you call the Death's Header, I shan't have lived in vain.' "

If a hive tolerates such arguments, it will sooner or later be smoked out by the bee-keeper, and its bees will die a shameful death; and the peoples who do likewise will also find their punishment at the hands of the Lord God of battles.

Many liberal critics have supposed that, because Kipling exalted the virtues of asceticism and discipline, he was hostile to the idea of liberty. That is mistaken. But he does believe that liberty is not lawlessness; on the contrary, that it is fundamentally dependent on respect for the laws and on obedience to the chief. At the cost of certain sacrifices, Kipling believes, man can become a noble and civilized crea-

ture; but in the natural state he is a violent and formidable animal, exposed by his bodily nature to the
temptations of fear and folly. Kipling's picture of
the human world has something biblical in it:

> The earth is full of anger,
> The seas are dark with wrath
>
> .   .   .   .   .   .
>
> From panic, pride, and terror,
> Revenge that knows no rein—
> Light haste and lawless error,
> Protect us yet again.

Even the most magnificently self-controlled of his
heroes are so only by conquest of themselves. Deep
inside, the dangerous brute lives on. As Andrè Chevrillon has put it: "He brings out the savage in man,
whether Englishman or Hindoo; he rouses and stirs
up the deep, vital, primary instincts, which he loves
because they are potent, because they strain and
shake up the whole of man's being and force out all
the energy that is in him. . . . The same murderous
jealousy waves a red rag before the eyes of the
Afridi and of the Yorkshireman. The soldier Lea-
royd, lying on the watch in the grass on a Himalayan hillside, awaiting the moment to fire his rifle,
tells his companions about his first love adventure;
in memory he sees again the face of the rival he
wanted to kill once in a Lancashire pit, and that
desire to kill revives in him; his speech becomes tense
and jerky; his mouth dry; he stammers; his eyes grow

bloodshot, and stare fixedly; his lips curl in a snarl over his yellow teeth and his flushed face is ugly to see."

And it is a matter of necessity that the Law and respect for the Law should impose a form on all these sins in fusion.

Even the Jungle has its law, and the animals respect it. When the wolf tribe, under the influence of the bad tiger, ceases for a few days to respect its old chief, Akela, the leaderless clan immediately suffers. Here are some of the wolves going lame through falling into traps; here is one dragging a leg shattered by a gunshot; others are mangy through eating tainted food; and when Mowgli brings them the tiger's striped skin one of the pack calls on him to be their leader: "Lead us again, O man-cub, for we be sick of this lawlessness, and we would be the Free People once more."

In fact, it is through law and obedience that disorder is made into order. Kipling describes the great charge at the conclusion of a military review in India, and the terrifying effect of that massed rush is to him symbolic of the terrifying power of popular masses, a power which, when disciplined, becomes a thing of beauty:

"Then I heard an old grizzled, long-haired Central Asian Chief, who had come down with the Amir, asking questions of a native officer.

"'Now,' said he, 'in what manner was this wonderful thing done?'

"And the officer answered, 'An order was given and they obeyed.'

" 'But are the beasts as wise as the men?' said the Chief.

" 'They obey, as the men do. Mule, horse, elephant, or bullock, he obeys his driver; and the driver his sergeant, and the sergeant his lieutenant, and the lieutenant his captain, and the captain his major, and the major his colonel, and the colonel his brigadier commanding three regiments, and the brigadier the general, who obeys the Viceroy, who is the servant of the Empress. Thus it is done.'

" 'Would it were so in Afghanistan,' said the Chief; 'for there we obey only our own wills.'

" 'And for that reason,' said the native officer, twirling his moustache, 'your Amir whom you do not obey must come here and take orders from our Viceroy.' "

There we can grasp Kipling's thought, in its purest and simplest form. Those who cannot provide themselves with a leader of their own will be subject to the leaders of others. Freedom, according to Aristotle, consists of ruling and being ruled. Races who refuse to be ruled will forfeit the right of self-rule. Here again, accordingly, Kipling is not hostile to liberty; but he sets forth its conditions, which are strict and binding. That Law with a capital L, of which he speaks so often, is in his eyes the natural outcome of the age-old wisdom of the races. It could not spring from the talky-talk of an assembly, nor from the votes of a crowd. It *is*. And it can be altered only by wise men who translate the law of hard fact into the written word.

The very idea of the vote has been frequently assailed by Kipling. Somewhere he remarks that there are two methods of governing: counting heads, or breaking them. And there are times when the reader wonders whether Kipling's natural preference is not for the second. He wrote one biting story about universal suffrage—*The Village that Voted the Earth Was Flat*—and also an extraordinary forecast of humanity being at last ruled by a reasonable, objective, silent council, and an American city revolting when it believes that the suffrage is going to be restored.

But although Kipling may have little respect for the electors in the mass, he has plenty for the man of the people regarded as an individual worker. He enjoys portraying, for instance, Hobden, whose family have owned and tilled the same soil, from father to son, for over a thousand years. The Roman, the Norman, the Saxon, the feudal lord and the modern financier, have all fancied that they were buying the farm. In point of fact they all obeyed the successive generations of the Hobdens. For it is only the man who works who keeps what he owns, and the deserving man what he commands:

Now this is the law of the Jungle—as old and as true
    as the sky;
And the Wolf that shall keep it may prosper, but the
    Wolf that shall break it must die.

As the creeper that girdles the tree-trunk the Law run-
  neth forward and back—
Yet the strength of the Pack is the Wolf, and the
  strength of the Wolf is the Pack.

Such is the Law of the Jungle, and such likewise
the law of the heroic society.

IV

WOMAN IN THE HEROIC SOCIETY

NATURALLY, in this Kiplingesque world, resembling
the world of Chivalry, the heroes hold a chivalrous
conception of woman and of love. The true hero
should, in the moment of action, be pure. The Parsi-
fal of the Indian Civil Service keeps himself inviolate
for some inaccessible maiden waiting for him in England. He is a "man's man," loyal to the service, to
the regiment, to friendship.

In the story of *The Man Who Would Be King*
there are two adventurers who, having resolved on
the conquest of a Himalayan Kingdom, make a con-
tract between them. Their agreement lays it down:
"(One) That me and you will settle this matter together; i.e. to be Kings of Kafiristan. (Two) That
you and me will not, while this matter is being settled, look at any Liquor, nor any Woman black,
white, or brown, so as to get mixed up with one or
the other harmful." And when the better of the two
breaks his vow and undertakes the conquest of a

woman, the enterprise collapses. "The Bible says that Kings ain't to waste their strength on women, 'specially when they've got a new raw Kingdom to work over."

Kipling's heroes, indeed, often seem to regard woman in the manner of certain primitive tribes, who see in her a sorceress, a focus of potent and perilous forces:

Man's timid heart is bursting with the things he must
    not say,
For the Woman that God gave him isn't his to give
    away;
But when hunter meets with husband, each confirms the
    other's tale—
The female of the species is more deadly than the
    male.

And even when she is the best of women, she is a terrible danger, by reason of the violence of the sentiments she inspires. Take Captain Gadsby: he has been the bravest officer in his regiment of Hussars, until the time of his marriage. His wife loves him; she does not want to hamper him in his profession; but she trips him up in it despite herself. His feelings become confused: the fear of losing her, the desire to live for their child, both conflict in Gadsby's mind with the problems of action, and he loses his aptitude for action. Consider the scene between Gadsby and his fellow officer, Captain Mafflin, in front of the Gadsbys' bungalow:

M. You look awf'ly serious. Anything wrong?

G. Depends on your view entirely. I say, Jack, you won't think more hardly of me than you can help, will you? Come farther this way.—The fact of the matter is, that I've made up my mind—at least I'm thinking seriously of—cutting the Service.

M. Hwhatt?

G. Don't shout. I'm going to send in my papers.

M. You! Are you mad?

G. No—only married.

M. Look here! What's the meaning of it all? You never intend to leave *us*. You *can't*. Isn't the best squadron of the best regiment of the best cavalry in all the world good enough for you?

G. (*Jerking his head over his shoulder.*) She doesn't seem to thrive in this God-forsaken country, and there's the *Butcha* to be considered and all that, you know.

M. Does she say that she doesn't like India?

G. That's the worst of it. She won't for fear of leaving me.

M. What are the Hills made for?

G. Not for *my* wife at any rate.

M. You know too much, Gaddy, and—I don't like you any the better for it!

G. Never mind that. She wants England, and the *Butcha* would be all the better for it. I'm going to chuck. You don't understand.

M. (*Hotly*). I understand *this*. One hundred and thirty-seven new horses to be licked into shape somehow before Luck comes round again; a hairy-heeled draft who'll give more trouble than the horses; a camp next cold weather for a certainty; ourselves the first on the roster; the Russian shindy ready to come to a head at five minutes notice, and you, the best of us all, backing out of it all! Think a little, Gaddy. You *won't* do it.

G. Hang it, a man has some duties towards his family, I suppose. . . .

M. (*Aside*). Couldn't conceive any woman getting permanently between me and the Regiment. (*Aloud*.) Can't say. Very likely I should do no better. I'm sorry for you—awf'ly sorry—but 'if them's your sentiments' I believe, I really do, that you are acting wisely.

G. Do you? I hope you do. (*In a whisper*.) Jack, be very sure of yourself before you marry. I'm an ungrateful ruffian to say this, but marriage—even as good a marriage as mine has been—hampers a man's work, it cripples his sword-arm, and oh, it plays Hell with his notions of duty! Sometimes—good and sweet as she is—sometimes I could wish that I had kept my freedom. . . .

Again, just as woman kills the man of action, so also she slays the artist. In *The Finest Story in the World* the young bank-clerk, Charlie, a great writer unconscious of his genius, reconstructs the life of privates who lived a thousand years ago, and quite naturally composes wonderful poems and the most convincing sailor-songs, until the day when, without a word, he shows his friend the photograph of a curly-haired girl with a soft, silly mouth. "Isn't it wonderful?" he whispered. . . . "It came like a thunderclap." From that moment Charlie has tasted the love of woman, which dissolves memory, and the finest story in the world will never be written.

In *The Light that Failed*, when Dick blasphemes against art and loses interest in his work, his friends conclude at once that he is involved in some folly over a woman. "She'll waste his time, and she'll marry him, and ruin his work for ever. He'll be a respectable married man before we can stop him, and—he'll never go on the long trail again."

Towards the courtesan, Kipling displays all the tolerance of the Hindus. She is necessary, part and parcel of the everlasting plan of human societies:

"Lalun is a member of the most ancient profession in the world. Lilith was her very-great-grandmamma, and that was before the days of Eve, as every one knows. In the West, people say rude things about Lalun's profession, and write lectures about it, and distribute the lectures to young persons in order that Morality may be preserved. In the East where the profession is hereditary, descending from mother to daughter, nobody writes lectures or takes any notice; and that is a distinct proof of the inability of the East to manage its own affairs."

But if he tolerates the courtesan, who, like a man, has her professional honour, he has a truly chivalrous detestation of the faithless wife. In his youth in India he observed and described the strange part which Delilah can play in male society. He realized the hidden reason for Potiphar Gubbins, who, despite his mediocrity of brain, was soon "at the top of the tree," and why Ahasuerus Jenkins, with his tenor voice, became a power to be reckoned with, thanks to Cornelia Agrippina, "who was musical and fat." At Simla he had seen ladies of mature age seducing young subalterns from loyalty to husbands and superiors; and he despised these ladies. He had observed the battles of women, and the hidden, mortal wounds which they inflict on one another.

And yet Kipling had such respect for technical excellence, for the good craftsman, that he extends this even to the coquette, provided that she plays her part to perfection. When he writes of Simla, his favourite is the terrible Mrs Hauksbee. He is afraid of her and her spells, but he admires her. When she is trying to rescue a greenhorn, newly arrived in India, from the fearsome talons of Mrs Reiver, another skilful and dangerous woman, and to restore the boy to his English fiancée, Mrs Hauksbee acts as a woman whose technique of femininity is perfect; and Kipling, as he watches this splendid duel, rejoices inwardly:

"At the beginning of August Mrs Hauksbee discovered that it was time to interfere. A man who rides much knows exactly what a horse is going to do next before he does it. In the same way, a woman of Mrs Hauksbee's experience knows accurately how a boy will behave under certain circumstances—notably when he is infatuated with one of Mrs Reiver's stamp. She said that, sooner or later, little Pluffles would break off that engagement for nothing at all—simply to gratify Mrs Reiver, who, in return, would keep him at her feet and in her service just so long as she found it worth her while. She said she knew the signs of these things. If she did not no one else could.

"Then she went forth to capture Pluffles under

the guns of the enemy. . . . This particular engagement lasted seven weeks—we called it the Seven weeks war—and was fought out inch by inch on both sides. A detailed account would fill a book, and would be incomplete then. Anyone who knows about these things can fit in the details for himself. It was a superb fight—there will never be another like it so long as Jakko Hill stands—and Pluffles was the prize of victory."

In the lists of love, however, women also suffer; and Kipling is not blind to their suffering. He has written that fine poem, *Mary, Pity Women!*, the agonizing plaint of the woman with her child, deserted by a sailor-lover:

What's the use o' grievin', when the mother that bore
    you
(Mary, pity women!) knew it all afore you?

And that refrain alternates with another, which recalls the furies of Hermione:

        I 'ate you, grinnin' there . . .
        Ah, Gawd, I love you so!

(On an analogous theme, *Love of Women* is a powerful and affecting story.) And there is also a dialogue, *The Hill of Illusion*, between a woman and the man she has planned to run away with, which is truly tragic, as fully charged with real sorrow as certain scenes in *Anna Karenina*. But, although Kipling understands women and feels for them, he seems always to be remembering that he is bent on displaying a heroic society, which he cannot allow to be ruined by caprice, passion, or jealousy and that only the hero's comrade has a legitimate place therein.

For naturally, in a chivalrous society, there is a place for the admirable woman, as there was in the mediaeval epics. Thus we find, firstly, the wife of the leader, who, like her husband, thinks only of action, such as the "William the Conqueror," who helps to fight the famine, enjoys listening to men who *do* things talking about their jobs, and to whom poetry (as the poet Kipling is delighted to record) means nothing but a headache. When "William" becomes engaged, she talks with her future husband about dams, canals, irrigation, children to be saved and famine in the eight districts: "and so Love ran about the camp unrebuked in broad daylight."

Likewise, there is the real soldier's wife, the steadfast wife who can be patient, cook rations, bandage the wounded:

> Now, if you must marry, take care she is old
> For beauty won't help if your rations is cold.

In the pages of Kipling we meet none of those intellectual and sensual Amazons such as we find in Wells or Huxley. Woman is either a dangerous, mysterious spell-binder, or a comrade in battle, the strong woman of the Scriptures. And it is made clear that in heroic effort, which demands from a man all the courage that is in him—whether it be the effort of a man of action or of a statesman—the woman who

[35]

cannot fight beside him will soon become an evil genius. It is a harsh message, but a true one.

V

THE ARTIST IN THE HEROIC SOCIETY

AND what place does this great artist reserve, in his heroic world, for artists? In nearly every writer who chooses to depict men of action, there is latent a thwarted man of action, filled with regrets. This is why a writer of this kind, in his stories, will set the man of action above the artist. And Kipling is such a writer. In one of his tales, *A Conference of the Powers*, he depicts a great writer, Eustace Cleever, being enthusiastically received by some admiring Anglo-Indian officers. These young captains and subalterns are grateful to him for having described their work and their country with such perfect accuracy, and Cleever, who is a lover of heroes, is touched by this admiration. But after listening to these young fellows, who have all been leaders and rulers and slayers of men, he is left for a long time silent:

"Then said Cleever, 'I can't understand. Why should you have seen and done all these things before you have cut your wisdom-teeth?'

"'Don't know,' said The Infant apologetically. 'I haven't seen much—only Burmese jungle.'

"'And dead men, and war, and power, and re-

[36]

sponsibility,' said Cleever, under his breath. 'You won't have any sensations left at thirty, if you go on as you have done. But I want to hear more tales—more tales. . . .'

". . . and when he departed, [I] asked him what he thought of things generally.

"He replied with another quotation, to the effect that though singing was a remarkably fine performance, I was to be quite sure that few lips would be moved to song if they could find a sufficiency of kissing.

"Whereby I understood that Eustace Cleever, decorator and colourman in words, was blaspheming his own Art, and would be sorry for this in the morning."

As for the man who has neither suffered nor created, who has lived only through books—Kipling leaves him to his pallid destiny, in a poem which is like a canto of Dante:

Now Tomlinson gave up the ghost at his house in
　　Berkeley Square,
And a Spirit came to his bedside and gripped him by
　　the hair—
A Spirit gripped him by the hair and carried him far
　　away,
Till he heard as the roar of a rain-fed ford the roar of
　　the Milky Way:
Till he heard the roar of the Milky Way die down and
　　drone and cease,
And they came to the Gate within the Wall where Peter
　　holds the keys.

"Stand up, stand up now, Tomlinson, and answer loud and high

"The good that ye did for the sake of men or ever ye came to die—

"The good that ye did for the sake of men on little earth so lone!"

And the naked soul of Tomlinson grew white as a rain-washed bone. . . .

"O this I have read in a book," he said, "and that was told to me

"And this I have thought that another man thought. . . ."

The good souls flocked like homing doves and bade him clear the path,

And Peter twirled the jangling Keys in weariness and wrath.

"Ye have read, ye have heard, ye have thought," he said, and the tale is yet to run:

"By the worth of the body that once ye had, give answer—what ha' ye done?"

Then Tomlinson looked back and forth, and little good it bore,

For the darkness stayed at his shoulder-blade and Heaven's Gate before:—

"O this I have felt, and this I have guessed, and this I have heard men say,

"And this they wrote that another man wrote of an earl in Norroway."

"Ye have read, ye have felt, ye have guessed, good lack! Ye have hampered Heaven's Gate;

"There's little room between the stars in idleness to prate!

"O none may reach by hired speech of neighbour, priest, and kin

"Through borrowed deed to God's good meed that lies
so fair within;
"Get hence, get hence to the Lord of Wrong, for the
doom has yet to run,
"And . . . the faith that ye share with Berkeley Square
uphold you, Tomlinson!"

Whereupon Tomlinson goes down from star to star even unto Hell; and, there at least, he hopes to be able one day to find admission. But even the Devil will have none of him; for to enter Hell, a man must have done something. Deedless, man does not even exist.

Then Tomlinson looked back and forth, and there was
little grace.
For Hell-Gate filled the houseless soul with the Fear
of the Naked Space.
"May, this I ha' heard," quo' Tomlinson, "and this was
noised abroad,
"And this I ha' got from a Belgian book on the word of
a dead French lord."
—"Ye ha' heard, ye ha' read, ye ha' got, good lack! and
the tale begins afresh—
"Have ye sinned one sin for the pride o' the eye or the
sinful lust of the flesh?"
Then Tomlinson he gripped the bars and yammered,
"Let me in—
"For I mind that I borrowed my neighbour's wife to
sin the deadly sin."
The Devil he grinned behind the bars, and banked the
fires high:

"Did ye read of that sin in a book?" said he; and Tom-
    linson said, "Ay!"
"And . . . the God that you took from a printed book
    be with you, Tomlinson!"

Is there, then, no salvation in the Kiplingesque universe for the artist, the man who only acts at one re-
move? Yes, there is one form of salvation: respect for
his craft. An artist *is* a man of action when, instead
of talking about Art with a capital A, he conscien-
tiously strives to master his craft, to be a good workman, and not to create Beauty with a capital B.
That is the great lesson that Dick teaches Maisie in
The Light that Failed: "Don't you understand, darling? Good work has nothing to do with—doesn't
belong to—the person who does it. It's put into him
or her from outside. . . . All we can do is to learn
how to do our work, to be masters of our materials
instead of servants, and never to be afraid of anything." Thus can the artist find his place in the Paradise of Heroes whither he will be led by the Anglo-
Indian Valkyries, sun-helmeted.

VI

THE INVENTOR OF MYTHS

A HEROIC conception of life—this was our first discovery in Rudyard Kipling. But a heroic pessimism,
if had been exhibited in an abstract philosophical
form, would never have touched men in their hearts.

RUDYARD KIPLING

The real secret of Kipling's hold is an instinctive and enduring contact with the oldest and deepest layers of the human consciousness.

We are men of the twentieth century; concerning the world about us we have formed certain modern and scientific ideas. But in a secret part of our thoughts and dreams we are also men of far older times. Within us all the successive religions of mankind lie superimposed. Forests remain to us as sacred woods, and towns as temples of the Emperor. Just as the developing embryo passes through all the stages of the species, so the human child, in the course of childhood and adolescence, recovers the magical beliefs of his ancestors. We have all passed through an age when the fairy world was the natural world. We have all, at some moment of our lives, worshipped animals as the Egyptians did. And thus any evocation of the youth of mankind will touch living and sensitive spots within our being.[1]

Now Kipling, through his twofold life in the East and the West, has become as it were a link between the gods of the East and the minds of the West. Although he has written that "East is East, and West is West, and never the twain shall meet," the twain *have* met—in himself. The gods are omnipresent in Kipling, as they are in Homer. And this is not so by a story-teller's artifice, or, if it really is so, the artifice is so perfect as to be almost imperceptible. Kipling is himself so near to the youth of humanity

[1] Regarding this, the reader should consult Alain's excellent book, *Les Dieux* (Paris. N.R.F.).

that, at the moment of his writing, he believes in the strokes of magic which he is describing. There Kipling seems to resemble his hero Kim. Like Kim, he would be tempted to yield to the Oriental's wild vision of the world, if he did not keep saying to himself, "I am a Sahib." As the Lama says very solemnly to Kim: "Perhaps in a former life it was permitted that I should have rendered thee some service. Maybe I freed thee from a trap; or, having caught thee on a hook in the days when I was not enlightened, cast thee back into the river." Thus runs the Oriental's thought, and in Kipling's finest Hindu stories we have a feeling that he too is thinking like a son of India, and that he believes in his myths.

Kipling's world is not the mechanical, over-regulated world of the Western determinist. It is a world positively thronged with gods, and constantly one hears their footsteps prowling round the paths of men. When a rising of the river Ganges forces the bridge-builder to take refuge on an island, the engineer Findlayson, there on that storm-swept strip of land, beset by rain and stream roaring in concert, beholds the gods themselves passing.

The brute beasts, in the pages of Kipling, speak: not as the animals of the fabulists, which are men, always intended to afford us lessons and examples, but simply, just because it is a fact that animals speak, because the bear and the panther and the serpent are thinking creatures with lives of their own. All this is so skilful and straightforward that it does not astonish us in the least. Through his *Jungle Book* Kipling gave a new mythology to a great portion of the human race, and it has engendered both symbols and ceremonies. The boys of England and France, Germany and Australia and Arabia, all go up to the Rock of Council, call themselves Wolfcubs, and learn the Law—because Kipling wrote the *Jungle Book*.

And he is not only capable of making animals come to life. Machinery, also, in his books, takes on an almost human life. In one of his stories, called .007, locomotives hold converse with each other; in another, *The Ship that Found Herself*, the countless parts of a new ship's hull and engines are shown working together for the first time during a maiden voyage.

He has invented new forms of the fantastic. The Englishman can glide without much difficulty into the realm of wonder; but Kipling more than any, as he lives in that shifting, narrow burning borderland between the worlds of reality and marvel. When he recites his multiplication-table to counteract a spell, the stern poetry of the West emerges to mask the poetry of the East, and "things that rode meaningless on the eyeball an instant before slid into proper proportion. Roads were meant to be walked upon, houses to be lived in, . . . and men and women to be talked to. They were all real and true—solidly planted upon the feet—perfectly comprehensible—clay of his clay, neither more nor less."

Real and true? Yes: but one instant of carelessness will let the sorcerer back, and by virtue of a capital letter an abstract sentiment will become a god, a locomotive will become a girl, the hive an empire in decay, and the humblest brook the Holy River of the Arrow. Just as the physicist, in certain elusive states of radio-active matter, can in a way be present at the metamorphosis of the atom, so, in Kipling's mind, we can grasp the instant when the marvellous is made flesh.

VII

KIPLING'S ART

DICK, the hero of *The Light that Failed*, is forever telling his friend Maisie that an artist's first duty is to master his craft. The creator of Dick has followed this advice throughout his life, and in Kipling's craftsmanship there is something prodigious. It is obvious at a glance that he is a real artist in words, that his vocabulary is amazingly varied and exact. Kipling has that air of omniscience which enables a great novelist to describe, with no apparent effort, the most diverse scenes and emotions. He can talk with accuracy about the Indian administration, about the Army as seen by an officer or by a private, about the sorts of machinery, about polo, about bee-hives, about live-stock. When he describes the construction of a bridge, he does not shock the skilled engineer, nor the Frenchman when he speaks about France. He talks only of what he knows, and he knows surprising and innumerable things.

Kipling knows that when the sea overhangs the sides of a sinking ship it is like a thread of silver, or a taut banjo string, which might remain there for centuries. He knows that when shellfire cuts swathes in an army, the empty avenues remind one of those ever-closing perspectives seen in the hopfields from a swiftly passing train. He knows that a wounded soldier falling with his rifle and equipment clatters like a poker falling in the hearth. He knows, or he divines, that in the galleys of the ancients, the sunlight filtered through between the oar and the hole, and fluttered this way and that with the vessel's movements.

True, H. G. Wells maintained, in *Mr Britling Sees It Through*, that English soldiers never spoke as Kipling's did. But Robert Graves counters this by saying that, between 1887 and 1914, all professional soldiers belonged only to one regiment, Kipling's Own, that Anglo-Indians adapted themselves to fit the picture which Kipling had made of them, learning from him that emotional constraint and that sense of imperial brotherhood with which he had endowed them.

Those of us who do not know India believe that Kipling's pictures are truthful, for we too have met soldiers and administrators, and recognize the *Man* when we meet him in a book. And in Kipling we meet him on every page. His skill in bringing people to life is particularly striking when he is depicting times past or future. No writer has a better understanding of the profound identity of human beings, of their passions and reactions, in all ages and all places. The first poem of his first book was already touching on that theme:

> We are very slightly changed
> From the semi-apes who ranged
> India's prehistoric clay.
>
> .   .   .   .   .   .
>
> We shall doubt "the secret hid
> Under Cheops' pyramid"
> Was that the contractor did
> Cheops out of several millions?
>
> .   .   .   .   .   .
>
> Thus, the artless songs I sing
> Do not deal with anything
> New or never said before.
> As it was in the beginning
> Is today official sinning,
> And shall be for evermore.

And he gladly reverted to this idea in *Puck of Pook's Hill*, where he drew Celts, Romans, Saxons and Normans as living men and women, our own kindred in their desires and feelings. Has the human body changed since Caesar's day, and have the passions links with the body changed any more? A little less ferocity there may be, a little more charity, a little more knowledge of the world: but the essence remains the same. Love, ambition, the qualities of leadership, the sufferings of the soldier—these all remain constant. Kipling paints the Romans in the days of their occupation of Britain as like the British soldiers in India. It is not anachronism (his artistry is too sensitive for that), it is a perfect transposition.

When the English children ask the centurion to tell them about his family, he replies: "Mother would sit spinning of evenings while Aglaia read in her corner, and Father did accounts, and we four romped about the passages. When our noise grew too loud the Pater would say, 'Less tumult! Less tumult! Have you never heard of a Father's right over his children? He can slay them, my loves—slay them dead, and the Gods highly approve of the action!' Then Mother would prim up her dear mouth over the wheel and answer: 'H'm! I'm afraid there can't be much of the Roman Father about you!' Then Father would roll up his accounts and say, 'I'll show you!' and then—then, he'd be worse than any of us!"

Above all, Kipling was able to realize that the technical necessities of certain callings remain for ever unaltered. Whether a non-commissioned officer has to handle men armed with javelins or men armed with machine-guns, there is an art of doing so which does not change: as *A Centurion of the Thirtieth* shows. Whether a sailor is bringing General Gordon or the apostle Paul from Africa to Europe, there is an art of sailing the Mediterranean which does not change: as *A Naval Mutiny* shows. A proconsul may be ruling a Roman province, or a Governor a British colony, but there is an art of organization which does not change: as *The Church that Was at Antioch* shows. Kipling, in fact, is one of those rare novelists who have realized that, in order to recreate the past, it does not suffice to read the documents, to heighten description with authentic objects, dead matter: it is in ourselves that the past lives. One recalls how Chesterton asked once why it was said that there were no Roman monuments in England, and answered, "We are all Roman monuments!"

By his power of suggesting truthful detail, Kipling succeeds in giving us a firm footing in the past, or in lands unknown to us. His air of assurance, his competence, the masterful tone of his narrative, all inspire us with confidence. His style of story-telling is very different from that of the great French masters. It was bound to be. A writer who has exalted the qualities of silence and self-restraint cannot put leisurely or complacent narratives in the mouths of his heroes. In Kipling the story is chopped small; it seems almost to be torn out of those who know it. Frequently he brings us to listen to a conversation in which there is talk of the story he wants to tell us, and which he assumes to be known. Nothing is explained; the characters allude to events without narrating them. Sudden flashes show us an aspect of the matter in hand, and then we are back in a tunnel. When we see the characters again, their attitude has changed, and Kipling leaves it to us to fill up the intervening spaces. Sometimes he even pretends to be ignorant of part of the story, and so heightens its credibility. A symbol takes the place of an explanation. Here, for instance, is a girl who does not want to marry a certain high official; she does not say so, but at the archery contest for which this powerful functionary has offered a diamond bracelet as prize, she deliberately shoots wide of the target, refusing bracelet and husband at the same time. The form is cunning, as it avoids flatness, preserves something of the mysterious slurring of actual life, and brings the reader himself into the course of the action. In all of his stories Kipling conveys a sense of knowing more about it than he chooses to tell. Every moment it looks as if a new episode were about to be hooked on to the main story. In his early stories he was constantly falling back on the device of saying that such-and-such was another story, to be told some other time.

Kipling's poetry would require a separate study. Some English critics maintain that Kipling is a great prose-writer but not a great poet. His poetry, ·certainly, is of a strangely rhythmic kind, popular in character and appeal, like Byron's poetry, and fashion in England looks askance at both. The celestial purity of Shelley and Keats has set the English stubbornly against other styles of poetry, which nevertheless have a beauty of their own.

An acute description of the feelings, in this connexion, of one Englishman of very sensitive taste, is to be found in Aldous Huxley's remarks about Byron and Poe in his essay on *Vulgarity in Literature*: "Poetry ought to be musical, but musical with tact, subtly and variously. Metres whose rhythms . . . are strong, insistent and practically invariable offer the poet a kind of short cut to musicality. They provide him . . . with a ready-made, reach-me-down music. He does not have to create a music appropriately modulated to his meaning; all he has to do is to shovel the meaning into the moving stream of the metre and allow the current to carry it along on waves that, like those of the best hairdressers, are guaranteed permanent."

The criticism would be just if it were not for the fact that in certain poets, such as Victor Hugo, Byron, or Rudyard Kipling, the alliance of emphatic rhythm with the content were not absolutely spontaneous. In Kipling the need for rhythm is so powerful and so primitive that sometimes he writes whole lines which are nothing but rhythmic beating, metrical onomatopœia, savage songs without articulate words. In his verse, as in folk song, the refrain rises spontaneously into life, and as in Hugo, the sense adapts itself to the rhythm with no visible effort. But perhaps there are Kipling's "better" poems, just as some of Chopin's nocturnes are lovelier than others, or certain symphonies of Beethoven grander than the rest. These the English reader knows by heart, and the result is that he judges as commonplace things which are merely too familiar.

VIII

THE POET OF EMPIRE

WE CAN now discern how much truth and how much falsity lie in the classic text-book definition of

Rudyard Kipling as "the poet of the British Empire." It is a narrow definition, which diminishes the true stature of this creature of myths and poet of a heroic conception of life. But the label is acceptable, inasmuch as Kipling has discovered in the qualities of his race an approximation of the eternal qualities which he requires in man.

Kipling has sometimes told his country harsh truths, but for a certain type of Englishman he has a manifest fondness. He has often taken pleasure in depicting him as silent, and as a man who dams up his deepest feelings, but terrible when the measure is filled to the brim. It is a theme to which he reverts whenever England passes through a grave crisis:

> It was not part of their blood,
> It came to them very late
> With long arrears to make good,
> When the English began to hate.
>
> Their voices were even and low,
> Their eyes were level and straight.
> There was neither sign nor show,
> When the English began to hate.

He is very proud of the English schools, admiring them for their ability to mould the men whom he likes: "Ten years at an English public school," he wrote in *The Brushwood Boy*, "do not encourage dreaming. Georgie won his growth and chest measurement, and a few other things which did not appear in the bills, under a system of cricket, football, and paper-chases, from four to five days a week, which provided for three lawful cuts of a ground-ash if any boy absented himself from these entertainments. He became a rumple-collared, dusty-hatted fag of the Lower Third, and a light half-back at Little Side football; was pushed and prodded through the slack back-waters of the Lower Fourth, where the raffle of a school generally accumulates; won his 'second fifteen' cap at football, enjoyed the dignity of a study with two companions in it, and began to look forward to office as a sub-prefect. At last he blossomed into full glory as head of the school, ex-officio captain of the games; head of his house, where he and his lieutenants preserved discipline and decency among seventy boys from twelve to seventeen; general arbiter in the quarrels that spring up among the touchy Sixty—and intimate friend and ally of the Head himself. . . . Above all, he was responsible for that thing called the tone of the school, and few realize with what passionate devotion a certain type of boy throws himself into this work. . . . Behind him, but not too near, was the wise and temperate Head, now suggesting the wisdom of the serpent, now counselling the mildness of the dove; leading him on to see, more by half-hints than by any direct word, how boys and men are all of a piece, and how he who can handle the one will assuredly in time control the other.

"For the rest, the school was not encouraged to dwell on its emotions, but rather to keep in hard condition, to avoid false quantities, and to enter the army direct, without the help of the expensive London crammer, under whose roof young blood learns too much."

It has pleased him to discover throughout the whole Empire traces of these English virtues. Long before broadcasting made it possible for such a gigantic dialogue to become an audible reality, he made Calcutta talk with Quebec in his verses, and Newfoundland with New Zealand. And England's reply to her sons and daughters was essentially Kiplingesque. England gave the Dominions their liberty, those children who were flesh of her flesh, bone of her bone:

The law that ye make shall be law and I do not press
    my will,
Because ye are sons of The Blood and call me Mother
    still.
Now must ye speak to your kinsmen and they must
    speak to you,
After the use of the English, in straight-flung words and
    few.
Go to your work and be strong, halting not in your
    ways,
Baulking the end half-won for an instant dole of praise.
Stand to your work and be wise—certain of sword and
    pen,
Who are neither children nor Gods, but men in a world
    of men!

Did he really find these virtues in the British Empire, or did he imagine them as being there? Here, certainly, there are very complex "actions and reactions." The Kipling spirit—that is to say, respect for the law, the sense of Empire, the desire for a heroic

Society—existed in England and long before Kipling. The "team spirit," self-effacement, the genius of obedience, have long been inculcated by the great public schools. Puritanism and sport have both contributed to the composition of this character; life at sea and in the colonies has also helped to shape it. In these last years of the nineteenth century Kipling could find many contemporary Englishmen who approached his ideal. From some of these, indeed, he doubtless formed that ideal. But it is no less true that he gave these men, as a class, more confidence in themselves, and that by painting them rather larger than life, he brought into existence imitators who sometimes even surpassed them. The moral influence of Kipling on a certain type of Englishman has been great, and we have already observed that the whole of the Boy Scout movement, a social phenomenon of high significance, is indebted to Kipling for a great part of its laws and strength.

But once again, it is the heroic society, not the British Empire, which counts for most in Kipling's work. If he discerns in other countries the qualities which he most admires, he is quick and eager to recognize them. And in particular, let it be said, he has written admirably about the virtues of France and the French.

IX

CONCLUSION

A BORN writer of books, reared by "the Famous Men" in a respect for the life that is not in books, finds himself at an early age, in India, in close touch with the life of men of action and the life of the native races. From these contacts he draws not only the subject-matter of stories which illustrate a Western philosophy of action, but also a truly Oriental sense of the marvellous. Thanks to him, the imagination of men bereft of the miracles of the East has been enabled suddenly to plunge into very deep layers of ancestral memory. Scratching at the surface of mere talk, he has been able to rediscover, underneath the man of the machine age, the man of the Bible and of Homer, underneath the subaltern of Gurkhas, the centurion of the legions. This doctrine has resulted in giving the British Empire "a mystico-literary justification." This is a historic fact, but an ephemeral accident: his enduring qualities are more deeply rooted. The things which he has described and sung are the eternal virtues which give a man the faculty of leadership and give a race the power of survival—

As it was in the beginning,
And shall be for ever more!

II

H. G. WELLS

H. G. Wells

THE prophet's trade is one which cannot be carried on at all times or in all places. Periods of stability and confidence have never needed prophets. In such times, writers are content to depict their own century and strive for perfection of form. But when human affairs tend towards disorder and anarchy, society turns to its artists and men of learning for the picture of a better world. To the chaotic, helter-skelter world of post-war years, H. G. Wells has been a psychiatrist as well as a novelist.

It will be our task to see whether the remedies he proposes are really suitable for the healing of our civilization, and whether his solutions solved the problems. Whether the answer is yes or no, one fact is certain: that these solutions have persuaded hosts of readers, and that Wells, in part of Europe and in the United States, will for some years have wielded an intellectual dominion comparable to that won and held by Voltaire in the eighteenth century. He has visited Franklin Roosevelt and Stalin; he has discussed affairs with the heads of states as with equals; he has often admonished the League of Nations. He himself, of course, was sternly admonished by the younger generation. But for the past decade and more, Wells has been a public institution. He expounds his mission and his ideas in an almost religious tone. He is serious, and is taken seriously. Does he really offer a coherent body of thought? Let us consider the prophet before we examine the prophecies.

I

THE MAKING OF H. G. WELLS

THE outline of Wells's life is fairly well known. There is an excellent narrative of his early life by Geoffrey West, and he himself has given us, in his lifetime, an autobiography which, in its first part at least, seems so frank that Rousseau's *Confessions* look cautious and maidenly in comparison. Perhaps it is only a semblance of truth; perhaps the sum total of the truth about a man is so complex and so incredible that it can never be told. Sometimes Wells interrupts his narrative to confess a distortion: "I realize how difficult an autobiography that is not an apology for a life but a research into its nature, can become, as I deal with this business of my divorce. . . . I have shown a disposition to simplify out the issue. . . . That makes a fairly acceptable story of it, with only one fault, that it is untrue. It is all the more untrue because like a bad portrait there is superficial truth in it." Whereupon he tries very hard to grasp the reality more firmly, but like many men of our time he feels that the idea of personality is confused. He

[60]

distinguishes between the "real person"; the *persona*, or the being that each of us imagines himself to be; and "the character," the being that other men see in us. The author of an autobiography describes the *persona*; the biographer examines "the character"; as for the "real person," nobody catches hold of this, and its nature is very vaguely apprehended. Whether Wells's autobiography gives us the ultimate truth, or, as Mauriac would say, the penultimate, material in plenty is provided by Wells for a future biographer. Let us try to pick out at least the most important strands.

Firstly: Wells is a man of the people, and he tells us about his difficult childhood simply and with dignity. His mother was a maid in a large country-house, where she later became housekeeper. She seems to have been a gentle little woman, religious, and respectful towards the established order. With her silk gowns and bonnets she did her best, in her later years, to resemble Queen Victoria. She had married the gardener on a neighbouring estate, Joseph Wells, a good cricket-player. He was a man very different from herself, who caused her a good deal of distress. The couple bought a small china shop at Bromley, in Kent; but Joseph Wells, whose tastes were those of a gardener, a naturalist, and a sports-man, did not take kindly to trade, and his customers consisted almost entirely of his cricketing friends. As a growing boy, Wells was later to appreciate the intelligence of his father, who had the same blue eyes as his son, and a mind of indefatigable freshness.

Sarah Wells longed above all things to make her son a respectable citizen. "What a pity," she would say to him, "that your father is not a gentleman!" It was her dream that he should become a salesman in a drapery shop, and into this calling, after a very summary schooling, she launched him. Wells has described the agonies of his early days in a provincial shop. "For a wretched couple of years in my boyhood I slept in one of those abominable dormitories, ate the insufficient food supplied and drudged in the shop. Then when I was fifteen I ran away one Sunday morning to my mother, and told her I would rather die than go on being a draper. That seventeen miles tramp, without breakfast, to deliver that ultimatum is still very vivid in my memory. I felt then most desperately wicked, and now I know it was nearly the best thing I ever did."

But this harsh boyhood left no bitterness in Wells, and when he portrayed it later in his novels, he did so with humour. To those years he owed a deep understanding of the working classes, and the advantage of having for a long time watched the upper classes from the outside. In the servants' hall of Up park, in Sussex, where as a boy he often sat in the evenings with his mother, the butler kept a list of the grammatical mistakes and historical inaccuracies perpetrated by those upon whom he waited at table. Wells, like this butler-grammarian, was soon making notes of the weaknesses of some of those who are the world's rulers. This country-house itself became a symbol to him: "Now the unavoidable suggestion of that wide park and that fair large house, dominating church, village and country-side, was that they represented the thing that mattered supremely in the world, and that all other things had significance only in relation to them. They represented the Gentry, the Quality, by and through and for whom the rest of the world, the farming folk and the labouring folk, the tradespeople . . . and the servants of the estate, breathed and lived and were permitted. . . . It was only when I was a boy of thirteen or fourteen that . . . I began to question the final rightness of the gentlefolk, their primary necessity in the scheme of things."

Society, it seemed to him, was badly fashioned. But his views of it were not that of a rebel, eager to destroy it all. From the first he had a sense of the comic which purged him of hatred. His feelings when he first came into touch with the ruling class were never those of a Julien Sorel; he did not find its members detestable; he thought them ridiculous, and he laughed chiefly at himself and his boyish efforts to resemble these people.

Secondly: the boy's natural bent was towards the sciences. When he was seven years old, a broken leg kept him laid up, and gave him the opportunity and the time to read. It often happens that in men's lives a mishap causes a rebound. "Probably I am alive today and writing this autobiography instead of being a worn-out, dismissed and already dead shop assistant, because my leg was broken." The reading habit was never lost by the young Wells, and the circle of his interests widened rapidly. In the days when he was employed in a store, an outraged overseer found him hidden in a cellar, writing rudimentary answers to such questions as, "What is matter? What is space?" Thanks to a schoolmaster who recognized his exceptional understanding, the youthful Wells, on leaving his shopkeeping, at once became an assistant master in a country grammar school.

Wells was then seventeen. While teaching, he prepared for his own examinations, applied for a pupil-teacher's bursary at the South Kensington College of Science, and one day received a magnificent blue document from the Board of Education informing him that he could henceforth live in London and would receive one guinea a week for attending lectures. Amongst the teachers at South Kensington, which he was about to enter, was the great Professor Huxley, the friend of Darwin, whose teaching was not only technical instruction but a discipline of the mind. "The study of zoology in this phase was an acute, delicate, rigorous and sweepingly magnificent series of exercises. It was a grammar of form and a criticism of fact. That year I spent in Huxley's class was, beyond all question, the most educational year of my life. It left me under that urgency for coherence and consistency, that repugnance from haphazard assumptions and arbitrary statements, which is

the essential distinction of the educated from the un-
educated mind."

At South Kensington Wells mixed with young
students of both sexes, very different beings from
any he had hitherto known. A great ferment was
taking place in his mind, one product of which was
an ill-written but ingenious essay, in which Wells
showed that it is only for convenience of expression
that we describe individuals as belonging to classes.
Actually, every individual and every phenomenon is
unique. It is only from the point of view of numeri-
cal law, and what might be termed statistical equilibrium, that an atom resembles an atom or a mammal
a mammal. The idea is sound, and thirty years later
it was to be followed up by the most eminent
physicists.

After leaving South Kensington, Wells was for
some time a teacher of natural science, and then suddenly began to spit blood. It was clear that he was
threatened by tuberculosis. A tubercular patient cannot teach. For a year or two he lived precariously,
just keeping himself afloat by journalism; and he had
hardly recovered from his illness when he put himself in even worse straits by marrying a cousin who
had been his love since boyhood.

About his sentimental life (at least in the earlier
years), Wells has spoken in his autobiography with
balanced objectivity, and something should here be
said about it as throwing light on some of the author's theories. His first marriage, a marriage of love,
was a failure. Wells had very little in common with

[65]

his first wife. "In my eagerness to find in her the mate of my imaginings, I quite overlooked the fact that while I had been reading and learning voraciously since the age of seven, she had never broken a leg and so had never been inoculated with the germ of reading. While I had gone to school precociously equipped, she had begun just the other way about as a backward girl, and she had never recovered from that disadvantage. It was a purely accidental difference to begin with, I am sure her brain was inherently as good or better than mine, but an unalterable difference in range and content was now established. Her world was like an interior by a Dutch master and mine was a loose headlong panorama of all history, science and literature. She tried valiantly to hang on to what I was saying, but the gap was too wide."

Meanwhile, in the course of his scientific work, Wells had met a young woman student who had become a friend and comrade to him. Here was the only woman with whom he wanted to share his life. At the time he was full of Shelley and believed in "free love." He left his wife. Before long he discovered, as have so many before him, that "free love" means too great a burden of difficulties for the woman, and after a divorce he married Catherine Robbins.

This second marriage was not altogether a success, judged by that blend of bodily and spiritual harmony which is the dream of all young people in the days of betrothal. But Wells was united to a woman whom he always held in the highest esteem, and if he did not attain to the perfect, superhuman harmony of his dreams, he found a conjugal compromise which ensured the duration of the marriage in spite of rather serious difficulties. "Having discovered that our private dreams of some hidden splendour of loving were evaporating, we were nevertheless under both an inner and an outer obligation to stand by one another and pull our adventure through. We refrained from premature discussion and felt our way over our situation with tentative and careful understatements. . . . She, even less than I, had that terrible fluidity of speech that can swamp any situation in garrulous justification and headlong ultimatums. And our extraordinary isolation, too, helped us to discover a *modus vivendi*. Neither of us had any confidants to complicate our relations by some potent divergent suggestion, and there was no background of unsympathetic values that either of us respected. Neither of us bothered in the least about what so and so would think. In many matters we were odd and exceptional individuals but in our broad relations to each other and society we may have come much nearer to being absolute and uncomplicated simple man and woman, than do most young couples. The research for a *modus vivendi* is a necessary phase of the normal married life today."

Thirdly, and consequently: Wells, who from boyhood had been shocked by the disorder of the social structure, is no less outraged, when once he has emerged from the first sentimental illusions, by the confusion in the relations of the sexes. As a young man he had followed Shelley in denying the necessity of marriage: "I had not the slightest wish for household or offspring at that time; my ambition was all for unencumbered study and free movement in pursuit of my own ends, and my mind had not the slightest fixation upon any particular individual or type of individual. I was entirely out of accord with the sentimental patterns and focussed devotions adopted by most people about me. In the free lives and free loves of the guardians of the *Republic* I found the encouragement I needed to give my wishes a systematic form. Presently I discovered a fresh support for these tentative projects in Shelley. Regardless of every visible reality about me, of law, custom, social usage, economic necessities and the unexplored psychology of womanhood, I developed my adolescent fantasy of free, ambitious, self-reliant women who would mate with me and go their way, as I desired to go my way. I had never in fact seen or heard of any such women; I had evolved them from my inner consciousness." And, as often happens, Wells was throughout his life to continue the search, in artistic creation, for this imagined woman, male in mind and female in body. Most of the heroines in his novels belong to this delectable, but alas unreal, class of intellectual Valkyries.

Fourthly: we must look at Wells as the political reformer. It is quite natural that a young teacher, struck by the chaotic state of society and believing

strongly in scientific intelligence, should be tempted
to dabble in politics. But from 1895 until 1902 Wells
was no more than a novelist, and very quickly a
famous novelist. He made his onslaught on the British
public by successive waves of books. The first consisted of scientific romances, such as *The Time Machine*, *The Island of Dr Moreau*, *The Invisible Man*,
and several others. But just when the critics were
beginning to label H. G. Wells as the ingenious and
prolific inventor of a new world of fantasy, he
launched his second wave: novels of humorous autobiography, in which he sketched his own beginnings
as a shop-assistant or teacher, and his early loves, all
in amusing and ironic style. This is the group of realistic novels which includes *Kipps*, *Love and Mr
Lewisham*, and *The History of Mr Polly*. The third
wave followed: novels of ideas, in which universal
reform is blended with the utopia of the senses: *The
New Machiavelli*, *Marriage*, *The Research Magnificent*, *The Passionate Friend*, and others. And
alongside there came books of doctrine such as *Anticipations* or *A Modern Utopia*. By the outbreak of
war in 1914, the celebrity of Wells, based on this
vast and various output of books, was more or less
equal to that of Kipling or Shaw.

The publication of *Anticipations* had brought him
into touch with a number of Liberal or Socialist reformers, particularly with Sydney and Beatrice
Webb, who formed the centre of the Fabian movement. In the Fabian Society, which fostered a non-
revolutionary Socialism, Wells met not only the

Webbs, but Bonar Law, Ramsay MacDonald, and others destined to be ministers of the Crown in Labour governments. He addressed meetings of the Society on several occasions, but very soon it was unmistakably clear that Wells and the Socialist movement had not many ideas in common.

The Socialist party regarded itself as representing a class, and a class which must take over power against other classes and other parties. But the young Wells was really concerned with the organization of all classes and all parties—soon he would be saying all countries—in a struggle against confusion and stupidity. He really did not hate that ruling class which he had so quizzically observed from the servants' hall where his mother worked; indeed, he believed that, with all their ridiculous qualities, they had remarkable virtues which could be used to great advantage in a plan of general organization. All his interests were fixed on scientific order and sound organization, and he hated the doctrine of the class war as something not only futile but dangerous.

He read a critical paper to the Fabian Society in which he pointed out the errors of their ways. It was a spirited performance, calculated to prick and prod his listeners into activity. He showed his resentment at the Society's family jokes, at its manner of aping and copying Shaw, and accused it of failing in all its duties, especially its propagandist duties. It was too small, too poor, too slow. To rouse it from its sleep he put forward proposals which were rejected, after a speech by Shaw, a better orator than Wells, who was left stricken on the field. In the end Wells left the Society. He had always wanted the Fabian Society to be something different from what it wished to be itself.

What Wells aimed at was not Socialism, but a universal Republic adapted to the totally new needs and conditions of mechanical and scientific civilization. This Wellsian Republic would not be an equalitarian democracy, but a state ruled by an aristocracy of intelligence. "I have never believed," he has said, "in the superiority of the inferior. . . . If I was in almost unconcealed revolt against my mother's deferential attitude to royalty and our social superiors, it was because my resentful heart claimed at least an initial equality with every human being; but it was equality of position and opportunity I was after, and not equality of respect or reward; I certainly had no disposition to sacrifice my conceit of being made of better stuff, intrinsically and inherently, than most other human beings, by any self-identification with people who frankly took the defeated attitude. I thought the top of the form better than the bottom of the form, and the boy who qualified better than the boy who failed to qualify . . . my biographical duty is to record that so it was with me. So far as the masses went I was entirely of my mother's way of thinking; I was middle-class,—'petty bourgeois,' as the Marxists have it."

Wells did not desire power for the masses; he wanted to see a government of samurai, or as Gobineau said, of "the sons of kings." In fact, that troubled lower-class childhood had formed, not a destroyer but a builder. Wells has spoken of his career as an advance from a backyard to cosmopolis. As he grew older, he reflected more, and became ever more convinced of the possibility of liberating man through science and organization; and he became more persuaded, too, that he, with a few others of his own kind, had a personal responsibility for the bringing of this new world into being.

The War was to prove a disconcerting ordeal to a writer who hated cruelty, disorder and waste. The sight of miserable humanity devoting so much bravery and science to self-destruction, when so much fruitful work was left undone, hurt Wells's mind to the quick. At the start he was content to "serve" as a journalist. He accepted the idea of this being "a war to end war," and believed that in this thunder of artillery the quest of world-peace was beginning. A sword drawn from its sheath, he claimed, was a sword drawn in the name of peace. In a war of this sort, nobody could wish to be a non-combatant. And in the pages of *Mr Britling Sees It Through*, Wells gave an excellent picture of the lives and thoughts of most intelligent Englishmen during 1914 and 1915. When he saw victory dawning, he hoped that now, at long last, the world could and would be refashioned: unless the next ten years proved pitiful and disastrous, he declared, they would be the greatest years in history.

Pitiful and disastrous they were. After a first flush of enthusiasm for the League of Nations, in which he imagined that he saw a draft plan of his new Republic and an organized world, Wells turned his back on it and slammed the door behind him, as formerly with the Fabian Society. Just as he had wished to entrust the ruling of the world to an aristocracy, so he would have liked to see the government of the World State in the hands of an aristocracy of nations. After 1920 he regarded the League of Nations as an obstacle to the world's peace, a diplomatic expedient to shelve all constructive proposals. (Now, in 1935, he must surely be changing his view on this point.)

Then Moscow, like Geneva, turned bitter in his mouth. There too, at first, he had hoped to see totally new men creating a world in accordance with his ideal. He saw Lenin, but after a conversation with Wells (if we are to believe Trotsky) Lenin vehemently exclaimed: "What a bourgeois! What a philistine!" Later, his visit to Stalin confirmed the lack of understanding between Wells and the new Russia. How could Wells hope to agree with a Marxist when he himself maintained that the doctrine which claims that the proletariat (or its representatives) are always right, is a doctrine opposed to any disciplined co-operation between the different types of intelligence needed by the nation? Wells attacked Stalin by criticizing the "old-fashioned" propaganda for class war, and the clumsy vocabulary which lumps together as "bourgeoisie" all sorts of types completely different from each other. Stalin replied with the classic formulas about the proletarian masses. The said proletariat, Wells declared, was nothing more than the old "sovereign people" beloved of democracies. The conversation was a stalemate for both parties.

But why, why was it impossible, then, to realize this dream of an organized planet, which to Wells had always seemed so reasonable? After the War he turned with frantic energy to the task of understanding this, and became as it were a new Encyclopaedist. He must first study the past, and he wrote his monumental *Outline of History*. He then proposed to compile a *Summa* of the present state of biological knowledge, and, with his son and Julian Huxley, he produced *Science of Life*. Finally he set out to examine the machinery of labour and commerce, and wrote a stout volume of political economy, *The Work, Wealth and Happiness of Mankind*.

These Wellsian encyclopaedias are intelligent, important books, on a large scale. One essential idea emerges from them, the conception of a world to be constructed according to a plan. "The truth remains," he wrote in his autobiography, "that today nothing stands in the way to the attainment of universal freedom and abundance but mental tangles, egocentric preoccupations, obsessions, misconceived phrases, bad habits of thought, subconscious fears and dreads and plain dishonesty in people's minds—and especially in the minds of those in key positions. That universal freedom and abundance dangles within reach of us and is not achieved, and we who are Citizens of the Future wander about this present scene like passengers on a ship overdue, in plain sight of a port which only some disorder in the chart-room prevents us from entering. Though most of the people in the world in key positions are more or less accessible to me, I lack the solvent power to bring them into unison. I can talk to them and even unsettle them but I cannot compel their brains to see."

In his dejection he wrote a new "anticipation," reverting in a way to his youthful longing to create new worlds. It was called *The Shape of Things to Come*, a history of the next two hundred years as it might be told in the school text-books which our great-grandchildren will be given in the year 2135.

Wells foretells a great war in the air, followed by a universal plague. The result of these twin calamities is to empty the cities, which become too dangerous. Humanity, about 1960, is living in small groups in the country. Means of transport and civilization gradually disappear. No more telephones, no more telegraphy. Wells quotes from the diary of a young man, Titus Cobbett, who traverses the South of France on a bicycle towards the end of the twentieth century. He finds the hotels in ruins, the roads broken up by trees. The only surviving cells of civilization are the aviation camps. And it is round these groups of technicians, pilots and chemists that the new society forms itself again, about the year 2160, a piece of perfect organization, that of the World State directed by "men like gods."

The whole of Wells's work since the War has been "a manual of deification." The axis of the system is his idea that mankind, with the means now at its disposal, can refashion the world, or, as Comte would have said, that the age of positive sociology has arrived. Wells thinks that the whole body of men capable of creating the World State, the intellectual aristocracy, should unite in an "Open Conspiracy," whose purpose would be to substitute intelligence for stupidity and the scientific spirit for collective passions in the conduct of human affairs. This doctrine we shall discuss later. Here, in concluding this brief survey of Wells's life, we must admire its consistency of direction, and the closeness of the bond between his doctrine, his novel-writing, and his life as a man.

II

THE IMAGINED UTOPIA

WELLS compares his own life to a musical fugue, with two interweaving themes. The primary theme is the steady growth of a brain, the adjustment of a mind. It is not only "from backyard to cosmopolis," it is from shop-assistant to prophet, from the haberdashery to the World Republic. "More and more consciously the individual adventurer, as he disentangles himself from the family associations in which he was engendered, is displayed trying to make himself a citizen of the world." The secondary theme may be stated thus: that the difficulty of solving the problem of the relations between the two sexes, especially in early life, is for most men a dangerous obstacle to happiness. The quest for a solution of the

sentimental problem should accompany, or even pre-
cede, that for a solution of the social one.

On these two themes Wells proceeds to build up
his work. Being dissatisfied with the world as it is,
he is tempted, as a very young man, to reconstruct it.
Men have always tried to imagine worlds which allow them to dream the things that are beyond their
powers in the existing world. In every epoch, the
marvellous takes on forms which are compatible with
the beliefs of the time. The Greeks had their gods,
their muses and nymphs, the Celts had their sorcerers and fairies, the Teutons their Nibelungs and
Valhalla. To a youth reared as Wells had been, and
subjected to the disciplines of science, the natural
mode of release would be in the form of imaginary
discoveries. The marvels of science can play the same
part as the marvels of fairy-tales. It makes reality of a
dream. But contemporary minds, reacting against the
fanciful, submit more readily to his suggestive power
because he takes into account their habits of mind.

Wells was particularly well equipped to create a
wonder-world for modern times. He combined two
qualities not often found together: on the one hand
extensive scientific knowledge, on the other, a dissatisfaction with the disorder of the world around
him which perpetually stimulated his imagination.
How did he come to be an inventor of futures? As
a child, he recalls, speculation about the future
seemed to him a joke in doubtful taste. He had started
life with ideas not unlike those once prevalent regarding the millennium. The world as we see it would

last for a certain time, and then, sooner or later, there would be trumpets and loud cries and celestial phenomena and the Last Judgement.

But his studies at South Kensington changed all this. He was left wondering what would happen to mankind if evolution continued. He first wrote a theoretical essay on what man would be like in the year 1000000. Shortly afterwards, when a magazine asked him for a long story, he had the idea of adapting this essay, which thus became *The Time Machine*, published in 1895. The "time machine" itself is rather vaguely described. The scientist in question is not concerned to be scientific in details. His interest is prophetic: what sort of society will his hero find in the year 802701, in the twilight of mankind?

In 802701 men have become so completely adjusted to their environment that the struggle for life has ended. Men are divided into two classes: the Eloi or "upper-worlders," and the Morlocks or "undergrounders." The Eloi are attractive little creatures, graceful and charming, with curly hair and large gentle eyes. They know nothing of pain and live on the surface of the earth. "You who have never seen the like can scarcely imagine what delicate and wonderful flowers countless years of culture had created." The Morlocks, a race of bestial habits, live underground, working endlessly, and have something inhuman and evil in them. The "time traveller" soon discovers that the Morlocks provide sustenance for the Eloi, but they do so rather as a sportsman feeds his pheasants, for every now and then they emerge

from their subterranean homes to carry off and de-
vour a certain number of Eloi. The traveller realizes
that the Eloi are the descendants of the rich, and
the Morlocks of the workers. "The Eloi, like the
Carlovingian kings, had decayed to a mere beautiful
futility. They still possessed the earth on sufferance:
since the Morlocks, subterranean for innumerable
generations, had come at last to find the daylit surface intolerable." In short, *The Time Machine* is a
parable or apologue, in the form of a projection into
the future.

The success of this book, and also his enjoyment
in writing it, led Wells to exploit this vein methodically for several years. He had only to let his mind
play on a theme, to find himself quickly in a position
to view mysterious and distant worlds, ruled by a
logical order, but different from one's ordinary conceptions. *The Wonderful Visit* grew out of a
remark by Ruskin to the effect that if an angel appeared on earth, it would certainly be shot by somebody. In Wells's book the angel, brought down by
the gun of a country vicar, lives among mortal men,
experiencing a degree of amazement at our manners
and morals which resembles that of Wells himself.

The Island of Dr Moreau is based on a surgical
conjecture of Wells, and on the idea that humanity
is merely the adaptation of the animal towards a
reasonable form. A great surgeon, Dr Moreau, has
discovered how to accelerate the process of evolution, and can make a man out of a beast within a
few days. He has accordingly treated pigs, bulls and

dogs, and given them some measure of human appear‹ ance and intelligence. But he can keep them up to this level only by constant discipline and by forcing them continually to repeat the Law. The symbolism is plain. We too are simply animals recently transformed into human beings. Pig and monkey and bull remain alive inside countless beings of human appearance, and only by making them recite the Law does society hold them in subjection. Here, for a moment, the pessimism of Kipling and the optimism of Wells touch hands.

The Invisible Man is at once a realistic story, and a tract on the danger of omnipotence in the hands of a man bereft of the brakes of morality. *The Invisible Man* marks a definite advance in Wells's technique: in *The Island of Dr Moreau* and *The Time Machine* the scientific aspect of the experiment was ill-defined, but here an effort is made to show us how the invisible man is at least conceivable.

The War of the Worlds is the story of the invasion of the earth by the inhabitants of Mars. *The Food of the Gods* has also a symbolic significance. Here a scientist invents a method of turning men into giants by giving them a particular food. But these creatures, who are stronger and more handsome than other men and should be welcomed with enthusiasm, are, on the contrary, rebuffed by everyone, even by their own families. It is an image of the world's treatment of the samurai and the prophetic mind. The world rejects man made perfect, even as it rejected the angel. This book, Wells says, "began with a wild burlesque of the change of scale produced by scientific men and ended in the heroic struggle of the rare new big-scale way of living against the teeming small-scale life of the earth. Nobody saw the significance of it, but it left some of its readers faintly puzzled. They were vastly amused and thrilled by my giant wasps and rats, but young Caddles was beyond them."

This element of symbolism makes it quite misleading to compare these early novels of Wells, as has often been done, with Jules Verne's romances. Jules Verne sought to prove nothing, whereas in Wells the marvellous is always utopian and satiric in essence, and there is always a moral intention. *The Time Machine*, we are told, suggests the responsibility of man towards humanity; *The Wonderful Visit*, the restricted horizon of most men's outlook, in contrast to that of a being free from all the normal constraints of humanity; *The Island of Dr Moreau* showed the bestial side of man's existence; *The Invisible Man*, the danger of power uncontrolled by moral sense; *The War of the Worlds*, the danger of intelligence being developed at the expense of sympathy.

Finally, Wells summed up all his ideas regarding the future, in a more didactic form, in a book entitled *Anticipations of the Reaction of Mechanical and Scientific Progress upon Human Life and Thought*. It is a remarkable book, for it appeared in 1901, and contains many forecasts of the world's future which have been justified by fact. When it appeared, an

English critic declared that it was the duty of the British Government to subsidize Mr Wells so that he could continue to prophesy, and that there should be a Prophet Laureate as well as a Poet Laureate.

And indeed if we turn the pages of *Anticipations*, we may observe that, in those days when motor-cars were grinding along at twenty miles per hour, with little certainty of reaching their destination, Wells was prognosticating the motor-truck for heavy transport, the struggle between this vehicle and the railway, and the probable victory of the motor. Furthermore: "parallel with the motor-truck, there will develop the hired or privately owned motor-carriage. . . . It will be capable of a day's journey of three hundred miles or more. . . . One will change nothing—unless it is the driver—from stage to stage. One will be free to dine where one chooses, hurry when one chooses, travel asleep or awake. . . ."

He foresaw the motor-train, and the motor-road: "The motor omnibus companies competing against the suburban railways will find themselves hampered in the speed of their longer runs by the slower horse traffic on their routes, and they will attempt to secure, and, it may be, after tough legislative struggles, will secure the power to form private roads of a new sort, upon which their vehicles will be free to travel up to the limit of their very highest possible speed. . . . It has been assumed, perhaps rashly, that the railway influence will certainly remain jealous and hostile to these growths. Assuredly there will be fights of a very complicated sort at first, but once one of these specialized lines is in operation, it may be that some at least of the railway companies will hasten to replace their flanged rolling stock by carriages with rubber tyres . . . and take to the new ways of traffic."

Finally, the chapter on warfare is one of the most astounding. Wells imagined the part to be played by the aeroplane, which at that date had not even flown: "I am inclined to think that the many considerations against a successful attack on balloons from the ground, will enormously stimulate enterprise and invention in the direction of dirigible aerial devices that can fight. Few people, I fancy. . . but will be inclined to believe that long before the year 1950, a successful aeroplane will have soared and come home safe and sound. Directly that is accomplished the new invention will be most assuredly applied to war." And he then describes a fight between aeroplanes which would not be laughable in a story of the war of 1914. And further, that in an article on "land cruisers," Wells described military tanks long before their invention, and the title of Prophet Laureate does not seem at all undeserved.

One important reservation, however, must be made. The human mind can sketch ordered forecasts in scientific discovery, and can point out the general trend of intellectual progress; but it cannot foresee the particular facts of history, the most important things of all to be known. So numerous are the possible combinations that our plans and our hopes are both betrayed by time, continually and equally. The future is hardly even an object of thought. But the building of imaginary worlds is a pleasing game. Wells was a master in it, because he played it with precision, a coherent imagination, a knowledge of science, and a characteristically English skill in blending the real with the marvellous. So dexterously did he add increasing measures of fancy to the dough of the novel, that it rose as if it were made of the pure flour of life.

III

THE POLITICAL AND SOCIAL UTOPIA

CONCERNING the art of the novel, Wells engaged in lengthy controversy with his friend Henry James. The older writer maintained that a novel should first and foremost be the portrayal, as truthful and lifelike as possible, of one character or of several. "The important point which I tried to argue with Henry James was that the novel of completely consistent characterization arranged beautifully in a story and painted deep and round and solid, no more exhausts the possibilities of the novel, than the art of Velasquez exhausts the possibilities of the painted picture. Competent critics have since examined this supreme importance of individualities, in other words of 'char-

acter' in the fiction of the nineteenth century and
early twentieth century. . . . With a certain justice these authorities ascribe the predominance of in-
dividuation to the example of Sir Walter Scott. But
more generally it was a consequence of the prevalent
sense of social stability, and he was not so much a primary influence as an exponent."

Accordingly, Wells treats with comparative disregard his humorous and quasi-autobiographical novels,
such as *Kipps*, *The History of Mr Polly*, *Love and
Mr Lewisham*. In these amusing and "truthful"
books, Wells has depicted the social rise of a young
man of working-class origin, and the hero's comical
struggles to mix in a higher class of society which
he soon discovers to be tedious and futile. These delightful books are scarcely mentioned by Wells in
his autobiography. On the other hand, he delights
in citing his "problem novels," in which the characters, with a few exceptions, are scarcely drawn at
all, but where the lengthy monologues of the chief
character enable Wells to express his ideas on politics, progress, or the future. In this category the best
books are *The New Machiavelli*, *Tono-Bungay*, *The
Passionate Friend*, *The Research Magnificent*, *The
World of William Clissold*.

In *Tono-Bungay*, regarded by many English critics
as the best of Wells's novels, the two elements of
ideas and character are combined in approximately
equal proportions. In *The New Machiavelli*, on the
other hand, the ideas are paramount, and for that

reason we may choose this novel as the type for this
class of Wells's books. Here we are given the autobiography of a politician, Remington by name, who
has believed (as Wells did in the early years of his
career) that by an alliance with Liberal or Fabian
semi-Socialists he could reform society. "My political
conceptions were perfectly plain and honest. I had
one constant desire ruling my thoughts. I meant to
leave England and the empire better ordered than
I found it, to organize and discipline, to build up a
constructive and controlling State out of my world's
confusions. We had, I saw, to suffuse education with
public intention, to develop a new better-living generation with a collectivist habit of thought, to link
now chaotic activities in every human affair, and particularly to catch that escaped, world-making, world-
ruining, dangerous thing, industrial and financial enterprise, and bring it back to the service of the general
good."

Quite soon Remington discovers the intellectual
weakness and inadequate courage of his political allies.
His wife Marguerite wants to see him pursuing the
normal career of a rising politician. He drifts apart
from her as he does from the ideas which she represents, and falls in love with an Amazon, Isabel, who
in turn becomes the symbol of the creative spirit.
But in a puritanical country unwedded love stands
condemned. Remington, who might well have been
a great rebuilder of society, finds himself elbowed
out of places of authority and condemned to leave

England with his Amazon. The book closes with a letter which he writes to his lawful wife: "There's this difference that has always been between us, that you like nakedness and wildness, and I, clothing and restraint. It goes through everything. You are always *talking* of order and system, and the splendid dream of the order that might replace the muddled system you hate, but by a sort of instinct you seem to want to break the law. I've watched you so closely. Now, I want to obey laws, to make sacrifices, to follow rules. I don't want to make, but I do want to keep. You are at once makers and rebels, you and Isabel too." And it is indeed as a maker and rebel that Wells likes to picture himself.

The general pattern of most of Wells's "intellectual" novels shows similar lines: the autobiography of a samurai, full of good intentions and eager to rebuild the world; by the side of this hero stands a half-Fabian, half-aristocratic Amazon; there is a war waged by the passionate couple, plebeian man and patrician woman, against the resistances of the world and the stupidity of its ruling class; victory falls to the world and stupidity, but there are vague hopes of better times to come. One of the most human of these novels is perhaps *The Passionate Friends*. But all are so intelligent, and so rich in remarkable discussion of interesting subjects, that we are often tempted to believe that Mr Wells is right, and that, alongside the novel of character, it is possible to write the adventure of a thought. And yet a novel by Stendhal or Balzac, a story by Mérimée or Tchekov, will move us more deeply. It may be that political doctrines are like religious teachings: to move us, they must be made flesh.

IV

THE DOCTRINE OF H. G. WELLS

WHAT goal does Wells propose for us?—The creation of an administrative and scientific paradise by an intellectual aristocracy. He has an almost physical horror of anarchy and violence. Impressed by the progress of science within our lifetime, he would like to see this progress extended to the social sciences. "When I think," he wrote in *The New Machiavelli*, "of the progress of physical and mechanical science, of medicine and sanitation during the last century, when I measure the increase in general education and average efficiency, the power now available for human service, the merely physical increment, and compare it with anything that has ever been at man's disposal before, and when I think what a little straggling, incidental, undisciplined and unco-ordinated minority of inventors, experimenters, educators, writers and organizers has achieved this development of human possibilities, achieved it in spite of the disregard and aimlessness of the huge majority, and the passionate resistance of the active dull, my imagination grows giddy with dazzling intimations of the human splen-

[88]

dours the justly organized state may yet attain. I glimpse for a bewildering instant the heights that may be scaled, the splendid enterprises made possible. . . ."

And who is to create the organized State? An élite, the samurais, the aristocracy which he depicts in *The Shape of Things to Come* as composed of air-pilots and chemists, the chivalry of experts (but any system of chivalry needs experts: only the technique has changed); and there is a code of chivalry of which he sometimes catches a prophetic glimpse in a troop of Boy Scouts: "There suddenly appeared in my world—I saw them first, I think, in 1908—a new sort of little boy, a most agreeable development of the slouching, cunning, cigarette-smoking, town-bred youngster, a small boy in a khaki hat, and with bare knees and athletic bearing, earnestly engaged in wholesome and invigorating games up to and occasionally a little beyond his strength—the Boy Scout. I liked the Boy Scout, and I find it difficult to express how much it mattered to me, with my growing bias in favour of deliberate national training, that Liberalism hadn't been able to produce anything of this kind."

Change the Boy Scout into a grown man, and you will find a Wellsian aristocracy. You will also find the present-day youth of Italy. It was not accidental that Wells gave one of his chief novels its title of *The New Machiavelli*: the Italian idea of the Prince, the idea that if great reforms are to be made victorious recourse must be had to great men, is an essential theme in Wells's philosophy. In this peculiar mixture he is at once Fascist and Liberal. "If you live in distress and confusion," he seems to be telling us, "it is because you will it so. To me, the cures are obvious: it needs only a little energy, and the entrusting of power to those fitted to exercise it. Science will henceforth allow us to control the universe, and if we applied its methods to human society, it would also enable us to control our political and financial differences. . . . I have drawn the main lines and conditions of man's future quite clearly, with no possibility of error, for myself and for others. I have shown that human life, such as we now know it, is only the raw material for a human life such as we might know. Our race could attain a fullness of life, a freedom and happiness which hitherto it has only dreamed. Humanity can muster its will and energy, and attain that ideal now. If it fails to understand its chance, then we are faced by cleavage, savagery, and perhaps a final collapse." And it will not be the first time in the history of a world that a race collapses and vanishes.

What would this happiness of the year 2200 be like? If we try to grasp it more firmly, or define it in terms of Wells's books, it fades away. It is not that of the Russians. It is not that of the Frenchman, because Wells is impatient of the peasant-farmer, the small tradesman, and, in a general way, of the average man. The mind of this designer seems more firmly knit in its critical than its constructive side. The

World State, to Wells, is far more of a mystical
aspiration than a clear idea.

V

CONCLUSION

A MAN of uncommon and wide intelligence, dis-
tressed by the absurdity of contemporary society and
impressed by the efficaciousness of scientific method,
desires to refashion the world. But once he begins to
imagine what the world *ought* to be, he is apt to be
blind to what it *is*. Utopia is his natural element. As
readers, we enjoy following him; as disciples, we
hesitate.

Wells takes credit to himself for not having taken
part in public life, and having thus preserved a free
mind. Free? The dove, feeling the pressure of the
wind under its wings, believes, as Kant says, that it
would fly better in the void. The solutions proposed
by Wells are always ingenious and generous; but
they do not solve the problems because they ignore
some of the data. The women of his novels, the societies of his forecasts, are beautiful but unreal: they
take no account of original sin. In Kipling, the gods
are everywhere; in the Wellsian universe, nowhere.
His idea of an "Open Conspiracy" of millionaires
and experts to take over the world and administer it
intelligently is a piece of fancy unrelated to the shape
of things as they are.

Wells's doctrine, in spite of its technical and scientific apparatus, is in fact a religion. He believes that human societies can attain to a state of lasting perfection, that this state is within sight, that the ship is lying just off the harbour, that sound education and goodwill would suffice to create this World Republic in which thousands of Wellses would direct the public services. It is a noble belief; but the world of flesh and blood, the world of soil and stone is not like that. The world is peopled by fallible, passionate, jealous creatures, capable of kindness and courage, folly and cruelty. Would they be capable of applying a World Plan of permanent equilibrium? Even granting that such a plan were conceivable, would it not still be necessary to allow for the conflicting passions of millions of men? But it is not conceivable. No single human brain can shape it. Plans beyond numbering are applicable in Utopia; on earth, we must live from day to day. Equilibrium could only be a stopping-place. Such is the lot of humanity.

But Wells, although he does not bring men temporal salvation, has nevertheless played a great and useful rôle for three decades past. Better than anyone he has demonstrated the absurdities of a society which has failed to adapt its functions to its powers. He has helped us to accept the inevitable transformations of that society. By suggesting hyperbolic plans he has prepared us to conceive of more modest, but practicable, plans. Above all, he has shown himself, in the best of his books, to be a great artist and the discoverer of new worlds of the imagination. It is not my own belief that, "when the sleeper wakes," this world of ours will have become like that of *A Modern Utopia*; but I should not be surprised if the people who inhabit it were not still reading *The Man Who Could Work Miracles* and *The Time Machine*.

III

BERNARD SHAW

Bernard Shaw*

* The author is particularly indebted to the biography by Dr. A. Henderson for material used in this essay.

WHEN Bernard Shaw came to the theatre as a playwright in the last decade of the nineteenth century he had the air of a bandit storming a fortress. And the theatre thus assailed was a Parisian theatre. It dominated all the stages of Europe with its formula of "the well-made play," settled for all time by Eugène Scribe. A young Scotsman named William Archer was its devoted champion among the London critics, and remained so to the day of his death. He was also a strenuous Freethinker. A young Irishman startled and amused him by sallies in freedom of thought which went quite beyond him and the two became friends.

Archer proposed that they should write a play in collaboration. Archer was to provide the plot and construct the plan on strict Parisian lines; and Shaw was to provide the dialogue. When the first act was completed and bore not the smallest resemblance to a Parisian "exposition," nor any recognizable relation to Archer's plot, the collaboration exploded with a violence which might have resulted in a life-long quarrel had it been possible to quarrel with Shaw. For he not only refused to see anything wrong with his first act, but blasphemed horribly against Archer's artistic faith. "Your art of playmaking," he said, "is not a living art; it is art of making wax flowers, clockwork mice, and rabbits on wheels which tap tambourines as you draw them along. Its figures are not human, they have no politics, no religion, no money troubles, and no sex. Yes, no sex, though they think that sex is the only subject that makes a play. But they know nothing about sex, they think that duels and divorce proceedings and marriage laws are sex. I leave such mechanical trash to the poor devils who cannot play the classic game, which is my game. A real play is not constructed; it grows like a flower. These Boulevardiers are always talking about art; they plaster all their street corners with their attempts at it; but they know nothing about it. I shall have to teach them from the ground up when I have finished with the English."

He has not yet had time, nor quite finished with the English, and this is doubtless the reason why Bernard Shaw, a great writer, serious in all his intentions but deliberately paradoxical, has never enjoyed in France the same success that he has in the Anglo-Saxon countries. Swift had to fall back on humour in order to attack the abuses of his age. Bernard Shaw has been able to demolish many British prejudices with impunity, because he pirouetted as he broke down the gates of the tabernacle.

BERNARD SHAW

I

LIFE

WHEN a journalist invited George Bernard Shaw, early in his career, to define himself, he replied: "Shaw is a bachelor, an Irishman, a vegetarian, a fluent liar, a social-democrat, a lecturer and debater, a lover of music, a fierce opponent of the present status of women, and an insister on the seriousness of art."

This early pirouette makes a good starting-point; it shows instantaneously our author's peculiar trick, which consists of obtaining a comic effect by stating the truth simply and cynically. For, in this reply, everything is true. An Irishman? Certainly. Shaw is an Irishman by his place of birth, which was Dublin, on July 26, 1856. He does not belong to the Catholic and Celtic majority in Ireland, but he is Irish in more respects than one.

Ireland is a land of controversy, and Shaw has been a life-long lover of controversy. His favourite maxims are in scrupulous opposition to those of the accepted wisdom of mankind: "Do not do unto others as you would that they should do unto you. Their tastes may not be the same.—Never resist temptation: prove all things: hold fast that which is good.—The golden rule is that there are no golden rules." Ireland, says Chesterton, is a land of saints, and throughout his life Shaw has been austere in life: whence the theoretic boldness of his ideas on morals, for it is only the sinner who really knows the dangers of sin. Finally, Ireland does not like sentimentalists, and Shaw has always matched his native Irish realism against the English sentimentality of which he makes game. His attitude in England has never been that of an Englishman talking to compatriots, but that of the member of a proud and conquered race addressing his conquerors.

It is important to realize, in trying to understand Shaw, that he is an Irishman; and no less to realize that he is a Protestant. He has remarked himself that the Irish Protestant is the only real one because he is the only one who protests; the Church of England has become a national church and lost the critical habit of Protestantism. Shaw enjoys making fun of those who reproach him with Puritanical instincts, but it is nevertheless a fact that, in his asceticism, he is akin to the Puritans. He is a teetotaler, and refrains even from tea or coffee. He regards any excitation of the brain as a crime against personality. He does not smoke and eats no animal flesh.

"I object," he wrote a few years ago, "to carnivorous diet, not only because I feel instinctively that it is abominable, but because it involves a prodigious slavery of men to animals. Cows and sheep, with their *valetaille* of accoucheurs, graziers, shepherds, slaughtermen, butchers, milkmaids, and so forth, absorb a mass of human labour that should be devoted to the breeding and care of human beings." He has always denied that he owes his perfect health to his vegetarianism, "firstly because his health is not perfect; secondly, because carnivorous people live as long and well as he, and finally because his vegetarianism is a diet for heroes and saints, not for vulgar persons." The only danger that he sees for society in vegetarianism is, indeed, the strength which it gives to its practitioners, from the bulls and the elephants to the Shelleys and Shaws. "Think," he advises us, "of the fierce energy concentrated in an acorn! You bury it in the ground, and it explodes into a giant oak. Bury a sheep, and nothing happens but decay." And just so, from the young vegetarian Protestant will emerge the explosive Bernard Shaw, who tried to blow up British society of the early twentieth century.

Shaw's family, as he describes it, was a typical product of the old feudal primogeniture system, which continually threw off younger sons with no money and younger sons' younger sons with less, but with unabated claims to be gentlemen of family. His father had been a government official. The abolition of his post as useless had left him with a pension which he capitalized to enable himself to become a man of business. He was not a success in that capacity; but he spoke of "the Shaws" as one might then speak of the Romanoffs or the Hohenzollerns. Bernard Shaw tells a story about him: "One evening I was playing in the street with a schoolfellow of mine, when my father came home. He questioned me about this boy, who was the son of a prosperous ironmonger. The feelings of my father, who was not prosperous, and who sold flour by the sack, when he learned that his son had played in the public street with the son of a man who sold nails by the pennyworth in a shop are not to be described. He impressed on me that my honour, my self-respect, my human dignity, all stood upon my determination not to associate with persons engaged in retail trade." It was in observing the life of his family that Shaw, like Stendhal before him, learnt how to despise; and the subject is one about which he has been brutally frank.

His father he says, was a remorseful drinker. "If you asked him to dinner or to a party, he was not always quite sober when he arrived; and he was invariably scandalously drunk when he left. Now a convivial drunkard may be exhilarating in convivial company. Even a quarrelsome or boastful drunkard may be found entertaining by people who are not particular. But a miserable drunkard—and my father, in theory a teetotaler, was racked with shame and remorse even in his cups—is unbearable. We were finally dropped socially." The tones are stern, but even the sentimental Dickens allowed himself harsh words of Mr Micawber.

Bernard Shaw's mother, who was twenty years younger than her husband, was a woman of intelligence. She was very musical, and took singing-lessons from a well-known Dublin musician. She played parts in the operatic performances which he arranged, and he lived under the Shaws' roof. From childhood Bernard Shaw sang operas and oratorios to himself, and it was to this early musical education that he was able, at the start of his literary career, to become a musical critic.

BERNARD SHAW

At sixteen he was taken away from school, in which he had found his school books unreadable, and entered an estate agent's office in Dublin, at a salary of eighteen pounds a year. He was soon promoted to a more responsible post and was seized with a dread that he would never escape from the office, which he hated. He endured four years of it, and then he threw over everything and went to London to join his mother, who had meanwhile left Ireland.

There he found himself in totally unfamiliar surroundings: "My destiny was to educate London, but I had neither studied my pupil nor related my ideas properly to the common stock of human knowledge." For a while he kept up some pretence of seeking commercial employment; but his destiny was to write, and it is almost incomprehensible why this highly intelligent man, who had from boyhood a really original style, could only earn a sum of six pounds sterling for his writing between the years 1876 and 1885; fifteen shillings for an article, five shillings for a poem, and five pounds for a chemist's advertisement. During this period he wrote five novels, all of which were rejected by the publishers. The first, *Immaturity*, was refused by George Meredith, as reader to Chapman and Hall, who simply wrote "No" in the margin. It waited fifty years for publication. The manuscript was thrown aside and nibbled by mice: "but even they could not get through it!" During these nine years Shaw was desperately short of money, and he shamelessly allowed himself, as he says, to be kept by his parents, hard pressed though they were to keep up appearances.

"The true artist," says Tanner in *Man and Superman*, "will let his wife starve, his children go barefoot, his mother drudge for his living at seventy, sooner than work at anything but his art. To women he is half vivisector, half vampire. He gets into intimate relations with them to study them, to strip the mask of convention from them, to surprise their inmost secrets, knowing that they have the power to rouse his deepest creative energies, to rescue him from his cold reason, to make him see visions and dream dreams, to inspire him, as he calls it."

In point of fact, Shaw did not suffer from his poverty. He has admitted that he never had much experience of poverty. Before he was able to earn anything with his pen, he says, he had "a magnificent library in Bloomsbury, a priceless picture gallery in Trafalgar Square, and another at Hampton Court, without any servants to look after or rent to pay." What did he want with money? Cigars and champagne were useless to him. If he had had smart clothes, he would simply have been asked out to dinner by the very people whom he took the utmost pains to avoid. In fact, he exclaimed, of what use would the paltry luxury of Bond Street have been to him, George Bernard Sardanapalus?

Socialism he embraced early, and at a time when it was decidedly a novelty in England. He was turned from religious scepticism to economics by a lecture by Henry George, and completely and finally converted to Communism by reading Karl Marx. He became one of the group of friends who, with Sidney and Beatrice Webb at their centre, founded the Fabian Society. Shaw has retained the friendship of the Webbs all through his life, and regards it as one of the most valuable he ever made. Unlike H. G. Wells, a later adherent to Fabianism, who moved swiftly from Socialism towards a kind of aristocratic doctrine, Shaw, though he made short work of Marx's obsolescences in abstract economics, and of his inexperience in practical administration, and laughs at the famous dialectic as a method of thought for British Islanders, remains in all essentials a convinced Marxist.

We must picture him as he was about the age of twenty-seven, young and unknown, with a bright red beard. His Socialist friends used to say he had nailed the Red Flag to his chin. It was quite usual, at public meetings, to see an irrepressible and brilliant young man rise in a corner of the hall and propound the most unusual questions. People asked who he was. And soon the name of Bernard Shaw became quite familiar in these "advanced" circles. Thanks to his friend, William Archer, he was at last able to make journalistic connexions, first as reviewer, and then as a critic of pictures, of music, and finally of the theatre. He arrested attention by his sparkling style and outspoken opinions. He was an advocate for what was then called "advanced" art: Wagner in music, the Impressionists in painting, Ibsen in the theatre. He made several signatures famous—"Corno di Bassetto" in *The Star*, but particularly his own initials, "G.B.S." in *The World*. He wrote a small book on Wagner's *Ring*: *The Perfect Wagnerite*, and another, *The*

POINTS OF VIEW

Quintessence of Ibsenism, as exegetist to the Norwegian anti-idealist.

With his very earliest articles he adopted a humorous tone. In order to make people listen to him, he has said, he had to pass himself off as a madman, to whom the privileges and freedom of a court jester were permitted. The orthodox elements in England were annoyed by this man who blew his own trumpet so blatantly. But he declared that he would gladly have gone about London with a barrel organ and dressed as a clown if that could have secured him a hearing; for, he argued, it is only the man with no message to give who scruples about banging the big drum at his shop door.

He had been influenced by Marx, Samuel Butler's denunciations of Darwinism, and by Ibsen. William Archer induced him to try his hand at playwriting. The first result, *Widowers' Houses*, achieved two semi-private performances in 1892, and created a scandal which is now quite unintelligible. Similar performances in coterie theatres by Stage Clubs followed; and two great box-office successes, one in America and the other in Germany, established him as a competent playwright; but in London his full theatrical success did not come until the creation of the Court Theatre in 1904, where his plays were given in succession. But the book publication of his *Plays, Pleasant and Unpleasant*, with the long expository prefaces, admirably written, had made him deservedly famous by the close of the nineteenth century.

pyright by the Fitzwilliam Museum, Cambridge

GEORGE BERNARD SHAW, BY AUGUSTUS JOHN

Simultaneously, with the steady growth of the dramatist Bernard Shaw, with his flow of invention, and his novel ideas, and his spirited gift for expressing them, there was also taking shape in the mind of the English public a very different character, whom Shaw himself styled "G.B.S." It was "G.B.S." who replied to interviewers in outrageous and comical fashion; it was "G.B.S." who headed the pages of the preface to his Cæsar play, "Better than Shakespeare?" Few noticed the mark of interrogation. Shaw was crammed with Shakespeare from his childhood, and delighted in him; but he was determined to break down the conventional "Bardolatry" of critics quite ignorant of their subject; and in the *Saturday Review* he wrote a series of iconoclastic articles, the burden of which was "Great is Ibsen and Shaw is his prophet. . . . Down with Shakespeare!"

It was "G.B.S.," likewise, who consistently and systematically insulted the English public and the American public. Throughout his life, apparently, Shaw has felt it to be at once his duty, and in his own interest, to cure the English of their dangerous self-conceit. From first to last in his writings, he has made fun of them. If he confronts an Englishman and an Irishman, in *John Bull's Other Island*, it is to show the Englishman as callow and ridiculous, but effective; the Irishman as subtle and positive but futile. If, in *Cæsar and Cleopatra* he introduces on Cæsar's staff a certain Britannus, who hails from the province of Britain, it is only to make English audiences laugh at themselves in his person. In *Saint Joan* he draws an English chaplain; it is to show him as childishly cruel and sincerely horrified at his own thoughtless work. To Americans also he tells the most unwelcome truths, with singular and unfailing zeal: "I myself have been particularly careful never to say a civil word to the United States. I have scoffed at their inhabitants as a nation of villagers. I have defined the 100-per-cent American as 99 per cent an idiot. And they just adore me and will go on adoring me until in a moment of senile sentimentality I say something nice about them, when they will at once begin to suspect me of being a cheap skate, after all, and drop me like a hot potato."

A French reader would have to be particularly careful, in estimating this factor, to take into account the difference between a Parisian and a London audience. Paris playgoers have lost the habit of tolerating plays like those of Molière, in which the chief comic element is a caricature of the French character. English audiences have reacquired this classic habit from Shaw's plays. They applaud them, firstly because they attach no great importance to ideas, secondly because these ideas are masked by Shavian humour, and finally because, as Shaw himself would admit, this English public is so sure of the absolute validity of its prejudices that no mockery can affect it. But the boutades of Bernard Shaw have altered the English public more than might have been thought possible, and his plays have helped to obliterate a great many Victorian modes of thought.

Shaw, then, has behaved skilfully in elaborating his cherished and serious ideas under a mask of the comical and outrageous. They are ideas for which in the slightly unreal aspect of the "G.B.S." character, the real Bernard Shaw would have found it difficult to secure a sympathetic hearing. As Louis Cazamian has remarked: "Bernard Shaw was an entertainer, but with no loss to his dignity. He ascended the stage, not booth boards. His manner is no grimace, but the practice of a mental hygiene. It is also an efficient practical policy. To charge him with gratuitous and systematic paradox, or self-advertisement—as is still too often done—is decidedly unjust, his thought is coherent and serious; he fights not for himself, but for his ideas."

II

THE ANTI-SENTIMENTAL

SENTIMENTALISM—there is the enemy! That might be Shaw's motto. Your sentimentalist is not the man who experiences strong and genuine sentiments, but the man who uses feigned sentiments to mask a real passion. At the time when Shaw was beginning to write, it was quite rare for anyone to dare to say openly that he was greedy, luxurious, ambitious, or cruel. The vices, in a respectable world, wore masks of virtue. And vice, transformed into sentimentalism, is as dangerous as a poison coated with sugar. In *The Man of Destiny* Shaw demonstrates how the middle classes, especially those of England, exploit a virtuous sentimentalism:

"*Napoleon*: There are three sorts of people in the

world, the low people, the middle people, and the
high people. The low people and the high people are
alike in one thing: they have no scruples, no morality.
The low are beneath morality, the high above it. I
am not afraid of either of them; for the low are unscrupulous without knowledge, so that they make an
idol of me; whilst the high are unscrupulous without
purpose, so that they go down before my will. Look
you: I shall go over all the mobs and all the courts
of Europe as a plough goes over a field. It is the middle
people who are dangerous: they have both knowledge
and purpose. But they, too, have their weak point.
They are full of scruples—chained hand and foot by
their morality and respectability.

"*Lady*: Then you will beat the English; for all
shopkeepers are middle people.

"*Napoleon*: No, because the English are a race
apart. No Englishman is too low to have scruples:
no Englishman is high enough to be free from their
tyranny. But every Englishman is born with a certain miraculous power that makes him master of the
world. When he wants a thing he never tells himself that he wants it. He waits patiently until there
comes into his mind, no one knows how, a burning
conviction that it is his moral and religious duty to
conquer those who have got the thing he wants. Then
he becomes irresistible. Like the aristocrat, he does
what pleases him and grabs what he covets; like the
shopkeeper, he pursues his purpose with the industry
and steadfastness that come from strong religious conviction and a deep sense of moral responsibility. He

is never at a loss for an effective moral attitude. As the great champion of freedom and national independence he conquers and annexes half the world, and calls it Colonization. . . . He makes two revolutions, and then declares war on our one in the name of law and order. There is nothing so bad or so good that you will not find Englishmen doing it; but you will never find an Englishman in the wrong. He does everything on principle."

Whenever one of Shaw's characters seeks to give the impression that he is better or braver or more generous than befits human nature, whenever he declares that he is a gentleman and will obey the sentimental conventions which form the gentleman's code, then the spectator versed in the Shavian theatre can be certain that this character is the traitor of the play. For anti-sentimentality, like sentimentality, has its own conventions.

This anti-sentimental convention was already full-grown in Shaw's mind by the time he wrote his first play, *Widowers' Houses*. A young English gentleman, Harry Trench, meets a young girl, Blanche Sartorius, when travelling, and becomes engaged to her. On his return to London he learns that the fortune of his future father-in-law comes from slum properties, and that his wretched tenants are mercilessly evicted whenever their rents are in arrears. Trench, who is capable of moral indignation, refuses to accept money from such sources; his own income will suffice for his wife and himself. But Mr Sartorius proves to him that his income also comes from a tainted source, as Trench's income is derived from a mortgage on Sartorius's houses. Trench is caught in the toils of capitalism, collapses and sulkily takes both money and daughter.

In *Mrs Warren's Profession* we find the same theme, the source of the money being even more base and the conclusion being the contrary one. Vivie Warren, a young student, has seen very little of her mother; she only knows that Mrs Warren is extremely rich and has always spent money liberally on her education. When she is about twenty years of age, Vivie, a well-educated, intellectual young woman, at last meets her mother, and finds her vulgar, but not unlikeable. Before long she discovers that her mother's wealth comes from her ownership of brothels in every part of Europe. Vivie refuses to touch this money, preferring a life of hard work and independence. But she sets up no moral superiority. Here is Vivie addressing Mrs Warren:

"You don't at all know the sort of person I am. . . . I don't think I'm more prejudiced or strait-laced than you: I think I'm less. I'm certain I'm less sentimental. I know very well that fashionable morality is all a pretence, and that if I took your money and devoted the rest of my life to spending it fashionably, I might be as worthless and vicious as the silliest woman could possibly want to be without having a word said to me about it. But I don't want to be worthless. I shouldn't enjoy trotting about the park to advertise my dressmaker and carriage-builder, or being bored at the opera to shew off a shopwindow-

ful of diamonds. . . . No: I am my mother's daughter.
I am like you: I must have work, and must make
more money than I spend. But my work is not your
work, and my way not your way. We must part.
It will not make much difference to us: instead of
meeting one another for perhaps a few months in
twenty years, we shall never meet: that's all."

Clearly, then, Vivie's cynicism is directed towards
preventing her mother from exploiting the sentiment
of daughterly respect. Shaw's cynicism is never
brought into play at the expense of genuine feelings,
but always to attack that kind of emotional blackmail-
ing, which is so potent in all amorous and social
relationships. Emmanuel Berl, the French critic, who
has analysed these matters in a contemporary light,
would say that genuine sentiment is killed by sentimental conformity, and this approximates to the
Shavian thesis.

Of all forms of sentimentality, the most dangerous
is that which women have so skilfully linked up with
the emotions of love. Amorous hypocrisy has been
unmasked by Shaw in several of his plays, and pre-
eminently in *Man and Superman*. He offers variations
on the Don Juan theme. But whereas in the old reper-
tory Don Juan is a hunter of women, Shaw's play
exhibits him as the prey pursued by women. Their
aim is to force Don Juan to renounce his freedom,
and to attain this they will unscrupulously make use
of the sentimental code which men have been foolish enough to accept.

By an amusing trick of the playwright, even the

names of the classic Spanish characters have been given an English shape. Don Juan de Tenorio becomes John Tanner. Doña Ana, whom he seduces and whose father he has killed, is now Ann, John Tanner's ward. Ann, strong and remorseless in the way of a woman who thinks she is on the track of her man, has resolved to conquer Tanner and marry him. Throughout the whole play she pursues him, and in the end forces him into the marriage which he at once dreads and desires. The most original act in the lengthy play is that in which, in a kind of dream, we pass from the plan of modern England into the Mozart's *Don Giovanni*, in the course of a descent into Hell, where we meet the Spanish Juan, the Statue of the Commander (who lives in Heaven but visits Hell to enjoy himself) and a *fin de siècle*, very Wildean, Devil, who is appropriately sentimental. The final tirade of Tanner, who consents to marriage with Ann, pushed to it against his reason by irresistible instincts, sums up the position of this Don Juan Despite Himself:

"I solemnly say that I am not a happy man. Ann looks happy; but she is only triumphant, successful, victorious. That is not happiness. What we have both done this afternoon is to renounce happiness, renounce freedom, renounce tranquillity, above all, renounce the romantic possibilities of an unknown future, for the cares of a household and a family. I beg that no man may seize the occasion to get half drunk and utter imbecile speeches and coarse pleasantries at my expense."

In fact, Ann and Tanner have neither of them
been anything but tools in the hands of the Life
Force, or the Instinct of the Species, which strives
to create the Superman. It is a play which interweaves
Bergson and Schopenhauer.

When Shaw, in the course of this play, transports
us to the Devil's realm, he shows us a Hell paved, not
so much with good intentions, as with fine sentiments.
Shaw's Devil is a cultured, respectable person. "I
know," he remarks, "that beauty is good to look at;
that music is good to hear; that love is good to feel;
and that they are all good to think about and talk
about. . . . Whatever they may say of me in churches
on earth, I know that it is universally admitted in
good society that the Prince of Darkness is a gentleman; and that is good enough for me." A cruel Devil
might be just endurable; but this highly respectable
Satan is an abomination.

Shaw seems to be saying to mankind: "Do what
you will; don't resist temptation; jilt women; kill
other men if you have to. But understand clearly
what you are doing, and don't pretend you are doing
the opposite. Heaven is simply the place where men
know what they are doing, and where the results of
their activities depend only on those activities; on
earth, human activities collide with the unpredictable
barriers of the created universe; in Hell, the shades
live on illusions. Over the gates of Hell are written
the famous words: 'All Hope Abandon, Ye Who
Enter Here.'—'What a relief!' sigh the weaklings
as they read the inscription. What is hope, if not a

form of moral responsibility? In Hell there is no hope; therefore, no duties, no work, nothing to be gained by prayer, nothing to be lost by doing just what one likes."

"Hell is the home of the unreal," says Don Juan in *Man and Superman*. "It is the only refuge from Heaven, which is, as I tell you, the home of the masters of reality, and from earth, which is the home of the slaves of reality. The earth is a nursery in which men and women play at being heroes and heroines, saints and sinners; but they are dragged down from their fool's paradise by their bodies. . . . But here you escape this tyranny of the flesh; for here you are not an animal at all, you are a ghost, an appearance, an illusion, a convention, deathless, ageless, in a word, bodiless."

Not to be oneself, to consent to live for one's mask and not for one's face, to renounce the body in order to make oneself the willing slave of one's own verbalism—that is Hell.

III

THE REALISTS

IF THE sentimental character, in Shaw's works, is always the traitor, the hero is always the antipathetic one, the realist. But what human beings are realists?

Firstly, the Irish. In the preface to *John Bull's Other Island*, Shaw explains at length that the Englishman is always a prey to his imagination, and that, in particular, he has created a mixed comic and poetic picture of the Irishman of which he cannot rid his mind, whereas the Irishman, on his side, sees the Englishman just as he is. Shaw delights in contrasting Wellington, the most Irish of Irishmen, with Nelson, the most typical of Englishmen, and argues that the Duke's scornful dislike of the theatrical side of Nelson, that self-conscious patriotic hero, was a natural and inevitable sentiment. Wellington's formula to deal with things of this kind was a familiar Irish phrase, "Sir, don't be a damned fool!" It is the formula applied by the Irish to all Englishmen. And if the Englishman retorts that the Irishman of legend is constantly to be met with in real life, the Irishman can answer, that of course he is; for so long as a degraded type of Irishman comes to England and finds the country full of romantic donkeys who tolerate his idling and boasting and drinking because he flatters their sense of moral superiority, degrading himself as well as his own country, so long will he learn the grimaces that dupe the English, and learn them even from the music-hall. But the genuine Irishman laughs at the Englishman's moral superiority.

Secondly, women are realists. They often appear to be defending sentimental love, but this is merely talk and cunning manœuvre. A woman's aim, often unknown to herself, but the single aim of every woman who is wisely seeking her essentially female happiness, is to marry and bear children. This is per-

fectly natural, because, in the distant division of the
species into two sexes, the more important share was
allotted to woman. It is she who devotes the best of
her strength during most of her life to prolonging
the surviving of the race. Having need of the male
to accomplish the most urgent task of nature, she
annexes him by natural right. So it is always the
woman who takes the initiative. True, men have
created a weak romantic convention by way of protection; the woman must wait, passively, until she is
asked with humility. But the pretence is so transpar-
ent that, even in the theatre, it deceives nobody. In
Shakespeare, the interest of the play is to see the
woman hunting the man. Certainly, she awaits the
devoted suitor, but awaits him as the spider does the
fly.

And so, in Bernard Shaw's version of Don Juan's
story, Don Juan will be the hunted, not the hunter.
He will struggle and resist. But his opponent is the
future mother, and in the conquest of the man she
needs, nothing will affright her; lies, tricks, impu-
dence, the sacrifice of all self-respect—she will risk
everything, and accept everything. Woman's love is
a sacrifice to a force more powerful than herself. She
sacrifices herself, and does not hesitate to sacrifice the
man. Indeed, Shaw sees the attachment of woman for
man as the attachment of the policeman for his
prisoner.

In this battle man is always the loser, because he
has too much imagination. Nearly all great artists
have been men, and they have accustomed man, their

brother, to live in a chimerical world. The musician teaches him the sweetness of sounds, the painter enriches his eyes, the poet teaches him to feel more deeply. When the Life Force drives him to love, he naturally confuses this new emotion with all the others he has previously experienced. He believes that in his love of a woman he will find all the romantic grace of the poets' loves. He thinks that the voice of his beloved will be the harmony of all songs, her face the beauty of all verses, her soul the passion of all dramas. Don Juan pursues this dream of making all the celestial joys incarnate in one fair woman. He finds her, he clasps her. He imagines he is loving some creature of coral and ivory with whom he might have lived outside of Time and Space. He loves a woman of flesh and blood, insistent on her rights, and for whom the story is beginning just where it is ending for him.

Marriage is an institution which seems indispensable for the maintenance of the species, because without it the female race would be always deserted by the race of Don Juans and the upbringing of children would become difficult. Besides, women, as guardians of racial continuity, have a paramount interest in honouring marriage and in binding the male by a sentimental convention. Cynical women betray their sex. True women wear the mask which they must wear, but Shaw, who is quite familiar with them, denounces them. They are consciously wearing moral masks in order to gain their real objectives. When they are sincere they are terribly practical and

POINTS OF VIEW

tenacious. In Shaw's plays the women nearly all belong to one of two types: the strong young woman who speaks her mind bluntly and refuses marriage (like Vivie in *Mrs Warren's Profession*), and the strong young woman who feigns helplessness in order to win the man's protection and marriage (like Ann in *Man and Superman*). The latter type, when a man is so bold as to tell her that she is a liar, like all women, is not upset; no, she smiles, and answers, "How did you guess?" But very few men see through the ruthless game of women. Only women understand the game thoroughly. No woman is ever the dupe of another.

And yet this strong creature has a weakness. The chink in her armour is seen when the woman, always maternal, even in love, allows her man's weakness to bring her tenderness into play. There is an example of this in *Arms and the Man*. During a war between Bulgaria and Serbia, Raina, daughter of a Bulgarian general, learns that her future husband, a young officer, has just swung the balance of victory by a heroic charge. When going to bed, she sees one of the vanquished fugitives coming into her room through the window. He is a Swiss, a professional soldier, the son of a hotel-keeper, who has taken service in the Serbian army as an instructor. He had been in command of the battery which had been so heroically charged by Raina's betrothed. But when the girl talks about her lover's exploit, Bluntschli, the real soldier, laughs bitterly: "Of all the fools ever let loose on a field of battle, that man must be the very maddest. He and his regiment simply committed suicide; only the pistol missed fire; that's all." And there one catches sight of one of Shaw's pet themes—the contrast between the romantic hero and the realist soldier.

But the young Swiss knows that he is lost unless Raina hides him. He is frightened, and worse still, he is hungry. He falls upon a bag of chocolates which she scornfully offers him, and then, overwhelmed with fatigue, he falls asleep on the bed. But when she could give him up, she saves him. Later on she breaks off her engagement on his account. Why? Because the woman always moves instinctively towards real strength, and also because, through a different instinct, she moves always towards apparent weakness. She loves Bluntschli, partly because he is a real soldier, with no talk about glory, but also because one night she rocked him like a child, because he is her "chocolate-cream soldier." . . .

This theme of the protective instinct which the woman feels in love is again handled in *Candida*. Two men love Candida: the poet Marchbanks, a real poet with the strength of a Shelley, and the Rev. Mr Morell, her husband, a powerful popular orator, self-intoxicated with his Christian-Socialist enthusiasm and his genius for preaching. The poet adores Candida, and really understands her; he would doubtless be capable of making her happy. The clergyman Morell has no suspicion of how much he owes to his wife, who has spoilt him with her devotion and her practical ability. He thinks he is protecting her, whereas it is Candida who looks after him. Placed in the position of choosing between these two men, Candida stays with her husband. Why? Because he is the weaker and because he needs her:

"*Candida (slowly recoiling a step, her heart hardened by his rhetoric in spite of the sincere feeling behind it):* Oh! I am to choose, am I? I suppose it is quite settled that I must belong to one or the other.

"*Morell (firmly):* Quite. You must choose definitely.

"*Marchbanks (anxiously):* Morell, you don't understand. She means that she belongs to herself.

"*Candida (turning on him):* I mean that, and a good deal more, Master Eugene, as you will both find out presently. And pray, my lords and masters, what have you to offer for my choice? I am up for auction, it seems. What do you bid, James?

"*Morell (reproachfully):* Cand— (*He breaks down: his eyes and throat fill with tears: the orator becomes a wounded animal.*) I can't speak ——

"*Candida (impulsively going to him):* Ah, dearest ——

"*Marchbanks (in wild alarm):* Stop: it's not fair. You mustn't shew her that you suffer, Morell. I am on the rack, too; but I am not crying.

"*Morell (rallying all his forces):* Yes, you are right. It is not for pity that I am bidding. (*He disengages himself from Candida.*)

"*Candida (retreating, chilled):* I beg your pardon, James; I did not mean to touch you. I am waiting to hear your bid.

"*Morell (with proud humility):* I have nothing to

offer you but my strength for your defence, my
honesty for your surety, my ability and industry for
your livelihood, and my authority and position for
your dignity. That is all it becomes a man to offer
to a woman.

"*Candida (quite quietly):* And you, Eugene?
What do you offer?

"*Marchbanks.* My weakness. My desolation. My
heart's need.

"*Candida (impressed):* That's a good bid, Eugene.
Now I know how to make my choice.

"*She pauses and looks curiously from one to the
other, as if weighing them. Morell, whose lofty confidence has changed into heart-breaking dread at
Eugene's bid, loses all power of concealing his
anxiety. Eugene, strung to the highest tension, does
not move a muscle.*

"*Morell (in a suffocated voice: the appeal bursting
from the depths of his anguish):* Candida!

"*Marchbanks (aside, in a flash of contempt):* Coward!

"*Candida (significantly):* I give myself to the
weaker of the two.

"*Eugene divines her meaning at once: his face
whitens like steel in a furnace.*

"*Morell (bowing his head with the calm of collapse):* I accept your sentence, Candida.

"*Candida.* Do you understand, Eugene?

"*Marchbanks.* Oh, I feel I'm lost. He cannot bear
the burden.

"*Morell (incredulously, raising his head and voice with comic abruptness)*: Do you mean me, Candida?

"*Candida (smiling a little)*: Let us sit and talk comfortably over it like three friends. . . . You remember what you told me about yourself, Eugene: how nobody has cared for you since your old nurse died . . . how you have had to live without comfort or welcome or refuge; always lonely, and nearly always disliked and misunderstood, poor boy!

"*Marchbanks (faithful to the nobility of his lot)*: I had my books. I had nature. And at last I met you.

"*Candida.* Never mind that just at present. Now I want you to look at this other boy here: my boy! spoilt from his cradle. . . . I build a castle of comfort and indulgence and love for him, and stand sentinel always to keep little vulgar cares out. I make him master here, though he does not know it, and could not tell you a moment ago how it came to be so. *(With sweet irony)* And when he thought I might go away with you, his only anxiety was—what should become of me! And to tempt me to stay he offered me *(leaning forward to stroke his hair caressingly at each phrase)* his strength for my defence! his industry for my livelihood! his dignity for my position! his—*(relenting)* ah, I am mixing up your beautiful cadences and spoiling them, am I not, darling? *(She lays her cheek fondly against him.)*

"*Morell (quite overcome, kneeling beside her chair and embracing her with boyish ingenuousness)*: It's all true, every word. What I am you have made me with the labour of your hands and the love of your

[124]

heart. You are my wife, my mother, my sisters; you are the sum of all loving care to me.

"*Candida (in his arms, smiling, to Eugene):* Am I your mother and sisters to you, Eugene?

"*Marchbanks (rising with a fierce gesture of disgust):* Ah, never. Out, then, into the night with me!"

The third class of realists is that of the artists. The artist is a realist for the same reasons as woman. The woman is unconsciously serving the instinct of the species, and sacrifices everything to its future; the artist sacrifices everything for his work of creation. He has no scruples. The great artist is never a gentleman. Dickens, Goethe, Shaw himself, are not gentlemen. Some will abandon women, others will brutally speak out all the truths which a gentleman conceals. Only their work matters to them. For that very reason it is great.

In *The Doctor's Dilemma* an artist, who in his temporal life has robbed and tricked his friends, dies without a pang of remorse. "I know," says Louis, "that in an accidental sort of way struggling through the unreal part of my life, I haven't always been able to live up to my ideal. But in my own real world I have never done anything wrong, never denied my faith, never been untrue to myself. I've been threatened and blackmailed and insulted and starved. But I've played the game. I've fought the good fight. And now it's all over, there's an indescribable peace. I believe in Michelangelo, Velasquez, and Rembrandt; in the might of design, the mystery of colour, the redemption of all things by Beauty everlasting, and the message of Art that has made these hands blessed. Amen. Amen."

And fourth come the men of action, realists also because they have their work to accomplish. Now, action in the world of reality does not admit of any illusions. If the man of action failed to understand human beings, if instead of seeing them as they are he imagined them as they ought to be, he would fail. If he sentimentally refused to lend himself to cruel but necessary actions, he would likewise fail. If he indulged in heroic and brilliant play-acting, in the rôle of the historic general, instead of carrying out the dull and difficult jobs of a real general, he would be neither Cæsar nor Wellington nor Napoleon. In *Arms and the Man* the hero is not the soldier, and that is the whole idea of the play. In *The Man of Destiny* we see Napoleon, at the moment of the battle of Lodi, sitting in a small Italian inn. He is expecting despatches from France. The officer who should be bringing them arrives, very crestfallen; he has had them stolen from him, and it is soon discovered that they were taken from him by a very pretty lady living in this very inn. General Bonaparte, who has no patience with feminine nonsense, is quite ready to lay hands on her to recover the papers. She then confesses that she stole them, not as a spy, but in order to save a woman, as the despatches included a letter denouncing this woman, with proof of her guilt. As Bonaparte presses her, she gives him to understand that the woman in question is Josephine, and that the letter gives proof of the liaison with Barras.

From that moment Bonaparte, determined not to be forced into admitting any knowledge of the wrong done him, is determined to prevent these letters from reappearing, and to make those who have wanted to bring this scandal home to him believe that he has never received this evidence of it. The subject here, it seems, is the total absence of ordinary human reactions in a man marked out by Destiny. The real man of action, like the real artist, becomes quite cynical as soon as his work is affected.

Here is the scene:

"*Napoleon.* Suppose I were to allow myself to be abashed by the respect due to your sex, your beauty, your heroism, and all the rest of it! Suppose I, with nothing but such sentimental stuff to stand between these muscles of mine and those papers which you have about you, and which I want and mean to have; suppose I, with the prize within my grasp, were to falter and sneak away with my hands empty; or, what would be worse, cover up my weakness by playing the magnanimous hero, and sparing you the violence I dared not use! would you not despise me from the depths of your woman's soul? Would any woman be such a fool? Well, Bonaparte can rise to the situation and act like a woman when it is necessary. Do you understand?"

Cæsar, in *Cæsar and Cleopatra*, is a great man, but not the hero of tradition. He says what others dare not say; he forgives because he has not time enough to bear grudges; he is generous because he does not desire the things coveted by ordinary men. When

Cleopatra tries to seduce him, he answers, "I have work to do, Cleopatra."

Even Saint Joan, in Shaw's play about her, is first and foremost a realist. In his preface, Shaw says: "She was one of the first apostles of Nationalism, and the first French practitioner of Napoleonic realism in warfare as distinguished from the sporting ransom gambling chivalry of her time. . . . She was never for a moment what so many romancers and playwrights have pretended: a romantic young lady. She was a thorough daughter of the soil in her peasant-like matter-of-factness and doggedness, and her acceptance of great lords and kings and prelates as such without idolatry and snobbery, seeing at a glance how much they were individually good for. . . . She talked to and dealt with people of all classes, from labourers to kings, without embarrassment or affectation, and got them to do what she wanted when they were not afraid or corrupt. She could coax and she could hustle, her tongue having a soft side and a sharp edge. She was very capable—a born boss."

We have tried to sketch the typical pattern of a novel by H. G. Wells: we might similarly outline the framework of the typical Shavian play. A group of sentimentalists and romantics is shown living surrounded by comfortable illusions, but in a dangerous fool's paradise. Enter a strong, unscrupulous character—woman, artist, Irishman, Cæsar—who observes the emotions in a mood of detachment and cynically speaks the truth. The sentimentalists, terrified at first by the idea of their naked features being visible, finally realize that their masks are suffocating them. And Truth is victorious.

IV

POLITICS

IN POLITICS, as in love, Shaw is determined to be the antiromantic.

"Idealism," he declares in an early preface, "which is only a flattering name for romance in politics and morals, is as obnoxious to me as romance in ethics or religion. . . . I can no longer be satisfied with fictitious morals or fictitious good conduct, shedding fictitious glory on robbery, starvation, disease, crime, drink, war, cruelty, cupidity, and all the other commonplaces of civilization which drive men to the theatre to make foolish pretences that such things are progress, science, morals, religion, patriotism, imperial supremacy, national greatness and all the other names the newspapers call them."

Shaw refuses to accept the fictions of Liberalism. In 1933 he addressed an audience of astounded Americans and attacked their republican Constitution: ". . . A final manifesto from the centuries of revolutionary Anarchism in which the struggle went on against the government as such, against government by feudal barons, by autocratic Kings, by the Pope and his cardinals, by the parliaments which have gradually ousted all these authorities, each of them

in turn being used to disable the others in the glorified cause of what people call Liberty, until, having
destroyed the Kings, the barons, the Church, and
finally all effective parliamentary governing power,
you found yourselves hopelessly under the thumbs
of your private racketeers, from the humble gunman
to the financial magnate, each playing for his own
hand without status, without national authority or
responsibility, without legal restraint and without any
sense of public government. You had perfected a Constitution of negatives to defend liberty, liberty, liberty—life, liberty and the pursuit of happiness—
against the only checks on anarchy that could secure
them, and fortified it by a Supreme Court which
dealt out nothing but prohibitions, and a political
party machinery of legislatures and senates, which
was so wonderfully devised that when you sent in
one body of men to govern the country, you sent
in another body of men along with them to prevent
their doing it. In your dread of dictators you established a state of society in which every ward boss
is a dictator, every financier a dictator, every private
employer a dictator, all with the livelihood of the
workers at their mercy, and no public responsibility."

Shaw is no sentimental champion of poverty. He
agrees that rich and poor are both detestable, that
he himself hates the poor and longs for their exter-
mination. Being slightly sorry for the rich, he is likewise forced to exterminate these; "and as there is
nothing to be said for the working-classes, the pro-

fessional classes, the wealthy classes or the ruling classes, none of them has any right to live."

But if Shaw is a revolutionary, setting out to transform the existing social order, he does not believe that a political revolution will suffice to do so. It will effect nothing, he declares, to change institutions—to set up an economic and scientific domination, in place of a military and ecclesiastical governance, to turn capitalistic rule into proletarian democracy, monarchy into republic. Nor will it suffice to turn romanticism into realism, realism into mysticism, or metaphysics into physics. But to make the wolf into the domestic dog, the fifteenth-century battle-horse into the racehorse, is something real; and if this can be done with wolves and horses, it can be done with men. To transform institutions is futile unless mankind itself is also transformed. The real change can only be an evolution towards the Superman. And there we leave the solid ground of morality for the more shifting stance of metaphysics.

V

METAPHYSICS AND UTOPIA

As soon as there is a question of the Superman, Shaw's cynicism vanishes; sarcasm is supplanted by a religious tone; the pirouetting stops, and he is seen in an attitude of prayer. But what kind of man will the Superman be? Will he be a healthy-looking philosopher-athlete, with a beauteous and healthy woman as his mate? Shaw has answered this question, in the course of his life, in two different ways. At the time of *Man and Superman* he was answering that the question was superfluous, since evolution towards the Superman was slowly going forward, without mankind knowing the goal towards which its instincts were guiding it. But later, when he wrote *Back to Methuselah*, he seemed to believe that man can consciously participate in the evolution of the species.

One thing certain is, that man must transform himself. Man as he exists today is no longer capable of survival, he is destroying himself; his political laws, his economic and international laws, betray him; his science betrays him. Either he must engender the Superman, adapted to social life and the scientific world, or, after a few wars and a few mortal crises, he will yield his place to species of less gross nature. Man, says Shaw, is not God's last word: if men cannot do the work demanded of them, He will produce a creature who can.

In every man and woman the Life Force, that impulse which transcends the individual, inspires actions which will help in the production of the Superman. Under its influence individuals cease to be egotists, and will act against their immediate interest, flaunting common sense, defying their most justifiable fears. "A father for the Superman!"—that is the secret cry of every woman; and often her conscious thought is stifled by that cry. From Butler, and perhaps from Bergson, Shaw learnt to disbelieve in the mechanical evolution of the Darwinian school; his belief is in creative evolution, in the effort of every separate creation to surpass itself. Life has created thousands of species: mouse and man, kangaroo and rhinoceros, are all more or less successful attempts to fashion the brute force of Life into individuals approaching closer and closer to perfection, the ideal individual being omnipotent, omniscient, infallible, devoid of illusions—in a word, a god. The God of Bernard Shaw is in course of creating Himself. Evolution is on the pathway of Divinity. Only in the fact that he has gone farther along that path does man differ from the microbe.

If, therefore, the human race wishes to survive, it must alter itself, or transcend itself. If men refuse to make the effort, Life will try a fresh experiment. What would it matter to Life? Infinity of time, infinity of numbers, are at its disposal. But, it may be said, does it depend on man to surpass himself?—Old Darwinian prejudices. . . . Just as the athlete in his training develops, and consequently creates his muscles, so a philosopher can make himself a brain. Will can do everything, and especially prolong the duration of life, but not conscious selfish will. The two people in *The Thing Happens*, who find themselves living for centuries, are a commonplace parson and a parlourmaid, who never consciously intended or believed in such a miracle. That is the sense of Shaw's "metabiological Pentateuch", *Back to Methuselah*.

Up to this point we all follow Shaw with sympathy. It is agreeable for man to learn that by a conviction of necessity he can prolong his life, develop his brain so that the earth is peopled with Goethes and Shelleys, and even engender a god. But we recoil when we come to the final term of this evolution. We cling to our world, our flesh, and our devil. The world of the Shavian patriarchs is an abomination to us. What are they doing with their lives? When Shaw, in the fifth part of his cycle, conveys us "as far as thoughts can reach," we see the Ancients of both sexes wandering about, bald, wise, and terrifying. Their bodies are abhorrent to them. Listen to them:

"*The She-Ancient.* The day will come when there will be no people, only thought. . . .

"*The He-Ancient.* And that will be life eternal."

And here we leave all real existence behind, to fall back into an extreme neo-Platonism and neo-Thomism. Shaw declares that intellect is a passion, and its satisfaction the most satisfying and permanent of all human enjoyments. He prophesies a development of this satisfaction into an ecstasy for transcending our carnal delights. The Ancients in *Back to Methuselah* look forward to discarding their bodies as they have discarded their tails. Their heaven is one in which they will be bodiless vortices of Life Force. This is *As Far As Thought Can Reach*, which is much too far for playgoers who still have more body than brains.

VI

THE ART OF BERNARD SHAW

PAUL VALÉRY once remarked to me that Shakespeare became famous because he had the apparently rash idea of making the actors, at the most tragic moments of his plays, declaim whole pages of Montaigne. "It happened," he added, "that this public liked moralizing speeches."

Nearly all publics like moralizing speeches in the theatre, provided they are intelligent and brilliant and deal with subjects of topical interest. Aristophanes and Molière both did equally bold things in different forms, analogous to Shakespeare's. Shaw was even more daring when he put scientific and philosophic conflicts on the stage, and gave his heroes long lectures to deliver on evolution, on the art of ruling the English, on Protestantism, on Ireland. He succeeded because these lectures were intrinsically original and interesting, because they were impassioned and had power to move an assembled crowd, and also because abstract speeches in the theatre are always made more concrete by the person of the actor. The presence of a human body almost automatically creates the illusion which a novelist has slowly and artfully to piece together.

The theatre depends on the spectator accepting a series of conventions. But he is willing to do so, and

that is why realistic settings and dialogue are superfluous to him. Shaw's dialogue would be highly im-
probable in real life, but the theatre is not real life.
Originally it is a religious ceremony, and as they
watch the stage men enjoy that meditation on the
things of eternity which the religious ceremony sets
before them. They also like to find in it an image of
the great dramas of secular life. Shaw, like his rival,
Shakespeare, enjoys trumpets and processions, and
great historical figures. He has a feeling for the
spectacular.

The comic element in Shaw is simple and rather
uniform in tone, but it is effective. It consists of making each character utter, not the words he would use
in actual life, but those which express his hidden and
heart-felt thoughts. This cynical device produces an
effect of surprise which might well be tragic, but it
remains comic because of an exaggeration of the effects and because of the general character of the vices
thus denounced. Of these, respectability is most often
the butt of Shaw's wit. This is another reason why
his success has never been notable in France. The
objects of his mockery are not those which call for
such handling amongst a realist and naturally disre-
spectful people. Frenchmen scarcely laugh at all, because, as the visitor said of the sermon he had listened
to, they "don't belong to this parish." The Shavian
plays most appreciated in France have been those in
a serious tone, like *Saint Joan*.

To the England of 1900 Shaw preached a very
salutary sermon. Upper-class morals were fairly free,
but the Myth of Respectability lay heavy on the

liveliest minds. Marx gave it its death blow and incidentally gave Shaw the necessary documentary evidence to *"épater le bourgeois"* with deadly conviction. If English youth now stands free from certain forms of hypocrisy, it is partly owing to Bernard Shaw. But if he has been a destructive power, he has had little creative influence. One could find very few people in England who have resolved, on Shaw's advice, to enlist deliberately in the service of the Life Force to create the Superman. Socialist converts he may have made; but here again the vague benevolence of the Socialist temperament recoiled from his remorseless precision. When he declared and proved Socialism, brought down to tin tacks, means equality of income, the Socialists were much more dismayed than the capitalists.

Has Shaw been the equal of Molière? Comparisons of this sort really have little meaning. Molière's voice, surely, is stronger, more direct and more sustained. His scenes are more workman-like in construction than Shaw's, though Shaw, who loves Molière, maintains that his technique is the same, and is the ancient technique of the clown and the ringmaster in the circus, slapstick and all. But Shaw, in the underworld act of *Man and Superman*, attains an intellectual poetry which is beautiful and all his own. Above all, some of his prefaces are masterpieces, alike in the stern boldness of their ideas and their vigorous, sparkling form. If a French comparison is necessary, it should rather be with Voltaire. He has the same encyclopædic intelligence, the same fusion of a light tone and serious content, the same vivacity of style and personality, the same vivid and laughing old age. Shaw, it may be, has more intellectual honesty than Voltaire: his notions of history are less distorted by fanaticism and anti-fanaticism; his view of Christianity is less unjust. Shaw's greatest misfortune as a political writer is that he writes in the language of a people which no longer persecutes ideas or sends writers into exile. Voltaire's books had the glamour of having been committed to the flames of the hangman; if the patriarch of Whitehall Court seeks the glory of Ferney, he should send himself into exile.

VII

IN THE sunset of the Victorian age, and after the defeat of Wilde, it was only violent and keen movement which could save a writer from the waves of treacly sentimentality which had invaded the theatre and the magazines. Shaw was brutal enough not to be made captive.

Mr Desmond MacCarthy tells how once he heard Bernard Shaw describe his mother's cremation with the most exhilarating joyousness. Shaw felt that MacCarthy was taken aback, and turning towards him he added, in a tone of apparent indifference: "Don't suppose that I am a man who forgets people easily."

It is a fine thing to reject vulgar sentimentalism out of respect for more secret, and more sincere, emotions.

IV

G. K. CHESTERTON

G. K. Chesterton

KIPLING, Wells and Shaw, each in his own way, are aristocrats. Kipling thinks that the right to command is conferred only by certain virtues; Wells believes in the privileges of intellect; Shaw awaits the reign of the Superman, who will be a hybrid of Shaw, Caesar and Methuselah. Chesterton, on the contrary, is a democrat; he upholds the average man, who digs in his garden and drinks beer at the public-house, and he has little affection for Wells's experts. Shaw and Wells, confronted by the failure of the nineteenth century, look for the salvation of mankind in the future. Chesterton hates the society engendered by machinery no less than they do, but sees the salvation of humanity in a return to the past. Kipling is a pessimist, Chesterton an optimist. Kipling calls upon the Lord God of hosts; Wells, upon the god of test-tubes and statistics; Shaw, upon the god of life; while Chesterton worships the Christian God as He is found in the Gospels. Wells and Shaw believe in progress; even Kipling shows a touch of admiration in describing the council of experts which one day will govern the earth; Chesterton is reactionary, brilliantly so, loudly and cheerfully so, and praises with intense admiration the freedoms of the Middle Ages. Wells describes imaginary worlds, and by sheer talent succeeds in making them seem real. Chesterton depicts the real world, and by sheer talent, manages to make it seem fantastic. In the history of English ideas at the opening of the twentieth century, Wells and Shaw are moderns, Kipling is the everlasting, Chesterton the anti-modern. This is a useful function.

I

LIFE AND WORKS

His life is uneventful, as befits a man who exalts the glamour of ordinary lives. Gilbert Keith Chesterton was born in London in 1874; during his school-days at St. Paul's School, he astonished masters and boys by his diversions and his precociousness. He was already writing poems, and the school magazine can show plenty of articles signed with the now famous initials, "G. K. C." Because he scribbled drawings in the margins of his note-books, his father supposed that he wanted to become an artist, and sent him to an art school. There he did very little, but found himself in the company of cynical young men, a circumstance which roused in him a defensive reaction and turned him towards religion and humility. This was in London, in the days of the so-called decadence, the *fin de siècle*, the disillusioned epigrams of Oscar Wilde. This atmosphere was repellent to Chesterton, and a reading of the poems of Walt Whitman consolidated his love of life, which was the sentiment natural to him. He has described himself as a pagan at ten years old and an agnostic at sixteen; at twenty he recovered a religious philosophy, and later discovered that this philosophy was that of Christianity.

On leaving school, he tried to make a living as an art critic. He published a few poems, praised by sound critics, but scarcely read. In 1899, Chesterton was a young journalist and poet in his twenties, quite obscure; in 1900, London was asking "Who is this G. K. C.?" It was the Boer War which suddenly made him famous. A certain number of Englishmen sided with the Boers, and took up an anti-Imperialist attitude: Gilbert Chesterton was one of them. But his position was original in this respect: that whereas many Nonconformists and Quakers showed hostility to this war, because they were hostile to all war and all nationalism, Chesterton affirmed his sympathy with the Boers *because of* his nationalism. He accused the Imperialists, not of being patriots, but of not being really patriots: because, he argued, if one believed in the idea of nationality, the idea of Empire is impossible, because it is a cosmopolitan idea tending to destroy the nationality of others. This doctrine Chesterton defended with astonishing skill, in a style that sparkled with imagery and antithesis. In a few months he was famous.

His personal appearance helped the rapid spread of this celebrity. He was a young giant, so large that Bernard Shaw said that, when one talked to Chesterton, half of his body was always out of sight. He wore a wide-brimmed felt hat and a very romantic cloak; he had a spontaneous, almost child-like, laugh. Highly imaginative, and believing, like Dickens, that adventure lurks at every corner of a London street, he perambulated Fleet Street armed with a sword-stick and a revolver. For the shortest journey he would take a hansom. In fact, his amusements, his jollity, his cult of taverns, his taste for detective stories, and countless other characteristics, made him a legendary creature.

How far did this legend fit the reality? The Chesterton whom we know nowadays is a plain, cheerful man, obviously enjoying life, who can reel off pages and pages of poetry, and talks with all the brilliance of his writing. Solemnity he knows not. "It is so easy to be solemn"; he says, "it is so hard to be frivolous. Let any honest reader shut his eyes for a few moments, and approaching the secret tribunal of his soul, ask himself whether he would really rather be asked in the next two hours to write the front page of the *Times*, which is full of long leading articles, or the front page of *Tit-Bits*, which is full of short jokes. If the reader is the fine conscientious fellow I take him for, he will at once reply that he would rather on the spur of the moment write ten *Times* articles than one *Tit-Bits* joke. Responsibility, a heavy and cautious responsibility of speech, is the easiest thing in the world; anybody can do it. That is why so many tired, elderly, and wealthy men go in for politics. They are responsible, because they have not the strength of mind left to be irresponsible."

G. K. CHESTERTON

G. K. CHESTERTON

Chesterton has always been strong-minded enough to be frivolous. From 1905 onwards he has published a weekly essay in the *Illustrated London News*, and despite this prodigious continuity of output, these essays, on every sort of subject, are nearly always worth reading. In them he has fought against the commonplaces of the day, which for the most part have been the "new" or "advanced" ideas: for there is a conventionality in rebellion against which Chesterton has always rebelled. In an age dominated by Wells and Shaw, G. K. C. declared himself a reactionary, savage and unashamed; in an age of temperance, he advocated the love of beer and wine; in an age of gloom, he preached gaiety: in fact, although not a Catholic by birth, he upheld Catholicism. In the vigour of his paradox and style, he is comparable to a Joseph de Maistre; but Joseph de Maistre was an aristocrat, Chesterton a democrat, a fact which at the time did not lack originality, as most of the 1905 reformers had lost faith in democracy.

Besides collections of essays and poems, he published lives of Browning and Dickens at an early age, and much later a life of Cobbett. His biographies were far from conventional in method. Chesterton could not refrain in them, apropos of his subjects' lives, from talking about all manner of things. He is continually quickening the reader's attention by his paradoxical statements. Such-and-such a poem, he will say, shows the characteristic trait of any youthful poem: it gives an impression of the author being a thousand years old. He will declare that the only basis for any optimism is—original sin. The idea concealed in such remarks is comparatively simple, but the elliptic form is a tonic to the mind. *Clarum per obscurius.*

The Dickens and Browning are both excellent books, in that Chesterton had the good sense to choose for his subjects, the lives of men whose natures were akin to his own. Dickens's love for the average man, his conviction that real tragedy and real romance are both to be found amongst ordinary men, are feelings inborn in Chesterton himself. Browning's optimism serves him as a pretext to describe his own: "Browning's optimism . . . was a result of experience—experience which is for some mysterious reason generally understood in the sense of sad or disillusioning experience. An old gentleman rebuking a little boy for eating apples in a tree is in the common conception the type of experience. If he really wished to be a type of experience he would climb up the tree himself and proceed to experience the apples. Browning's faith was founded upon joyful experience, not in the sense that he selected his joyful experiences and ignored his painful ones, but in the sense that his joyful experiences selected themselves and stood out in his memory by virtue of their own extraordinary intensity of colour."

With regard to Browning, too, Chesterton expounds for the first time a theory to which he has wisely been constant throughout his life—that of the simple and ageless quality of man's fundamental emotions. "Robert Browning was unquestionably a thoroughly conventional man. There are many who think this element of conventionality altogether regrettable and disgraceful; they have established, as it were, a convention of the unconventional. But this hatred of the conventional element in the personality of a poet is only possible to those who do not remember the meaning of words. Convention means only a coming together, an agreement; and as every poet must base his work upon an emotional agreement among men, so every poet must base his work upon a convention. Unless he is describing an emotion which others share with him, his labours will be utterly in vain. If a poet really had an original emotion; if, for example, a poet suddenly fell in love with the buffers of a railway train, it would take him considerably more time than his allotted three-score years and ten to communicate his feelings.

"Poetry deals with primal and conventional things —the hunger for bread, the love of woman, the love of children, the desire for immortal life. If men really had new sentiments, poetry could not deal with them. If, let us say, a man did not feel a bitter craving to eat bread; but did, by way of substitute, feel a fresh, original craving to eat brass fenders or mahogany tables, poetry could not express him. If a man, instead of falling in love with a woman, fell in love with a fossil or a sea anemone, poetry could not express him. Poetry can only express what is original in one sense—the sense in which we speak of original sin. It is original, not in the paltry sense of being new, but in the deeper sense of being old; it is original in the sense that it deals with origins."

We encounter these ideas again in two books of greater importance than the biographies, which are books of doctrine. The first, entitled *Heretics*, was an attack on the writers whom he regarded as tainted with modernism, and especially on the most gifted, and therefore the most dangerous, namely Bernard Shaw and H. G. Wells. This polemical work made his adversaries ask for his own ideas, and he thereupon wrote *Orthodoxy*, the outline of a positive doctrine. To these we shall return.

Meanwhile, there are his novels. These are not real novels, but allegories, in which the characters stand for representative Chestertonian themes. *The Man Who Was Thursday*, which the author describes as "a nightmare," is the story of six men who have been given in common the task of fighting anarchy in the world, knowing each other only by their pseudonyms, which are the names of the days of the week, and receiving their orders from a mysterious chief named Sunday. The voice, the great voice of Sunday occasionally gives them their commands, in dark rooms, but they have never seen the man who thus instructs them. Ultimately they come face to face with Sunday, a monstrous giant, and then discover that their supreme leader is none other than the head of the anarchists whom they have always pursued. Criminal and policeman are one and the same man.

The symbolism is visible. If Sunday is at once the Great Anarchist and the chief of the Powers of

Order, it is because God has created all things, evil
as well as good, and that in Him the contraries are
reconciled. *The Man Who Was Thursday* is not a
novel but a refutation of the manichaean idea, a defence of the oneness of nature and of divine unity.

The final scene, where Sunday and the six police-
men converse, is a discussion between the Creator
and his creatures: " 'We will eat and drink later,' he
said. 'Let us remain together a little, we who have
loved each other so sadly, and have fought so
long. . . . I sent you out to war. I sat in the darkness,
where there is not any created thing, and to you
I was only a voice commanding valour and an unnatural virtue. You heard the voice in the dark, and
you never heard it again. The sun in heaven denied
it, the earth and sky denied it, all human wisdom
denied it. And when I met you in the daylight I
denied it myself.'

"There was complete silence in the starlit garden,
and then the black-browed secretary, implacable,
turned in his chair towards Sunday, and said in a
harsh voice—

" 'Who and what are you?'

" 'I am the Sabbath,' said the other without moving. 'I am the peace of God.'

"The Secretary started up, and stood crushing his
costly robe in his hand.

" 'I know what you mean,' he cried, 'and it is
exactly that that I cannot forgive you. I know that
you are contentment, optimism, what do they call
the thing, an ultimate reconciliation. Well, I am

not reconciled. If you were the man in the dark room, why were you also Sunday, an offence, to the sunlight? If you were from the first our father and our friend, why were you also our greatest enemy? We wept, we fled in terror; the iron entered into our souls—and you are the peace of God! Oh, I can forgive God His anger, though it destroyed nations; but I cannot forgive Him His peace.' . . .

" 'Have you ever suffered?'

"As he gazed, the great face grew to an awful size. . . . It grew larger and larger, filling the whole sky; then everything went black. Only in the blackness before it entirely destroyed his brain he seemed to hear a distant voice saying a commonplace text that he had heard somewhere, 'Can ye drink of the cup that I drink of?' "

The other Chesterton novels are similarly allegories. *The Napoleon of Notting Hill* demonstrates that only by a return to the local patriotism of the Middle Ages can mankind be saved. *The Ball and the Cross* is a long theological discussion, the Ball being a symbol of scientific knowledge in opposition to the Cross. And *The Innocence of Father Brown* is a collection of short detective stories of the Sherlock Holmes genre, in which the detective is a Catholic priest who understands and unravels the most complicated mysteries because he approaches them with a perfectly simple mind. It is curious that Chesterton, who is so fond of the ordinary man, finds himself incapable of depicting one in his novels. Nearly all his heroes are, or become, philosophers

[150]

and theologians, and the novel itself is hardly more than a marginal drawing to illustrate doctrine. It is, in fact, on the doctrine that we must fix our attention in a study of Chesterton. To round off the sketch of his life, it need only be said that he married in 1901, and since then he has lived in the charming town of Beaconsfield. He has long been an intimate friend of Hilaire Belloc; and these two men have not only been friends, but also fellow-fighters for more or less common causes. So much so, that Shaw, who has fought against them both, has affected to regard them as one single monster, which he called "the Chesterbelloc." It was perhaps under Belloc's influence that Chesterton finally became a convert to the Catholic Church in 1922. The logic of his thought was certainly leading him to Rome, and between the books preceding and following his actual conversion there is very little difference.

II

MAGIC

CHESTERTON's doctrine may be approached by way of an apologue which he has given us in the form of a comedy. It gives, I think, the clearest introduction to his ideas. This play, *Magic*, is a work of beauty, poetic and far-reaching.

The scene is laid in the English countryside, in the drawing-room of a ducal mansion. The Duke has

a nephew and a niece, both of them highly strung
and delicate, threatened by a dangerous inheritance
of madness. The nephew has been brought up in
America, believes only in science, and stands for the
modern world. The Duke also has two guests, a doctor and a clergyman, who represent science and religion; whilst he himself is an eclectic, a broadminded man—and therefore, Chesterton would say,
a very narrow-minded man. He tries to see good in
all doctrines, which results in his understanding none;
he does his best to please everybody, and actually
pleases nobody. The Duke makes a gift of fifty
pounds towards the building of a new village inn, and
at the same time subscribes fifty pounds to the com-
mittee which is opposing the building of the new
inn.

In order to amuse his newly arrived nephew and
niece, the Duke invites a conjurer, who is also a symbolic figure. He is the fake miracle-worker, half-way
between the two worlds of science and religion.

"Doctor. The Duke is indescribable . . . put two
or three facts or ideas before him, and the thing he
makes out of them is always something that seems
to have nothing to do with it. Tell any other human
being about a girl dreaming of the fairies and her
practical brother from America, and he would settle
it in some obvious way and satisfy someone. Now
the Duke thinks a conjurer would just meet the case.
I suppose he vaguely thinks it would brighten things
up, and somehow satisfy the believer's interest in
supernatural things and the unbeliever's interest in

smart things, as a matter of fact the unbeliever thinks
the conjurer's a fraud, and the believer thinks he's
a fraud too. The conjurer satisfies nobody. That is
why he satisfies the Duke."

Enter the conjurer, a huge black cape wrapped
round him. When he has laid out his apparatus on
the table, the young American goes through them,
explains all the tricks in advance, and makes fun
of them. Then, pointing to a red lamp away at the
end of the avenue, which marks the doctor's house,
he tells the conjurer that it would be a real surprise
if he could change that red into blue. . . . And at
that moment, far off down the avenue, the lamp turns
blue. A miracle has happened.

The onlookers are stupefied. The young American
breaks the silence, gasping: "'Wait a bit! Wait a
bit! I've got you! I'll have you! . . . You put a wire
. . . no, that can't be it. . . .'

"'Well, well, just at this moment we need not en-
quire.'

"'No, Priest, I will not let it alone. Could it be
done with mirrors? You have a mirror. . . . I've
got it! Mixture of lights! Why not? If you throw a
green light on a red light. . . .'

"'You don't get blue.'"

How was the trick done? The doctor begs the
conjurer to explain, as it would be dangerous to
leave this unbalanced young man in such a state of
excitement. But the conjurer *cannot* explain anything.
He does not know himself how the trick was done;
he willed it strongly; the light changed colour. It is

magic, it is a miracle. But as the young man is beginning to show unmistakable signs of mental derangement, the doctor and the magician agree to invent a false and apparently scientific explanation which will soothe him, for, so absurd is modern man, he can be reassured only by a denial of the evidence. The real fanatic is the materialist, as Flaubert discerned long ago.

So runs this parable. It prepares us for understanding Chesterton's philosophy, which is in essence a reaction against the excesses of materialistic teachings.

III

HERETICS[1]

IN THE Middle Ages, says Chesterton, a heretic was a man who prided himself on not being heretical. He regarded himself as the one orthodox man. It was the rest of the world who denounced the heretic's religion as a heresy. But the heretic would have thought himself mad if he did not believe that he was professing the true faith. It was not until modern times that men not only took to calling themselves heretics, but even took pride in doubting, and held that the cosmic theories, man's idea of the universe, are not things of prime importance.

"Atheism itself is too theological for us today.

[1] In these two sections I have attempted a brief summary of the ideas in Mr Chesterton's *Heretics* and *Orthodoxy*. But his readers will appreciate how severely I have been obliged to abridge. A. M.

Revolution itself is too much of a system; liberty itself is too much of a restraint. We will have no generalizations. Mr Bernard Shaw has put the view in a perfect epigram: 'The golden rule is that there is no golden rule.' We are more and more to discuss details in art, politics, literature. A man's opinion on tramcars matters; his opinion on Botticelli matters; his opinion on all things does not matter. He may turn over and explore a million objects, but he must not find that strange object, the universe; for if he does he will have a religion, and be lost. Everything matters—except everything."

From this fear of deciding, this refusal to choose, sprang the extraordinary doctrine of art for art's sake, the doctrine of Oscar Wilde. "Literature has purposely become less political; politics have purposely become less literary. General theories of the relation of things have thus been extruded from both; and we are in a position to ask, 'What have we gained or lost by this extrusion? Is literature better, is politics better, for having discarded the moralist and the philosopher?'" Writers, since Flaubert and Wilde, have come to talk, not about the principles of things but about the principles of their art. This is not a sign of vigour; the healthy man does not talk about his health. Vigorous organisms are concerned with their activity, not their functions. And Chesterton does not only ask artists to be great artists; he insists on taking into account their views on the essential subjects: "I am not concerned with Mr Rudyard Kipling as a vivid artist or a vigorous personality; I am concerned with him as a Heretic—that is to say, a man whose view of things has the hardihood to differ from mine. I am not concerned with Mr Bernard Shaw as one of the most brilliant and one of the most honest men alive; I am concerned with him as a Heretic—that is to say, a man whose philosophy is quite solid, quite coherent, and quite wrong." And then Chesterton picks up, one at a time, all the leading heretics of his age.

The Wellsian heresy? This lies in a renunciation of the human and of the present in favour of Utopia. Wells claims to be a scientist, and often refers to the humility of the man of science, but where is the humility of Mr Wells?

"Mr Wells began his literary work with violent visions—visions of the last pangs of this planet; can it be that a man who begins with violent passions is humble? He went on to wilder and wilder stories about carving beasts into men and shooting angels like birds. . . . Since then he has done something bolder than either of these blasphemies; he has prophesied the political future of all men; prophesied it with aggressive authority and a ringing decision of detail. Is the prophet of the future of all men humble? . . . It is the humble man who does the big things. It is the humble man who does the bold things. . . . And the weakness of all Utopias is this, that they take the greatest difficulty of man and assume it to be overcome, and then give an elaborate account of the overcoming of the smaller ones. They first assume that no man will want more than his share, and then are very ingenious in explaining whether his share will be delivered by motor-car or balloon."

They assume that no being will violate the pacts, and then show the utmost ingenuity in the art of anticipating everything, except the one fact that men will be men. Wells believes that a World State would abolish war, but fails to see that inside a World State there would be terrible civil wars and local wars.

Chesterton recalls Wells's amusing story, *The Food of the Gods*, in which he tells of men growing as big as trees; but he argues that there is no reason to expect that we should have any particular regard for such creatures of excessive size. To be interesting, they must keep within our scale of measurements. *The Food of the Gods* is the story of Tom Thumb told from the giant's point of view, and doubtless the giant killed by Tom Thumb regarded himself as a superman. Probably he saw Tom Thumb as a limited, narrow-minded creature, static and non-dynamic, trying to check the onward march of life. Like Wells, the modern world sides with the giants, but the unchanging paradox is that only the weak can behave. The morality of the giants is too simple, and it certainly is not ours. The Wellsian samurai may be perfect (which is unlikely because they are, after all, men), but they do not know the average man. As the social problem lies in how best to govern a mass of average men, the samurai are incompetent. In practice, they have always failed.

The Shavian Utopia, in spite of an apparent incompatibility with the Wellsian, is of very similar character. Shaw wishes to create the Superman. He is generally represented as a brilliant acrobat, a master of intellectual clowning. Really he is a perfectly consistent man defending a theory, and doing so by amusing methods and with great skill: he is a dangerous heretic. Shaw, who has seemingly been making fun of the beliefs of the past, has actually discovered a new god in an unimaginable future; he has been mocking all idealism, only to uphold the most extravagant ideal of all, that of the new being. Shaw can never have seen things as they are in reality, or he would have dropped on his knees before them. He has not ceased from comparing humanity with something unhuman, with the sage of the Stoics, with the economic man of the Fabians, with Julius Caesar, with Siegfried, with the Superman; and it is fallacious to judge men by comparison with something not human, with a divinity looming vaguely in the twilight of the future.

The one element lacking in Shaw's greatness, according to Chesterton, the only objection that can be urged against his claim to be a great man, is that he is not easily satisfied. He cannot understand that the most loved and valued thing we know is not the Superman, but just the man, the man who drinks beer, the maker of religions, the fighter, the sinner, the sensual man. Those things which are founded on this real creature endure everlastingly. Things founded on the chimera of the Superman died with the moribund civilizations which alone gave them birth. Empires and kingdoms have crumbled because of this inherent and continual weakness, because they were founded by strong men and upon strong men. The Christian Church was founded on weakness, and for that reason is indestructible. No chain can be stronger than its weakest link.

As regards Rudyard Kipling, we have already indicated the line of attack. Of all the Chestertonian excommunications this is the least fair. True, he thoroughly appreciated that Kipling was not a "militarist," as so many superficial critics have urged, "for in so far as his work is earnestly understood the military trade does not by any means emerge as the most important or attractive. He has not written so well about soldiers as he has about railway men or bridge-builders, or even journalists. The fact is that what attracts Mr Kipling to militarism is not the idea of courage, but the idea of discipline." In fact, what attracts Kipling in strife is not the idea of battle, but the idea of discipline. "So far from having merely preached that a soldier cleaning his side-arm is to be adored because he is military, Kipling at his best and clearest has preached that the baker baking loaves and the tailor cutting coats is as military as anybody."

But Chesterton maintains that in his obsession with this multiple vision of power, Kipling is naturally cosmopolitan. He happens to pick his examples in the British Empire, but almost any other empire would serve him equally well. "That which he admires in the British army he would find even more apparent in the German army; that which he desires in the British police he would find flourishing in the French police. . . .

"The great gap in his mind is what may be roughly called the lack of patriotism, that is to say, he lacks altogether the faculty of attaching himself to any cause or community finally and tragically; for all finality must be tragic. . . . He admires England because she is strong, not because she is English." There follows an attack on the exoticism of Kipling; and Chesterton concludes that the world really is being diminished by exploration and conquest. Steamships and telegraph cables make the world smaller, only the microscope makes it larger.

As against exoticism, Chesterton upholds the village, the small town, which hold advantages over the large modern State which a man must be blind to ignore. The man living in a small community is really moving in a much bigger world; he has a better knowledge of the human race, with the hostility of its different species and the incompatibility of its variants. It is in our own family, our own street, that we can really get to know human beings. "And it is the whole effort of the typically modern person to escape from the street in which he lives. First he invents modern hygiene and goes to Margate. Then he invents modern culture and goes to Florence. Then he invents modern imperialism and goes to Timbuctoo." We make our friends, we make our enemies, but God makes our neighbour. And for that reason

G. K. CHESTERTON

the neighbour is a natural being, a natural advantage
upon which we should not look askance.

Just as the principle applies to the Empire, to the
nation within the Empire, to the town within the
nation, and even to the street in the town, so it applies to the house in the street. The institution of the
family is to be praised for the same reasons as the institution of the nation or town. It is good for a man
to live a family life, just as it is good and pleasant for a
man to be snowbound in a street. These experiences
force him to understand that life is something within,
not without, himself. Modern critics of the family
have suggested that it is not a good institution because
it is not always harmonious, but the family is a good
institution for the very reason that it is not harmonious. It is sound because it contains so many divergent and varied elements, and it is an adventure
because it is a gamble.

Life becomes truly romantic when a man is obliged
to undergo experience, active and passive; the life
of the rich is fundamentally dull and uneventful because the rich can choose what will happen. The rich
are bored because they are omnipotent; they are incapable of creating adventure because they contrive
it in this one way. Life is made interesting by that
great limitation of nature which forces us to undergo
the unexpected.

And so the great flaw in the modern conception
of intellectual progress is that, ever since the eighteenth century, it has been concerned with pushing

beyond the boundaries, breaking down obstacles, abolishing barriers, rejecting dogmas. Man cannot live without dogmas. Materialism is the dogma of those who fancy they have escaped from dogma. If there can be such a thing as intellectual progress, it is a progress in the building of a dogmatic philosophy of life.

"Now of all, or nearly all, the able modern writers," says Chesterton in summing up, "whom I have briefly studied . . . they do each of them have a constructive and affirmative view. . . . There is nothing merely sceptically progressive about Mr Rudyard Kipling. There is nothing in the least broadminded about Mr Bernard Shaw. . . . Even the opportunism of Mr H. G. Wells is more dogmatic than the idealism of anybody else." And for that reason they are great writers. The aesthetes of the eighteen-nineties used to tell us that art should produce only pieces of fine writing, that to write well was the one important thing, that ideas can only spoil a work of art, that the artist must in no measure be a moralist. These rules of taste having been pointed out to the generation of 1900, that generation was satisfied by three moralists—Kipling, Wells, and Shaw. The fact is that every man, every average Englishman, stands in need of his metaphysical system and is forced to hold firmly to it. So let us be deaf to the aesthetes; the age of Wilde is dead; the age of the theologians has returned. Let us dig deeper and deeper until we have unearthed our own opinions.

Such, roughly, is the general sense of *Heretics*.

IV

ORTHODOXY

It was only natural that the man who had written this book should at once be challenged to exhibit his own orthodoxy. One critic remarked how he would begin to worry about his philosophy when Chesterton had shown what his own was, adding that this was perhaps a rash remark to make to someone who was only too ready to reply with a book at the slightest provocation.

Orthodoxy begins with an apologue. "I have often had a fancy for writing a romance about an English yachtsman who slightly miscalculated his course and discovered England under the impression that it was a new island in the South Seas." This, he explains, is exactly what the course of his own mind had been. He set out to discover a doctrine; and after studying all the new and unusual aspects of his discovery, he saw that he had simply rediscovered the catechism. Our generation, through its anxiety to be a few years ahead of its time, was eighteen hundred years behind.

What philosophy had Chesterton thus rediscovered? It may be sketched in brief outline.

First: *Reason, as an instrument of thought, is admirable, provided that its material is taken from reality. If it works in the void, it turns to madness.* "Poets do not go mad; but chess-players do . . . when a poet really was morbid it was commonly because he had some weak spot of rationality on his brain. Poe, for instance, really was morbid; not because he was poetical, but because he was specially analytical. . . . The madman is the man who has lost everything except his reason." A lunatic's explanation of something is in a certain sense rational and satisfying; but the lunatic is confined within the clear, exact prison of one idea, and lacks the complexity of a healthy being. A healthy being lives through the body, and it is in the body and by virtue of the body that abstract ideas lose their importance and their danger.

Now, modern thinkers are admirably gifted with the power of reasoning, but are very limited in common sense. They do not think of the real, solid things of life, of struggling peoples, of the pride of mothers, of a young man's first love. They are above and beyond these realities, in a realm of abstract words. If they forced themselves to write only in words of one syllable, in concrete terms, most of their ideas would be inexpressible. Materialism, for instance, is a mental aberration: it denies the evidence. It seeks to explain thought and the soul by actions of the brain, but cannot; and if it had the slightest measure of common sense, it would understand that the spirit, which contains everything, could not be itself entirely contained in one of the little agglomerations of matter which it contains.

The determinist is likewise insane. He denies free will in the name of a process of reasoning, but will is a fact, and in any case the determinist does not himself believe in his own system. If he did so believe, he would not be free to praise or blame, to be grateful, to justify himself, to exist, to pardon sinners or blame tyrants, nor even to say "thank you" when someone passed the mustard. All these creatures of system are mad. Madness is simply reason placed in the void; men are made spiritually sound only by mysticism. By destroying the mystery, a morbid state is created, and the ordinary man is healthy only because he believes in the mysteries. He has always been concerned about what is true, not about what is logical; when he sees two truths apparently in contradiction, he accepts both truths and the contradiction as well. The world has laws, and that is science; sometimes these laws are suspended, and that is a miracle. If the young American in *Magic* had accepted these two manifest truths, he would not have gone out of his mind.

It is not at all Chesterton's intention to attack reason: on the contrary, he is eager to defend it. What he maintains is that human reason is engaged in a process of self-destruction. Determinism, pragmatism, Nietzscheism, are just so many forms of suicide. Reason collapses if it consents merely to make patterns of ill-defined words, which do not correspond to physical, perceptible realities. It is an excellent tool when it is used to work on real facts. But if it denies reality, if it seeks to be rationalistic, in opposition to what is traditional, to the solid universe of churches and houses, it becomes harmful and absurd. It is like the office of the factory claiming superiority over the factory, or like the theorist of the battery who believes that the shell has been at fault because his calculations were perfectly correct.

Second: *Among the realities which reason should respect and take into account, a foremost place must be given to tradition and legend.* "The things common to all men are more important than the things peculiar to any men . . . a legend . . . ought to be treated more respectfully than a book of history. The legend is generally made by the majority of people in the village, who are sane. The book is generally written by the one man in the village who is mad. . . . Tradition . . . is the democracy of the dead."

Now, amongst the traditions of every human society, a foremost place is held by fairy-tales. Every human life starts with belief in the world of fairy-tales, and this shows that the belief is a real need. And it may well be that the fairy world is simply the real world. What are its rules? First and foremost, that there magic is a possibility. Cinderella's godmother can change the pumpkin into a coach and the mice into horses just as, in the real world, the acorn turns into an oak and the egg into a bird. The materialist will retort that this is quite different, that the real world has its fixed laws. "But is it any the less magical for that?" Chesterton will reply. "All the towering materialism which dominates the

modern mind rests ultimately upon one assumption;
a false assumption. It is suppposed that if a thing
goes on repeating itself it is probably dead; a piece
of clockwork. People feel that if the universe was
personal it would vary; if the sun were alive it would
dance."

"The sun rises every morning," says Chesterton.
"I do not rise every morning; but the variation is due
not to my activity, but to my inaction . . . it might
be true that the sun rises regularly because he never
gets tired of rising. His routine might be due, not to
lifelessness, but to a rush of life. . . . It is possible
that God says every morning, 'Do it again' to the
sun; and every evening, 'Do it again' to the moon.
It may not be automatic necessity that makes all
daisies alike; it may be that God makes every daisy
separately, but has never got tired of making them."

A second point at which modern thought clashes
with the tradition of humanity is the supernatural
sense of boundaries and strict conditions. In fairy-
tales there are always rules which limit the actions
of mankind. . . . You cannot live with the king's
daughter unless you show her an onion. . . . These
rules and conditions are not explained. . . . Why
should I leave the ball at midnight? Why can you
stay there until midnight? This dialogue is a symbol
of life, the dialogue between Man and God. It is,
in a different form, the same dialogue that we over-
heard in *The Man Who Was Thursday* between
creature and Creator. "Why am I sometimes un-

happy?" asks the man. "Why are you sometimes happy?" might be the answer to him. And to both questions the reply is the same—that such are the conditions laid down for you. Now, in the books of Wells and many of the moderns these conditions disappear. Man becomes a god. But this is fallacious: man is not a god; man must respect the conditions of the fairy world, which is also the human world, and it is well that things should be so.

Chesterton was never able to join the younger generation of his time in a general sense of revolt. To him, both optimism and pessimism seem absurd. Such general judgements on the world would be comprehensible if you could change your world as you change your house; but we have only one world, and we owe it a measure of loyalty. The primary patriotism is a love of the universe. If you belong to Hammersmith, you must not be for Hammersmith or against it: you must love Hammersmith. If you are bound up with this earth, you must love this earth.

Such were Chesterton's spontaneous feelings, he says; such were his intellectual needs; and in this way did he accept the terms of the supernatural. And so, when he encountered Christianity, he found that these ideas and needs, this joyful acceptance, fitted in wonderfully with his doctrine. "It was as if I had been blundering about since my birth with two huge and unmanageable machines, of different shapes and without apparent connection—the world and the Christian tradition. I had found this hole in the world:

the fact that one must somehow find a way of loving the world without trusting it. . . . I found this projecting feature of Christian theology, like a sort of hard spike, the dogmatic insistence that God was personal, and had made a world separate from Himself. The spike of dogma fitted exactly into the hole in the world—it had evidently been meant to go there— and then the strange thing began to happen. When once these two parts of the two machines had come together, one after another, all the other parts fitted and fell in with an eerie exactitude."

Christianity is often illogical, but the world itself is illogical. If one key fits a lock, you know that to be the right key. Christianity, after the ancient wisdom, was a new attitude of the wise man: much more complex and less rational than the wisdom of the Greeks, but all the more true. Paganism had been, as it were, a marble pillar standing upright by its symmetrical proportions. Christianity is like a huge, rugged, romantic rock, which, although it may oscillate at a touch, stands balanced there for thousands of years because of the equilibrium of its shapelessness. And this is the compelling romanticism of orthodoxy.

To which the agnostic replies: "Well and good. So you have harmonized fairy-tales with Christian theology? Very well. You have found a practical philosophy in the doctrine of the Fall? Very good. But granting that there are certain truths in these doctrines, why cannot you take the truths, accept the good points of Christianity, all that you can define as morally valid, and leave aside the dogmas, which are by their very nature incomprehensible?"

"But why not accept Christianity in its entirety?" answers Chesterton. "What reasons are there for not believing?" Some men refuse to believe because they accept a theory of evolution and regard mankind as simply a species of the animal world. Others refuse because they hold that primitive religion springs from ignorance and fear; others again because of the "bitterness and darkness" which priests have brought into the world. To all of these arguments, says Chesterton, there is one answer: that they are false. If you consider mankind and animals, you will be struck, not by the fact that man resembles the beasts, but that he is different from them. When I began to study modern ideas regarding prehistory, I found that modern science knows nothing at all about prehistoric man, for the very good reason that he is prehistoric. In *The Eternal Man* Chesterton sets out to show, like Kipling, that man has always been man.

The agnostic has doubts because the Middle Ages were "barbarous"; but they were not (and Chesterton wrote a whole history of England to show it). Or because Darwinism is proved; but it is not. Or because miracles do not happen; but they do. Because monks were idle; but they were very industrious. Because nuns were unhappy; but they were cheerful. Because Christian art was sad and insipid; but it delighted in brilliant colours and gold. Because modern science has left the supernatural behind; but it is moving towards the supernatural at express speed.

There remain the objective phenomenon of the supernatural, the belief in miracles, and in the creation of the world of God. In these, says Chesterton, "I believe . . . as I do in the discovery of America. The believers in miracles accept them . . . because they have evidence for them. The disbelievers in miracles deny them because they have a doctrine against them. . . . If I say, 'Mediaeval documents attest certain miracles . . .' they answer, 'but the mediaevals were superstitious.' . . . Iceland is impossible because only stupid sailors have seen it; and the sailors are only stupid because they say they have seen Iceland.

"The Christian Church . . . is a living teacher. It not only certainly taught me yesterday, but will almost certainly teach me tomorrow. When your father told you, walking about the garden, that bees stung or that roses smelt sweet, you did not talk of taking the best out of his philosophy. When the bees stung you, you did not call it an entertaining coincidence. When the rose smelt sweet you did not say 'My father is a rude, barbaric symbol, enshrining . . . the deep delicate truths that flowers smell? No: you believed your father, because you had found him to be a living fountain of facts, a thing that really knew more than you; a thing that would tell you truth tomorrow as well as today."

Such, in summary, is the Chestertonian faith, as he presented it in *Orthodoxy*, a book which, in its forcible thought and dazzling style, is unique.

V

CONCLUSION

THE capital sin of the past two centuries has been
pride. Human intelligence, drunk with its own successes, has reached the point of ignoring the restraints
of reality and scorning the traditions of the race. In
the end it has imprisoned itself, like a larva, in a determination of its own secretion, in a web of its own
weaving, and it has let itself be ruled by monsters of
its own creation. Chesterton, with wonderful vigour
and brilliance, has striven to reconcile intelligence
with tradition. Against Shaw and Wells he is an in-
dispensible counterpoise, and, as he would say himself with a smile, a massive one, and therefore an effective one.

He can be accused of sometimes being the victim
of his own virtuosity. The physicist works out symmetrical formulas and finds in these the laws of the
universe because God is a geometrist; similarly Chesterton, by setting paradox alongside paradox, builds
up a picture of reality because reality is a totalling
of paradoxes. But sometimes this juggling with formulas exhausts the reader, who is left with an uneasy
feeling in his mind. He sees so clearly that Chesterton is brilliant that he no longer sees how profound Chesterton is. In the ballet of his words we do
not always recognize the ordinary life which he

[172]

would have us love, and which we are continually touching as we read Dickens or Tolstoy. In his novels Chesterton attains the peak of vivid intelligence, but it lacks life; and this is serious for a writer who wants to lead us back from the intellect to life itself. Even in *Orthodoxy*, it is only when we have ceased to be dazzled by the outward glitter that we discover the beauty of the doctrinal structure.

But here let us apply to Chesterton what he himself said about Dickens. There are critics who wish that Dickens had been different; and there are visitors to the Zoo who gaze at the hippopotamus or the elephant and think that these giant creatures would be more nearly perfect if they were different. But the hippopotamus and the elephant are facts. Dickens and Chesterton are facts. Without his paradoxes, without his jokes, without his rhetorical switchbacks, Chesterton might perhaps be a clearer philosopher. But he would not be Chesterton. It has often been supposed that he is not serious because he is funny; actually he is funny because he is serious. Confident in his truth, he can afford to joke. Tyrants and prophets of woe are often men who are afraid. Certainty breeds serenity.

During an age of morbid rationalism, Chesterton reminded men that reason is indeed a wonderful tool, but a tool that needs material to work on, and produces nothing if it does not take the existing world as its object. His fable to explain Browning's conception of the universe may also serve to make his own understood:

"Browning's conception of the Universe can hardly be better expressed than in the old and pregnant fable about the five blind men who went to visit an elephant. One of them seized its trunk, and asserted that an elephant was a kind of serpent; another embraced its leg, and was ready to die for the belief that an elephant was a kind of tree. In the same way to the man who leaned against its side it was a wall; to the man who had hold of its tail a rope, and to the man who ran upon its tusk a particularly unpleasant kind of spear. This, as I have said, is the whole theology and philosophy of Browning. But he differs from the psychological decadents and impressionists in this important point, that he thinks that although the blind men found out very little about the elephant, the elephant was an elephant and was there all the time."

To Chesterton as to Browning, the universe stands constant, solid and wondrous, under all the theories built up by intelligence, each as different from the others as were the reports of the blind men on the elephant. In that universe, with Chesterton's help, we can grow deep, spreading roots, and the shifting winds of the mind cannot drag us out of the soil for those brief and glorious flights that end in a quick fall.

V

JOSEPH CONRAD

Joseph Conrad

"JOSEPH CONRAD," wrote Paul Valéry, who knew him well, "spoke French with a good Provençal accent, but English with a dreadful accent which caused me much amusement. To be a great writer in a language which one speaks so poorly is something rare and outstandingly original." But everything is surprising when one examines the career of Conrad. He was admired by sensitive writers, passionately concerned with form, like Valçry and Gide in France, Virginia Woolf and Desmond MacCarthy in England, no less than by a muscular poet like Paul Claudel and a great host of readers. Speaking Polish like the Pole that he was, French like a man who had learnt it from childhood and spent his youth in Marseilles, and yet encountering the English tongue only late in life, he set about writing in English, and not only "added graces" to this adopted language, but expressed a certain Anglo-Saxon ideal better, perhaps, than any other man of letters.

In the group of "messages" which we are here trying to decipher, Conrad's appears as the most direct expression of a stoic philosophy of life, that of the British man of action. This foreigner has proved himself, more exactly even than Kipling, the interpreter of what is best in the English soul. The work of

Kipling is peopled often by the gods of the East, and the powers of Evil prowl in its jungles, at the gates of Indian cities, round the camps of the Sahibs and alongside the workshops of the bridge-builders. In Conrad's books, man stands alone facing the universe; his finest tales describe the battles of man with the sea, that is to say, the age-long struggle which has fashioned the most characteristic Englishmen.

More than a poet of the sea, he preaches the virtues engendered by the sea. He propounds a rule of life which is an active pessimism, akin to that of Tchekov, but more romantic perhaps, because the sailor will always be less of a realist than the physician. It is this philosophy which we shall try to set forth. But we should first of all describe the life which illuminates the work.

I

His full name was Joseph Conrad Korzeniowski, and he was born in Russian Poland in 1857, the son of a Polish patriot in life-long revolt against the Russian domination. After the abortive insurrection of 1863 against the Tsar's government, he was condemned to exile and sent off into northern Russia. There is in existence a photograph of the little boy Conrad, on the back of which he has written: "To my dear grandmamma, who helped me to send presents to my poor papa in prison, a Pole, a Catholic, a gentleman, July 6, 1863."

Madame Korzeniowski, a frail and charming

woman, soon followed her husband into exile, and took with her this five-year-old son. He had hitherto been brought up like the well-to-do children of these great country houses which we know so well through the novels of Tolstoy or Turgenev. On the steps of the house, to bid him farewell, stood his old nurse, the housekeeper, and the French governess, a worthy but plain lady, who cried tearfully to him at the moment of departure: "Don't forget your French, darling!"

In years to come, Conrad was annoyed when the critics, who had accepted his first novels unreservedly as coming from an English novelist, discovered that he was a Pole and sought to explain his talent in terms of the Slav temperament. Nothing, he protested, could be more foreign to the Polish temperament than what the critics called "the Slav soul." Poland, a country purely Western in spirit, moulded by Italy and France, had a tradition of free government, a chivalrous code of morals, an almost exaggerated respect for the rights of the individual. He further protested against an attempt to explain certain characters in his books by the fact that he was reputed to be the son of a revolutionary. This was incomprehensible: the Polish rising was a patriotic revolt against a foreign tyranny.

Conrad's father, indeed, was essentially a conservative. He was a man of culture, who had translated Victor Hugo into Polish, and was himself a creative writer. After the death of his wife, who was tuberculous and could not stand up to exile and the change of climate, he undertook the education of his son. "I take up my life again, which is entirely centred upon my little Conrad. I teach him what I know, but that, unfortunately, is little. I shield him from the atmosphere of this place, and he grows up as though in a monastic cell. . . . We shiver with cold, we die of hunger. . . . Such is our life." Reading, to these proscribed victims, was the only possible mode of escape; and at a very early age Conrad read Hugo's novels in his father's translation, Walter Scott, Fenimore Cooper, and (above all) Dickens, of whom he was always fond. His health then became so much undermined that the boy had to be removed from this chilly climate and sent to live with an uncle. "Conrad," his father wrote, "is at his uncle's in the country, and we are both unhappy. The child is so stupid as to grieve for my loneliness and to regret an existence in which the only distractions were my doleful countenance and my lessons." The mingled fondness and bitterness in these words enable us to imagine what the boy's childhood was like. Surrounded by Russians, whom he regarded as enemies, with no friend other than a sick father, he could only form a pessimistic view of life; but he could also derive a lofty idea of the aristocratic virtues, as displayed by his father. When M. Korzeniowski died the city of Cracow gave him a solemn burial, as to a national hero. To his son, youth though he was, they gave the freedom of the city.

The lad's sole remaining relative was his maternal uncle. He was rather a stage uncle, crabbed but kind at heart, and advised Conrad not to go on living in an oppressed Poland, where as a patriot's son he would have no future. He even encouraged him in an idea of becoming a naturalized Frenchman, so as to lose the nationality of his father's persecutors. The strange thing is that this young fellow, brought up far away from any seacoast, in the heart of Europe, even then had a passionate longing to become a sailor. But where and how could he do so? The simplest idea seemed to be to live in France, whose language the young Korzeniowski spoke and where there was a long-standing tradition of Polish friendship.

At the age of seventeen he arrived in Marseilles, with an introduction to a resident who was able to bring him into touch with sailors, pilots, and the curious world of ship-chandlers. We catch a glimpse of him sailing one night in the vessel of one of his new friends and holding the tiller for the first time, heading over in the darkness to the Château d'If. He thought of *Monte Cristo*, which he had read long ago with his exiled father. "Keep her in the wake of the moon," said the Captain, sitting down on the lowered sails and feeling for his pipe. It may have been on that night that the writer Conrad was born.

Not until he was twenty-one did he set foot in England. He knew nobody there, and did not speak the language. He first began to learn it from North Sea fishermen, and a wild and stormy school he said it was. But England pleased him immediately because of what he described as a certain chivalrous aspect of its characters. He always protested against the view that he might just as well have become a writer in some other language. "The truth of the matter is that my faculty to write in English is as natural as any other aptitude with which I might have been born. I have a strange and overpowering feeling that it had always been an inherent part of myself. English was for me neither a matter of choice nor adoption. The merest idea of choice had never entered my head. And as to adoption—well, yes, there was adoption; but it was I who was adopted by the genius of the language, which directly I came out of the stammering stage made me its own so completely that its very idioms I truly believe had a direct action on my temperament and fashioned my still plastic career."

He studied for the examinations for the British Mercantile Marine, became naturalized, and, by dint of his energy, obtained a mate's certificate after a spoken examination in this foreign tongue. For twenty years thereafter his life was spent at sea. He was a professional seaman, and knew the ocean's peace. "A sailor," he said, "finds a deep feeling of security in the exercise of his calling. The exacting life of the sea has this advantage over the life of the earth, that its claims are simple and cannot be evaded." According to his official papers, Conrad was an excellent ship's officer. He was always deeply and legitimately proud—far more so than of his literary fame—because he had been judged a good sailor by seafaring men.

In time he became first mate, and then captain; and in the course of long voyages in the South Seas he

JOSEPH CONRAD, FROM A CHALK DRAWING BY SIR WILLIAM ROTHENSTEIN

became familiar with the astounding world of sailors, brokers, traders, adventurers, rajahs, Dutchmen, Chinese and Malayans which, in later years, he was to describe. *The Nigger of the Narcissus*, one of his best novels, is the authentic story of a voyage that Conrad made in 1884; *Almayer's Folly* is the story of a man whom he came across in the same way. Almayer was a half-caste Dutchman about whom there were sailors' tales everywhere from Dongola to Singapore. Captains and rajahs alike laughed when Almayer's name was mentioned. Conrad had seen his strange shape for the first time from the deck of his ship, standing out against the palms and bamboos, the stout man in flowery cotton pyjamas, with huge yellow petals. He was told the story of this pathetic, romantic failure, and it interested him. Perhaps it even inspired him for the first time with the desire to compose a story. If he had not known Almayer so well, Conrad said, he would probably never have had a line put into print. And we may picture Conrad writing the chapters of this first novel of his on board a two-thousand ton vessel lying alongside the quays of Rouen, while he evokes the shade of Flaubert leaning over him before the Theatre des Arts, and while his companions, rather puzzled and inquisitive, open the door of his cabin and ask: "What is it you're always scribbling there?"

Conrad did not answer, and in any case he only wrote in his spare time, so that *Almayer's Folly*, begun in 1887, was not completed and published until 1894. When John Galsworthy, then an unknown young man, travelled in a sailing-ship with Conrad, the latter made no mention at all of his manuscript. "Very dark he looked in the burning sunlight, tanned, with a peaked brown beard, almost black hair, and dark brown eyes, over which the lids were deeply folded." With the crew he was popular, with the young officers friendly and companionable, and with his old whiskered captain, respectful. He spoke about life, not books.

As a matter of fact Captain Korzeniowski was then going through the inner crisis which he described in *The Shadow Line*. "One goes on. And the time, too, goes on—till one perceives ahead a shadow-line warning one that the region of early youth, too, must be left behind.

"This is the period of life in which such moments of which I have spoken are likely to come. What moments? Why, the moments of boredom, of weariness, of dissatisfaction. Rash moments. I mean moments when the still young are inclined to commit rash actions, such as getting married suddenly or else throwing up a job for no reason."

One day without any reason, Conrad left his ship, as if he had seen a vision, just as a bird, for no visible reason, will leave its branch and fly off to migrate to some far region of the earth. The sailor became an explorer on land, and left for a journey to the Congo. As a little boy of nine, looking at a map of Africa, he had put his finger on a space which in those days was blank, a *terra incognita*, and said: "When I'm big, I shall go there." He went there, and lost his

health. On his return from Africa he was a different
man, gouty and partly disabled, and felt unable to
resume a seafaring life. Illness is often the cruel and
powerful fairy who determines the vocation of
writers. It was this which slew Captain Korzeniowski.

When he left the sea at the age of thirty-seven,
in 1894, he sent the manuscript of *Almayer's Folly*
to a London publisher, Fisher Unwin. Three months
later he learnt that his book was accepted. It had the
good fortune to be read by Edward Garnett, one of
the finest judges of literature in England, and a man
who has lavished his help most generously on the
talented young writers of this generation. Garnett
was so much struck by the manuscript of *Almayer's
Folly* that he asked if he could meet its author. He
gave Conrad advice and encouragement. Conrad
then wrote another novel, *The Outcast of the Islands*,
and then his third, *The Nigger of the Narcissus*.

Thenceforward his life became that of a professional writer, but a writer working in peculiarly difficult circumstances. He had married, he was poor,
and he needed money. Throughout those long years
of making a start, he wrote under the spur of the
sternest need. Writing to Mrs Galsworthy in 1909, he
said: "Excuse this discordant strain; but the fact is
that I have just received the accounts of all my publishers, from which I perceive that all my immortal
works (13 in all) have brought me last year something under five pounds in royalties. That sort of
thing quenches that *joie de vivre* which should burn
like a flame in an author's breast and in the manner

of an explosive engine drive his pen onward at 30 pages an hour."

Furthermore, he was struggling with a strange language, and worked very slowly. He was stricken with rheumatism, and seated at his desk he was often in bodily pain; but he resolved to be as good a craftsman of letters as he had been a model sailor. All his letters offer glimpses of a studious, hard-pressed life: "In the last 23½ months, I have written 187,000 words, of which 130,000 of the novel. I sit 12 hours at the table, sleep six, and worry the rest of the time, feeling age creeping on and looking at those I love. For two years I haven't seen a picture, heard a note of music, had a moment of ease in human intercourse—not really.

"Sixteen months for a long novel nearly done and some 57,000 words of the other work is not so bad—even for a man with his mind at ease, with his spirits kept up by prosperity, with his inspiration buoyed by hope. There's nothing of that for me! I don't complain, dear Jack, I only state it as an argument, for when people appraise me later on with severity, I wish you to be able to say: 'I knew him—he was not so bad.' By Jove, all the moral tortures are not in prison-life. I assure you I feel sometimes as if I could drop everything."

Desmond MacCarthy, who saw him about this time, describes his black eyebrows and curving nose, his humped-up shoulders, the extreme quietness of his voice and gesture, and his rather deliberate courtesy. He struck this English observer as "foreign," but he was magnificently dignified, and obviously he expected other people not only to respect that dignity but to have something of it themselves. No writer led a life more hidden or more proud. "Possibly his early training in the merchant service taught him the difference in value between, say, the mate's views on navigation and those of the intelligent passenger. He seldom parted with his signature in any cause, and he respected his own craft so sincerely that he did not think it necessary for his manhood publicly to express strong views on the problems of London traffic, diet, or foreign exchanges. . . . Men of letters have lost by his death that heartening thing—a living example."

It might have been thought that Conrad would find a home within sight of the sea; but he had seen too much of it. Like the sailor who takes care not to let the sea-air into his bunk when he is in it, Conrad always lived well inland. The sea could not be the friend of a man who knew its temper all too well. He was reluctant to speak about his past life. His seafaring memories were now only material to be worked into shape. The sea was like an old lover, cast off, and in the hall of his house there was only one engraving, the picture of a splendid sailing-ship, to evoke a twinge of longing memory. "Don't look at that," he said to André Gide; "let's talk about books."

From the time of his abandoning his career as a sailor, Conrad's life was one of constant and exacting literary toil, carried on through ceaseless physical suffering. His letters are full of references to his work being behindhand, and his brain being tired.

He died in 1924, quite suddenly, of a heart attack. The whole of the previous day he had spent working at his desk. More than once he had described with a touch of envy the death of sailors who went down battling. "Nobody can say with what thoughts, with what regrets, with what words on their lips they died. But there is something fine in the sudden passing away of these hearts from the extremity of struggle and stress and tremendous uproar—from the vast, unrestful rage of the surface to the profound peace of the depths, sleeping untroubled since the beginning of the ages."

II

THE NOVELIST OF SAILORS

ONE period in the life of any novelist can generally be singled out as that of what may be called "recording." In the course of this the writer is learning, through his own painful experience, and that of other people, the nature of the human passions and the mechanism of human society. The classic example of this is Balzac. After the period of acquisition comes one of gestation, during which the acquired experience ripens, and lastly comes the time when the creative work is produced, often quite brief, but during which the seeds already sown germinate and bring

forth the literary fruits. In the lives of certain novelists there are wide overlappings which make these successive stages hard to distinguish. But in the case of
Conrad the dividing line is sharp and clear. Nearly
all the subjects of his best books are taken from memories of his life between seventeen and thirty-seven,
when he was active and not writing. They can be
classed in two categories: first, stories in which Conrad was a participant, or of which he was a witness,
and second, those which had been told to him. We
shall see how these stories at second-hand gave certain of Conrad's novels their peculiar and complex
form.

The Nigger of the Narcissus is the very simple
story of a ship's crew, a voyage, a storm. There is no
plot, but all the types are shown as forming a human
group—the captain, the mate, the average run of humanity, the dregs, and a strange character, the nigger himself, who shams illness, rouses false sentiments,
and spoils the whole ship's company. *Typhoon* is
the adventure of a vessel carrying Chinese coolies
who begin to murder each other in the midst of a
terrific storm on account of some missing money.
Storm and mutiny would lose the ship if it were not
for the thick-skinned apathy of Captain MacWhirr.
Youth, again, is the story of a ship on fire at sea.
The young officer who tells of the disaster recalls
how it was his first command, and how, when so
near to death, his feelings were of loyalty and happiness.

Lord Jim, the finest of Conrad's novels, is also a

story of the sea. The vessel *Patria*, laden with Indian pilgrims, has struck a piece of floating wreckage and sprung a leak; the officers, a poor lot, abandon her and violate the code of the sea by taking to the boats and leaving the pilgrims to their fate. But the ship does not sink. She is brought to port by a French vessel, and the guilty officers have to face a court of judges. The young mate, Jim, the only Englishman of decent birth amongst them, cannot understand how he came to fail. Might not any man have done the same in these circumstances under the orders of bad superiors? But he cannot forgive himself. The stain on his career tortures him. He spends his life trying to obliterate it, and in the end dies for a point of honour.

Would it be accurate to describe these books as fine sea stories? Conrad did not think so. "I won't bore you," he wrote, "with a discussion of fundamentals. But surely those stories of mine where the sea enters can be looked at from another angle. In the *Nigger* I give the psychology of a group of men and render certain aspects of nature. But the problem that faces them is not a problem of the sea, it is merely a problem that has arisen on board a ship where the conditions of complete isolation from all land entanglements make it stand out with a particular force and colouring. In other of my tales the principal point is the study of a particular man, or a particular event. My only sea book, and the only tribute to a life which I have lived in my own particular way, is *The Mirror of the Sea*."

Now, *The Mirror of the Sea*, although it has fine passages, is really one of Conrad's less satisfactory books. The truth of the matter is that pure description of natural spectacles should never be the essential object of a writer. Critics admire the great storms that Conrad describes in *Typhoon* or *The Nigger of the Narcissus*; and magnificent storms they are. But they are tedious, like paintings of naval battles. Vainly the painter strives to preserve the movement; but a movement caught and fixed is no longer alive. The writer, for his part, uses the time element. His hurricanes move *crescendo*, but nothing is more monotonous or harder to maintain than a continuous *crescendo*. Even Beethoven failed in that; and as a way out he had the explosion of a perfected harmony. But a literary *crescendo* has no adequate resolving chords. "I become confused. . . . I forget how overwhelming the last wave but one was compared with the one I see coming. The little cup of my imagination was full long ago, but the waterfall goes on pounding into it."

Conrad himself would not have liked to be regarded as primarily a man who could describe storms. He was far too honest to assume any sentimental love of the sea. We might almost say that if he liked a seafaring life it was not from any love of the sea, but from love of the battle against the sea. "For all that has been said of the love that certain natures (on shore) have professed to feel for it, for all the celebrations it has been the object of in prose and song, the sea has never been friendly to man. At most it has been the accomplice of human restlessness, and playing the part of dangerous abettor of world-wide ambitions. . . . As if it were too great, too mighty for common virtues, the ocean has no compassion, no faith, no law, no memory. Its fickleness is to be held true to men's purposes only by an undaunted resolution and by a sleepless, armed, jealous vigilance, in which, perhaps, there has always been more hate than love."

If a man cannot love the sea, he can love a ship as he does a garden or a workshop, because these are man-made things, with the marks of the toil and sacrifices of men. All Conrad's captains are proud of their ships. "She was small, but she was good. . . . No other ship could have stood so long the weather she had to live through for days and days. . . . She was fairly worn out, and that's all. You may believe me. She lasted under us for days and days, but she could not last for ever. . . . I am glad it is over. No better ship was ever left to sink at sea on such a day as this." In these words he makes an old captain, with pious affection, utter the funeral oration of his ship.

In *Youth*, just when the sailors are forced to abandon their blazing vessel, the young officer who is telling the story says: "She burned furiously, mournful and imposing like a funeral pile kindled in the night, surrounded by the sea, watched over by the stars. A magnificent death had come like a grace, like a gift, like a reward to that old ship at the end of her laborious days." And analysing this feeling more closely, we find that what interests Conrad is not so much the ship, as the love that men bear their ship.

Conrad is not so much a novelist of the sea as a novelist of certain moral themes. And he knew it. He said to Galsworthy that, whatever you do, people look beyond your art to find your ideas, and that it is these ideas which must be stressed if contemporary judgements are to be guided. And here, too, we must stress these moral themes if we are to understand the essential Conrad.

III

STOIC PESSIMISM

JEAN AUBRY, Conrad's friend and biographer, records that in a volume of French poetry Conrad particularly admired this quotation:

> Dans l'air froid, belisé par des feux innombrables,
> La terre, vaisseu triste au vieux mât pourrissant,
> Mène, sans timonier, vers des ports improbables
> Son grand rêve de gloire, obscur et impuissant.

That Conrad should have relished these lines is comprehensible, for, as he wrote to the author, "my name for nearly sixty-five years now has been amongst those of the crew of that old, enchanted ship gliding with no helmsman across the unknown, into whose splendour and shame you have looked so finely, with the noble clearsightedness of a poet."

The battle between the man of action and the blind forces seemed to Conrad not always hopeless, but always unequal. The crew of the burning ship does what it can, struggles to quench the flames, toils bravely at the pumps; but in the end it is the fire that wins. In Conrad, the forces of annihilation are often the winners. True, in life itself they always triumph in the end. Men die, ships founder, civilizations fall. The sea is not the only power of darkness.

Almayer has married the daughter of a native potentate, a girl captured and adopted by a rich planter. By her he has had a daughter, whom he adores and wishes to Europeanize. But his native wife, who hates him, regains her dominion over the girl and in the end draws her back into savagery. Almayer is left alone, face to face with this inhuman nature, and becomes half-mad. The dark forces have won.

Heart of Darkness has more or less the same subject, or rather the same theme. Marlowe, the character who acts as observer in most of Conrad's novels and is perhaps simply a projection of the author, makes a trip to the Congo, and there hears about a certain Kurtz, a European, a kind of saint living in the jungle amongst the natives, where he does much good. Marlowe is curious about the man and sets out to find him. At last he reaches the village where Kurtz has been living, only to find that he has died a mad-man, after causing himself to be worshipped as a god by the natives in the course of savage and cruel orgies. So here too the dark forces, this time represented by the forests instead of the sea, have conquered reason and goodwill.

In Conrad's eyes the crowd, the people, are like the ocean or the jungle—foes for the hero. In *Nostromo* he depicts a South American country where all the evil passions are kindled by the discovery of a silver mine. As in *The Nigger of the Narcissus*, and as in Kipling's novels, humanity is shown divided into two quite distinct classes. On one side stand the leaders, the masters and foremen, the men born to command because they have a sense of honour (they may be ordinary sailors or workmen: it is a question of soul, not of caste). In the other camp are the underlings, the ruck, the ignoble animal that man becomes when he is not held by the bonds of honour. The character of *Prince Roman* is typical in his freedom from illusions. He did not depend on his imagination, but on long experience of the political atrocities which seemed fated to occur in the life of a state; to him the ordinary course of public institutions consisted of a series of disasters which befell the citizens, each of them logically producing another, unchained by hatred, vengeance, folly and greed, as if they were the dispensation of a divine will. His pessimism is also Conrad's. He believes in the essential badness of man in the mass.

But even the men of honour, even the born leader, can sometimes fall before the powers of darkness. Jim came of good stock; he was, Conrad says, "one of us." But who can answer for not knowing the day when the universe piles up errors so that even the strongest soul is strained to breaking-point? "And it's easy enough to talk of Master Jim, after a good spread, two hundred feet above the sea-level, with a box of decent cigars handy. . . . Of course there are men here and there to whom the whole of life is like an after-dinner hour with a cigar; easy, pleasant, empty, perhaps enlivened by some fable of strike to be forgotten before the end is told—before the end is told—even if there happens to be any end to it."

In *Lord Jim* there is a French naval officer, the rescuer of the derelict pilgrims, who tries hard to judge Jim fairly. "'The fear, the fear—look you—it is always there.'. . . He touched his breast near a brass button, on the very spot where Jim had given a thump to his own when protesting that there was nothing the matter with his heart. I suppose I made some sign of dissent, because he insisted, 'Yes! yes! One talks, one talks; this is all very fine; but at the end of the reckoning one is no cleverer than the next man—and no more brave. Brave! This is always to be seen. I have rolled my hump (*roulé ma bosse*)', he said, using the slang expression with imperturbable seriousness, 'in all parts of the world; I have known brave men—famous ones! *Allez!*' . . . He drank carelessly. . . . 'Brave—you conceive—in the Service —one has got to be—the trade demands it (*le métier vent ça*). Is it not so?' he appealed to me reasonably. '*Eh bien!* Each of them—I say each of them, if he were an honest man—*bien entendu*—would confess that there is a point—there is a point—for the best of us—there is somewhere a point when you let go everything (*vous lâchez tout*). And you have got to live with that truth—do you see? Given a certain combination of circumstances, fear is sure to come. Abominable funk (*un trac épouvantable*). And even for those who do not believe this truth there is fear all the same—the fear of themselves. Absolutely so. Trust me. Yes. Yes. . . . At my age one knows what one is talking about—*que diable!*'"

Yes, some will be honoured, and others will leap, as Jim did, into that bottomless pit into which men bereft of honour fall and from which they can never climb out again. But, Conrad reflects, there is scant justice in this meting out of destinies. It is a matter of luck; there are thousands upon thousands of chances shaping the lives of each one of us. He considers the case of his Captain MacWhirr, and wonders what could have driven this son of a little Belfast grocer to run away to sea when he was only fifteen. And the example suggests the idea of some vast, powerful, invisible hand always ready to descend on the ant-heap of our earth, to grasp any one of us by the shoulder, bang our heads together, and hurl us in unforeseen directions and towards inconceivable flights.

IV

THE HUMAN VIRTUES

A TRAGIC vision of the universe! But it would be misleading to describe Conrad as simply a pessimist and fatalist. The truth is more complex. Although Conrad is a pessimist as regards the results of action, and although he believes that the best of men can promise neither success nor salvation, he is an optimist as regards the qualities engendered by action itself. Men often wage a desperate battle; captains have to let their best ships go down; the jungle swallows up the finest of men; the mob hunts down the greatest leaders; and in any case, victory itself is always imperfect and was not worth all the trouble, as one finds when the triumph is achieved. The treasure of *Nostromo*, saved at the cost of great sacrifice, brings only evil in its train; to wrench that fortune out of the mine was all in vain. But these unavailing struggles are the cause of sentiments excellent in themselves—devotion to a leader or a group, loyalty, honour. Conrad's conclusion seems to be that man is the only treasure.

"Those who read me know my conviction that the world, the temporal world, rests on a very few simple ideas; so simple that they must be as old as the hills. It rests notably, amongst others, on the idea of Fidelity." The material world, the world of storms and crowds, has no stability; the world of men can be stable only through loyalty, that is to say, through a self-given vow not to abandon the group to which one has deliberately bound oneself. A man of honour is a man whose promise, once given, can be counted on, even to death. Jim ought not to have jumped into the boat. A character in *Nostromo* declares that he gave Don Carlos his word not to let the mine fall into the bandits' hands. It does not so much as enter Captain MacWhirr's head that a sailor *could* think of his personal safety in the storm. The sentiment is as old as the hills, and it is found in the history of every ancient race; but it is one without which no human society is possible. How can a man live, how can he fight, if the comrade alongside may betray him?

Any sacrifice to honour is comparatively easy, so long as one is living amongst one's own kind, amongst men who feel the same sentiments. As a motto for *Lord Jim* Conrad chose a reflection of Novalis: "It is certain my Conviction gains infinitely, the moment another soul will believe in it." If Jim broke down under the stress of danger, it was because the mean and common spirits of the men about him had no sense of honour.

"'Man is born a coward (*l'homme est né poltron*). It is a difficulty—*parbleu!* It would be too easy otherwise. But habit—habit—necessity—do you see?—the eye of others—*voilà*. One puts up with it. And then the example of others who are no better than yourself, and yet make good countenance. . . .'

"His voice ceased.

"'That young man—you will observe—had none of these inducements—at least at the moment,' I remarked.

"He raised his eyebrows forgivingly: 'I don't say; I don't say. The young man in question might have had the best dispositions—the best dispositions,' he repeated, wheezing a little.

"'I am glad to see you taking a lenient view,' I

said. 'His own feeling in the matter was—ah!—hope-ful, and . . .'

"The shuffle of his feet under the table interrupted me. He drew up his heavy eyelids. Drew up, I say—no other expression can describe the steady delibera-tion of the act—and at last was disclosed completely to me. I was confronted by two narrow grey circlets, like two tiny steel rings around the profound black-ness of the pupils. The sharp glance, coming from that massive body, gave a notion of extreme effi-ciency, like a razor-edge on a battle-axe. 'Pardon,' he said punctiliously. His right hand went up, and he swayed forward. 'Allow me . . . I contended that one may get on knowing very well that one's courage does not come of itself (*ne vient pas tout seul*). There's nothing much in that to get upset about. One truth the more ought not to make life impossible. . . . But the honour—the honour, mon-sieur! . . . The honour . . . that is real—that is! And what life may be worth when'. . . he got on his feet with a ponderous impetuosity, as a startled ox might scramble up from the grass . . . 'when the honour is gone—*ah ça par exemple*—I can offer no opinion—because—monsieur—I know nothing of it.'"

It is when Jim once more finds himself among men of his own sort and tradition that he realizes how he has lost caste. His life henceforth will be devoted to regaining it.

If Conrad liked England so well, it was chiefly because he found there a setting favourable to the cultivation of such loyalties. "I know his appearance;

JOSEPH CONRAD

he came from the right place; he was one of us. He
stood there for all the parentage of his kind, for
men and women by no means clever or amusing, but
whose very existence is based upon honest faith, and
upon the instinct of courage. I don't mean military
courage, or civil courage, or any special kind of
courage. I mean just that inborn ability to look
temptations straight in the face . . . a power of resistance, don't you see, ungracious if you like, but
priceless—an unthinking and blessed stiffness before
the outward and inward terrors, before the night of
nature and the seductive corruption of men—backed
by a faith invulnerable to the strength of facts, to the
contagion of example, to the solicitation of ideas.
Hang ideas! They are tramps, vagabonds, knocking
at the back door of your mind, each taking a little
of your substance, each carrying away some crumb
of that belief in a few simple notions you must cling
to if you want to live decently and would like to die
easy!"

Conrad had not much belief in the part played in
the conduct of life by intelligence. His favourite
hero is Captain MacWhirr, the taciturn man, quietly
sure of himself, having just enough imagination to
carry him on from one day to the next. Captain
MacWhirr is not the whole of England, but he is
astonishingly like the self-portrait which Englishmen
have been taught to respect. His refusal to think into
the future is the same as Joseph Chamberlain's. The
barometer's dropping. . . . All right, it is dropping.
. . . That is a fact. . . . When other facts turn up,

they will be noted and action will be taken. As for trying to foresee the future, or acting according to theories, or trying to sail round a storm, Captain MacWhirr can think of nothing more foolish. He has the same horror for the high-falutin as Kipling's schoolboys have. When his second officer is angry at being obliged to sail under the Siamese flag, Mac-Whirr is literally incapable of understanding his repugnance.

"The first morning the new flag floated over the stern of the *Nan-Shan* Jukes stood looking at it bitterly from the bridge. He struggled with his feelings for a while, and then remarked, 'Queer flag for a man to sail under, sir.'

" 'What's the matter with the flag?' inquired Captain McWhirr. 'Seems all right to me.' And he walked across to the end of the bridge to have a good look.

" 'Well, it looks queer to me,' burst out Jukes, greatly exasperated, and flung off the bridge.

"Captain MacWhirr was amazed at these manners. After a while he stepped quietly into the chart-room, and opened his International Signal Code-book at the plate where the flags of all the nations are correctly figured in gaudy rows. He ran his finger over them, and when he came to Siam he contemplated with great attention the red field and the white elephant. Nothing could be more simple; but to make sure he brought the book out on to the bridge for the purpose of comparing the coloured drawing with the real thing at the flag-staff astern. When next Jukes,

JOSEPH CONRAD

who was carrying on the duty that day with a sort of suppressed fierceness, happened on the bridge, his commander observed.

" 'There's nothing amiss with that flag.'

" 'Isn't there?' mumbled Jukes, falling on his knees before a deck-locker and jerking therefrom viciously a spare lead-line.

" 'No. I looked up the book. Length twice the breadth and the elephant exactly in the middle. I thought the people ashore would know how to make the local flag. Stands to reason. You were wrong, Jukes. . . .'

" 'Well, sir,' began Jukes, getting up excitedly, 'all I can say—' He fumbled for the end of the coil of line with trembling hands.

" 'That's all right.' Captain MacWhirr soothed him, sitting heavily on a little canvas folding-stool he greatly affected. 'All you have to do is to take care they don't hoist the elephant upside-down before they get quite used to it.' "

To take facts as they come, and to turn them to the best account, is the simplest and most noble form of duty. "Work is the law. Like iron that lying idle degenerates into a mass of useless rust, like water that in an unruffled pool sickens into a stagnant and corrupt state, so without action the spirit of men turns to a dead thing, loses its force, ceases prompting us to leave some trace of ourselves on this earth."

It is in action that human destiny, so poor a thing in relation to the greatness of the universe, recovers its own nobility. "The sight of human affairs deserves admiration and pity; they are worthy of respect too, and he is not insensible who pays them the undemonstrative tribute of a sigh which is not a sob, and of a smile which is not a grin. Resignation, not mystic, not detached, but resignation open-eyed . . . is the only one of our feelings for which it is impossible to become a sham.

"Not that I think resignation the last word of wisdom. . . . But I think that the proper wisdom is to will what the gods will. . . ."

V

ARISTOCRAT AND REALIST

THESE cherished virtues Conrad found amongst sailors rather than landsmen. For the latter he had a certain scorn, and declared that they did things badly because they had too much safety in life and not enough responsibility. They know that, whatever they may do, their little town is not going to capsize, or spring a leak and sink, with their wives and families. Only at sea is the leader a leader, master beneath God, severed from all social or sentimental ties, freed from the false leaders who become powerful on land through plotting and eloquence but would not stand up five minutes in a typhoon.

In real danger, every man desires and respects the real leader. When Mr Jukes is on the point of yielding in the storm, he finds profound comfort by

meeting the imperturbable MacWhirr in the black-
ness: "'Don't you be put out by anything,' the Captain continued, mumbling rather fast. 'Keep her facing it. They may say what they like, but the heaviest
seas run with the wind. Facing it—always facing it—
that's the way to get through. You are a young sailor.
Face it. That's enough for any man. Keep a cool
head.'

"'Yes, sir,' said Jukes, with a flutter of the heart.

"In the next few seconds the Captain spoke to the
engineroom and got an answer.

"For some reason Jukes experienced an access of
confidence, a sensation that came from outside like a
warm breath, and made him feel equal to every de-
mand. The distant muttering of the darkness stole
into his ears. He noted it unmoved, out of that sudden belief in himself, as a man safe in a shirt of mail
would watch a point."

Like every philosophy of a man of action, like
Kipling's, for instance, to which it is akin, the philosophy of Conrad is aristocratic. He admires the common seaman, of course, if he serves with action and
obedience, as much as he admires the captain; but
like Kipling, Conrad detests the man who is always
thinking of his rights and never of his duties. That
type of man he has portrayed in the character of
Donkin in *The Nigger of the Narcissus*: "They all
knew him! He was the man that cannot steer, that
cannot splice, that dodges the work on dark nights;
that, aloft, holds on frantically with both arms and
legs, and swears at the wind, the sleet, the darkness;

[205]

the man who curses the sea while others work. The man who is the last out and the first in when all hands are called. The man who can't do most things and won't do the rest. The pet of philanthropists and self-seeking landlubbers. The sympathetic and deserving creature that knows all about his rights, but knows nothing of courage, of endurance, and of the unexpressed faith, of the unspoken loyalty that knits together a ship's company. The independent offspring of the ignoble freedom of the slums full of disdain and hate for the austere servitude of the sea."

There is no demagogic flummery in Conrad, and he can certainly never be accused of having tried to attract readers by such means. "At a time when nothing which is not revolutionary in some way or other can expect to attract much attention, I have not been revolutionary in my writings. The revolutionary spirit is mighty convenient in this, that it frees one from all scruples as regards ideas. Its hard, absolute optimism is repulsive to my mind by the menace of fanaticism and intolerance it contains."

Conrad does not believe that democracy can free us from war. Quite the contrary: "The era of wars so eloquently denounced by the old Republicans as the peculiar blood guilt of dynastic ambitions is by no means over yet. They will be fought out differently, with lesser frequency, with an increased bitterness and the savage tooth-and-claw obstinacy of a struggle for existence. They will make us regret the time of dynastic ambitions, with their human absurdity moderated by prudence and even by shame,

JOSEPH CONRAD

by the fear of personal responsibility and the regard paid to certain forms of conventional decency. For, if the monarchs of Europe have been derided for addressing each other as 'brother' in autograph communications, that relationship was at least as effective as any form of brotherhood likely to be established between the rival nations of this continent, which, we are assured on all hands, is the heritage of democracy. In the ceremonial brotherhood of monarchs the reality of blood-ties, for what little it is worth, acted often as a drag on unscrupulous desires of glory or greed. Besides, there was always the common danger of exasperated peoples, and some respect for each other's divine right. No leader of a democracy, without other ancestry but the sudden shout of a multitude, and debarred by the very condition of his power from even thinking of a direct heir, will have any interest in calling brother the leader of another democracy; a chief as fatherless and heirless as himself."

Regarding women, as regarding peoples, Conrad is a pessimist. A sailor has one thing in common with the knight-errant, in that he spends much of his life far from home. Distance makes him idealize women. He conjures up a vision of romantic, chivalrous love, and so is much more painfully disappointed by actual women than is the classic novelist who, like Molière or Shaw, expects her to be no more than a woman. Conrad's heroes, like Kipling's, are often terrified of women. The classicist can write dispassionately that women have no morality, but depend for their morals

[207]

simply on those whom they love. The romantic sailor is surprised to find them devoid of the male virtues. But in the end he understands, realizing that honour is a noble heritage from the Middle Ages, which has never belonged to women. In principle, he thinks, women always get what they desire, and we can only suppose that honour is not a thing they desire. Prudence also, the reasoned prudence in which a man takes pride, is foreign to them. Feeling, sensation at any price, is their secret motto; and as all the virtues do not suffice them, they crave also for every crime. Why? Because *power*, over and above all the rest, is still the sensation which they prize.

VI

CONRAD'S ART

His view of life enables us to imagine Conrad's methods of work. Respecting the good craftsman, despising the pedant and the chatterbox, Conrad would speak only about what he knew. He trained himself rigorously to speak of it with perfect accuracy. The artist, like the scientist, he thought, must seek the truth and only the truth. The duty of a writer seemed to him akin to that of the sailor: he should do his work as well as possible, paint exactly what he saw, keep his sentences as flawless as a scrubbed deck, and expect no reward but the unspoken respect of his peers.

His mode of narration is peculiar to himself. Henry James was amazed by the complexity of his stories: "It places Mr Conrad absolutely alone as a votary of the way to do a thing that shall make it undergo most doing." The "alone" is amusing, for Henry James was the most successful and constant practitioner in this method. But it is true that, in Conrad, it is rather more surprising, in that it seems to be less the considered choice of a literary artist than the natural movement of an honest man.

Conrad wrote once that the prime virtue of a writer should be an absolute loyalty to his emotions and sensations, even in the very fever of creation. Precise adherence to what has been seen, felt or heard; the imbuing of these sensations with emotion and poetry; the scrupulous refusal to heighten that emotion or force that poetry—such was his literary ideal.

That story of the Malayan planter was told him one day by a colonial journalist in a Singapore office. That story of Lord Jim he got to know gradually, through a succession of narratives. He might have transposed it as Stevenson would have done. He might place the centre of the work inside the hero by adopting an autobiographical form, in the Defoe manner. But that would mean inventing sensations, which was exactly the thing he forbade himself. The storm came to him in the form of a narrative, and in narrative form he would render it. Thus we have a plot on two planes—the depiction of the narrator by

Conrad, and then the depiction of the characters by this narrator.

Nor is that all. Even the narrator, who puts Conrad on the track of a subject, does not himself know all its aspects. Sometimes he breaks off his story to introduce someone else with fresh subsidiary information; sometimes the author himself goes off in search of witnesses who can throw light on a new facet of the same history. In this way the reader finds the novel being presented to him exactly as it was presented to the novelist. The reader is given the impression that the subject is there, somewhere, but hidden, in the midst of a walled arena round which the author is moving, only occasionally able to give a rapid glance at aspects of the details which are never the same.

Will that difficult artistry find imitators? At present the best of the young English novelists seem to have wisely laid aside these exacting exercises. Nothing could be more simple or straightforward than the stories of David Garnett or Aldous Huxley. Besides, literary technique is not the most important aspect of Joseph Conrad. The essential matter is his deep awareness of a certain form of human grandeur.

VII

"Man is but a faint gleam in the storm, but that gleam persists and that gleam is everything." These words

JOSEPH CONRAD

of Henri Poincaré might be taken as a summary of Conrad's philosophy. Obviously, his picture of the world is very different from that of Wells, who sees human intelligence as a shining light in which, if we exercise sufficient will, we could for ever bathe our planet. Everyone judges from his own experience, and the philosophy of a man of action cannot resemble that of a laboratory student. Conrad, like Kipling, has lived among men who wage war, with others beside them, against the storms of the skies or of men. More than Kipling, he was one of them. Uprooted from his native soil, and doubly uprooted because the sea kept him so long from even his adopted land, Conrad was perhaps indebted to that impoverished mode of life for the power of perceiving certain human virtues in their pure state. He wrote once that those who read him would know his deep conviction that the temporal world rests upon a few very simple ideas, so simple that they must be as old as the hills, and that it rests, amongst others, on fidelity. There indeed is the essence of the human societies so exactly symbolized by the group sailors, isolated amid the waves on their few wooden boards.

VI

LYTTON STRACHEY

Lytton Strachey

THE case of Lytton Strachey is one of the most remarkable within our purview. Here, in fact, is a writer who attained fame, and very extensive fame, with three historical studies, at a time when the world of literature seemed to be ruled by the novelists. We should be less surprised if the success of this historian had been made by historians. But, on the contrary, the English universities were for a long time somewhat hostile towards Strachey, because, although he showed himself a man of praiseworthy erudition, and skilled in sniffling out details, he denied that history was a science, and made so bold as to reinstate Clio among the Muses. In which, moreover, he succeeded with ease, because he was a great artist, and perhaps one of the best prose-writers of this century. We must seek out the causes of the worldly success thus won by an essayist whose writings did not seem, *a priori*, destined to interest a wide public.

I

WORKS AND STYLE

ABOUT Strachey's life there is little to say. The biography of the biographer has not yet been written: it awaits an artist worthy of the subject. Suffice it to say here that he was born in 1880, a son of Sir Richard Strachey, a famous Anglo-Indian administrator. He studied at Cambridge, and in 1912 published a small, but excellent and brilliantly written, manual entitled *Studies in French Literature*. About this time he was contributing articles on French subjects to certain of the English reviews. And to give a first impression of Strachey's style, we can hardly do better than take a passage from his essay on Racine, the least appreciated in England of all the great French writers. With remarkable subtlety Strachey analyses the causes of this lack of comprehension. "Owing mainly, no doubt, to the double origin of our language, with its strange and violent contrasts between the highly-coloured crudity of the Saxon words and the ambiguous splendour of the Latin vocabulary; owing partly, perhaps, to a national taste for the intensely imaginative, and partly, too, to the vast and penetrating influence of those grand masters of bizarrerie—the Hebrew prophets—our poetry, our prose, and our whole conception of the art of writing have fallen under the dominion of the emphatic, the extraordinary, and the bold. No one in his senses would regret this, for it has given our literature all its most characteristic glories, and, of course, in Shakespeare, with whom expression is stretched to the bursting point, the national style finds at once its consummate example and its final justification. But the result is that we have grown so unused to other kinds of poetical beauty, that we have now come to believe . . . that poetry apart from 'le mot rare' is an impossibility. The beauties of restraint, of clarity, of refinement, and of precision we pass by unheeding; we can see nothing there but coldness and uniformity; and we go back with eagerness to the fling and the bravado that we love so well. It is as if we had become so accustomed to looking at boxers, wrestlers and gladiators that the sight of an exquisite minuet produced no effect on us. . . . But let us be patient, and let us look again.

> *Ariane ma soeur, de quel amour blessée,*
> *Vous mourûtes aux bords où vous fûtes laissée.*

Here, certainly, are no 'mots rares'; here is nothing to catch the mind or dazzle the understanding; here is only the most ordinary vocabulary, plainly set forth. But is there not an enchantment? . . . Is there not a flow of lovely sound where beauty grows upon the ear, and dwells exquisitely within the memory? Racine's triumph is precisely this—that he brings about, by what are apparently the simplest means, effects which other poets must strain every nerve to produce. The narrowness of his vocabulary is in fact nothing but a proof of his amazing art."

The man who could so justly and accurately define the poetic quality of a foreign writer was certainly a great critic, and there were a few people who knew as much, even in those days. In London a small group of remarkable minds, most of whom were later to become famous, had collected round Strachey: Virginia Woolf, the novelist, Clive Bell, the art critic, Maynard Keynes, the economist, and the charming Francis Birrell, who died in 1935, formed part of the group. But until 1918 Strachey's fame scarcely extended beyond what is called Bloomsbury.

In May 1918 there appeared from his pen a book of four essays which made a great stir. Its very title, *Eminent Victorians*, was a challenge; for the persons portrayed therein, Cardinal Manning, Florence Nightingale, Dr Arnold, General Gordon, had hitherto been regarded by most Englishmen as very eminent Victorians indeed, almost sacred characters, already embalmed by legend for the everlasting edification of the faithful. Strachey rejected legend; beneath the ritual gestures of the mummy he ventured to discover the memory of a living, fallible being, and showed that these "eminent" personages had just been men and women, having plenty of characteristics in common with the ordinary run of mankind. A great many minds in England had been chafing under the historical convention which had so long shielded the Victorians. Strachey's book came to them as a deliverance, all the more freely relished as

LYTTON STRACHEY, FROM THE PAINTING BY HENRY LAMB

LYTTON STRACHEY

its irony was veiled with an appearance of candour, and the mischievous lines grouped into an exquisite form.

The method was no less original than the tone. Until Strachey entered the field, English biography, especially in the nineteenth century, had a decidedly heavy air about it. "Those two fat volumes," wrote Strachey himself, "with which it is our custom to commemorate the dead—who does not know them, with their ill-digested masses of material, their slipshod style, their tone of tedious panegyric, their lamentable lack of selection, of detachment, of design? They are as familiar as the *cortège* of the undertaker, and wear the same air of slow, funereal barbarism. One is tempted to suppose, of some of them, that they were composed by that functionary, as the final item of his job."

This was a stern judgement, and quite unfair on some of the best Victorian biographies; but it exactly described some of them. The family of a deceased Victorian celebrity, at the time of his death, would select a respectful scholar, entrust him with the papers, and counsel prudence. The scholar, as happy in this flood of documents as a crab in its pool, printed the greatest possible number of letters, unpublished fragments, and diaries, linking up these texts with a desultory commentary; and having completed this labour, he believed he had achieved something "scientific."

Strachey, for his part, regarded such a compilation as a means, not as an end. These long, conventional biographies, clumsy and one-sided, but packed with facts, were to become the mines from which he would extract the ore for his own accounts. He perceived that even the dullest of these panegyrics contained, all unbeknown to their authors, rich strands of truth, irresistible themes of satire. And it was in these books of his predecessors that he carefully, patiently sought out the traits of character which, grouped and ordered by a real artist, were to renovate the portraits of the Victorians.

Renovate? Perhaps it would be better to say "touch up." Or better still, to say that Strachey once more thrust history into the mists which are necessary to it. Before him (excepting such memoir-writers of genius like Boswell, Retz, or Saint-Simon), historical characters seem over-simplified. Strachey draws his characters as a great novelist might, with an eye on the movements of the body, stressing an unconsidered remark, and coming nearer and nearer to life with each recorded feature.

Look up, for instance, at the portrait of the extraordinary Lord Hartington, later the Duke of Devonshire, in whom the ordinary Englishman had for so long an absolute trust, and observe how much closer the portraiture is to La Bruyère, or even to Proust, than to Macaulay: "For indeed he was built upon a pattern which was very dear to his countrymen. It was not simply that he was honest: it was that his honesty was an English honesty. In Lord Hartington they saw, embodied and glorified, the very qualities which were nearest to their hearts—impartiality, solidity, common sense—the qualities by which they themselves longed to be distinguished, and by which, in their happier moments, they believed they were. If ever they began to have misgivings, there, at any rate, was the example of Lord Hartington to encourage them and guide them—Lord Hartington who was never self-seeking, who was never excited, and who had no imagination at all. Everything they knew about him fitted into the picture, adding to their admiration and respect. His fondness for field sports gave them a feeling of security; and certainly there could be no nonsense about a man who confessed to two ambitions—to become Prime Minister and to win the Derby—and who put the second above the first. They loved him for his casualness—for his inexactness—for refusing to make life a cut-and-dried business—for ramming an official despatch of high importance into his coat-pocket, and finding it there, still unopened, at Newmarket, several days later. They loved him for his hatred of fine sentiments; they were delighted when they heard that at some function, on a florid speaker's avowing that 'this was the proudest moment of his life,' Lord Hartington had growled in an undertone, 'the proudest moment in *my* life, was when my pig won the prize at Skipton fair.' Above all, they loved him for being dull—with Lord Hartington they could always be absolutely certain that he would never, in any circumstances, be either brilliant, or subtle, or surprising, or impassioned, or profound. As they sat, listening to his speeches, in which considerations of stolid plainness succeeded one another with complete flatness, they felt involved and supported by the colossal tedium, that their confidence was finally assured."

Or better still, at that very subtle portrait of Queen Elizabeth, in *Elizabeth and Essex*, where each sentence seems to pick up a part of what was stated in the one before, and moves forward in this groping way towards a complicated truth: "Nor was it only her intellect that served her; it was her temperament as well. That too—in its mixture of the masculine and the feminine, of vigour and sinuosity, of pertinacity and vacillation—was precisely what her case required. A deep instinct made it almost impossible for her to come to a fixed determination upon any subject whatever. Or, if she did, she immediately proceeded to contradict her resolution with the utmost violence, and, after that, to contradict her contradiction more violently still. Such was her nature—to float, when it was calm, in a sea of indecisions, and, when the wind rose, to tack hectically from side to side. Had it been otherwise—had she possessed, according to the approved pattern of the strong man of action, the capacity for taking a line and sticking to it—she would have been lost. She would have become inextricably entangled in the forces that surrounded her, and almost inevitably, swiftly destroyed. Her femininity saved her. Only a woman could have shuffled so shamelessly, only a woman could have abandoned with such unscrupulous completeness the last shreds not only of consistency, but of dignity, honour, and common decency, in order to escape the appalling necessity of having, really and truly, to make up her mind. Yet it is true that a woman's evasiveness was not enough; male courage, male energy, was needed, if she were to escape the pressure that came upon her from every side. Those qualities she also possessed; but their value to her—it was the final paradox of her career—was merely that they made her strong enough to turn back, with an indomitable persistence, upon the ways of strength."

Strachey's style is finely shaded, to the point sometimes of preciousness. He sketches, he tests, he scores out, he glosses. He masters the indefinite and the complex. His best portraits are those of characters like Prince Albert or Robert Cecil, whom he can paint as they should be painted, in grey against grey: such as Bacon, "The detachment of speculation, the intensity of personal pride, the uneasiness of nervous sensibility, the urgency of ambition, the opulence of superb taste—these qualities, blending, twisting, flashing together, gave to his secret spirit the subtle and glittering superficies of a serpent"; or such as Gladstone, ". . . 'the elements' were 'so mixed' in Mr Gladstone that his bitterest enemies (and his enemies were never mild) and his warmest friends (and his friends were never tepid) could justify, with equal plausibility, their denunciations or their praises."

Nearly always his dissections lead, not to conclusions but to questionings. His favourite words seem to be *subtle* and *perhaps*. When he is just about to drop a character, in despair of getting any closer to him, he still has twinges of regret or repentance, and he will add one last paragraph, generally beginning with "And yet. . . ." There, with marvellous skill, he will undo the new-made joints of the structure he has so patiently erected. The name of Proust has already occurred, and it is just in this feeling for the infinitely small in the order of passion and character that Strachey often reminds one of Proust. From Proust also he seems to have that rare and delicate touch of style which blends familiarity with perfection and nonchalance with vigour. Like Proust, too, Strachey is above all a poet, that is to say, a man who, by fresh images, can recreate a living world. There is a truly poetic beauty in Strachey's description of the death of Queen Victoria, the last stanza of a completed poem; it might call to mind the funeral march of Siegfried, the recurring themes of the cycle, at the end of the *Götterdämmerung*.

II

ART OR SCIENCE?

WHERE has our analysis led us, so far? To a historian with a genius for writing, seeking to adorn history with all the charms of style and poetic creation. But we should pause to examine the problem of history. What should history be? Strachey had no doubts: it is an art. But many historians would protest, and declare that it is a science. What's more, it ought to be no more than a science.

The issue is one which was lately revived in France by Paul Valéry. "History," he has said, "is the most dangerous product compounded by the chemistry of the intellect. Its properties are well-known. It causes dreams, it intoxicates whole peoples, engenders in them false memories, exaggerates their reflexes, keeps their old wounds open, torments their rest, leads them to megalomania or a persecution complex, and makes the nations bitter, intolerable, and vain."

But has history no certainty in dictating conduct to the peoples? None. History is unknowable. The historians of the French Revolution agree with each other exactly as Danton agreed with Robespierre, albeit with less drastic consequences, for "the guillotine, happily, is not at the disposal of historians."

Still, there exist historical facts concerning the authenticity of which all historians are agreed. Charlemagne was crowned Emperor in the year 800, and the battle of Marignan was fought on September 14, 1515. We possess the texts of treaties, and statutes, and the verbatim reports of parliaments. Well and good: but freedom to *choose* from among these events and documents allows the historian to narrate his story in accordance with his own prejudices and preferences. History justifies whatever it is required to justify. It gives no precisely drawn lesson, because it contains everything and offers examples of everything. In Valéry's view, it is absurd to talk of the "lessons" of history. From history can be extracted every political doctrine, every morality, every philosophy.

Against the scientific view of history Lytton Strachey took his stand as vigorously as Valéry. "What are the qualities that make a historian? Obviously these three—a capacity for absorbing facts, a capacity for stating them, and a point of view. The two latter are connected, but not necessarily inseparable. The late Professor Samuel Gardiner, for instance, could absorb facts, and he could state them; but he had no point of view; and the result is that his book on the most exciting period of English history resembles nothing so much as a very large heap of sawdust. But a point of view, it must be remembered, by no means implies sympathy. One might almost say that it implies the reverse. At any rate it is curious to observe how many instances there are of great historians who have been at daggers drawn with their subjects. Gibbon, a highly civilized scoffer, spent twenty years of his life writing about barbarism and superstition. Michelet was a romantic and a republican; but his work on mediaeval France and the Revolution is far inferior to his magnificent delineation of the classic and despotic centuries."

Most historians would rise in protest against both the criticism of Valéry, and the allied view of Strachey. Fustel de Coulanges, for instance, has maintained in masterly fashion that the reading of documents would be futile unless done with preconceived ideas. He indicted the scholars of a bygone age for having sought in documents the title-deeds of monarchy, and Montesquieu for having claimed thus to find the justification of liberty: "The friends of the parliamentary system sincerely believed that in our ancient documents they found a system of national assembly, and nearly the whole of parliamentary practice. Others have claimed to discover there the origins of the modern jury. French scholars infuse history with their party spirit, Germans with racial self-esteem. Both are altering the truth. An interested party cannot read a text truthfully, seeking in it the confirmation of his own thesis. He is blind to anything in it that contradicts his thesis. He believes himself to be scanning the documents, whilst actually he is gazing only at the reflection of his own mind."

A little further, and we might almost think that Fustel de Coulanges was anticipating a reply to Strachey: "There are some who think it good and useful for a writer to have preferences, ruling ideas, dominant conceptions. These, it is claimed, give his work more life and more charm, and provide the salt to correct the insipidness of fact. To think thus is to be profoundly mistaken as to the nature of history. It is not an art; it is a pure science. Possibly a certain philosophy may emerge from this scientific history, but it must emerge naturally and unaided, almost independently of the historian's will."

To which Lytton Strachey would have replied— and indeed did so reply, when once I put this passage from Fustel de Coulanges before him—on lines approximately as follow:

(a) However numerous may be the documents consulted, we shall never possess them all, especially in the case of a remote age. So, in spite of the historian's conscientiousness, the truth can still elude him: all the more so because frequently the essentials are not contained in documents. There have been conversations of which no record is extant, but which have altered the face of the earth.

(b) Documents are so numerous, and also so contradictory, that it becomes absolutely necessary for the historian to make a choice, and that act of choice in itself involves a breaking of the objectivity insisted upon by Fustel de Coulanges.

(c) It is an incorrect use of terms, said Strachey, to use the word "science" in speaking of history, because the particular attributes of science—namely, the possibility of making experiments, of verifying a general law, and of observing as often as one pleases the accuracy of relationships already ascertained—are here completely absent. A historian can be conscientious and honourable; he cannot be a scientist in the true sense of the word, as a physicist or an astronomer can be.

To these points an adversary could in his turn retort that as regards modern history nearly all the documents are extant, that although mistakes may be made in consulting them, far greater errors will result from neglecting to consult them, and that even if criticism consists, in effect, of choosing between certain documents, that choice itself should be guided by the traditional method of the historian.

If I myself were permitted to intervene in this debate, I should say that I do not understand why, once the spadework is completed and the truth established (so far as we can ever approach to truth), the most scrupulous criticism and the most systematic care for detail should prevent our trying to make a history a work of art.

III

THE HISTORIAN'S ATTRIBUTES

BUT our concern here is not to ascertain whether Valéry or Strachey, in this problem of history, wins or loses against Fustel de Coulanges. It is to find out what Strachey was. Let us therefore take the three attributes of the historian as he enumerated them, and try to see in what degree they were his.

The first amounts to an aptitude for absorbing facts. But which facts? Strachey accumulates facts unnumerable. He enjoys detail. True, on occasion he permits himself a general picture, a wide painting of a period, but first and foremost he is a good reader of memoirs, in which he hunts out minute and truthful details. "Clio is one of the most glorious of the Muses; but, as everyone knows, she (like her sister Melpomene) suffers from a sad defect: she is apt to be pompous. With her buskins, her robes, and her airs of importance she is at times, indeed, almost intolerable. But fortunately the Fates have provided a corrective. They have decreed that in her stately advances she should be accompanied by certain apish, impish creatures, who run round her tittering, pulling long noses, threatening to trip the good lady up, and even sometimes whisking to one side the corner of her drapery, and revealing her undergarments in a most indecorous manner. They are the diarists and letter-writers, the gossips and journalists of the past, the Pepyses and Horace Walpoles and Saint-Simons, whose function it is to reveal to us the littleness underlying great events and to remind us that history itself was once real life."

Nothing is more enjoyable in writing a biography, or even a work of history, than to set off in pursuit of the living details in the thickets of memoirs and letters. Sometimes we may read hundreds of pages without finding anything but general ideas, and disputable at that. Then suddenly the turn of a sentence brings life into view, and the faithful reader holds it caught. It is delightful, for instance, to find that D'Orsay had a loud laugh, with a "Ha! Ha!" and grasped his friends too tightly by the hand. Strachey is admirable at this game. He knows that the little Princess Victoria, as a child, learned from the governess how to make little cardboard boxes tricked out with gilt paper and painted flowers, or that Prince Albert, before leaving Germany, listened with melancholy to *Der Freischutz* being played by the ducal orchestra, and that on his deathbed he repeated the words *"Liebes Fräuchen, gutes Weibchen."* He can show us an evening at Windsor, the family circle at the round table, the Queen's albums of engravings, with the Prince Consort playing endless games of chess with three of his gentlemen. He regards history as consisting more of such things than of great projects and wide plans. "An international conference," he once said to me, "is simply so many men, each with his fixed character, his habits, his neuralgia, his good or bad digestion. The history of the conference, if it could be written, would be not only the analysis of the great confronted interests, but a picture of the mutual reactions of these temperaments on each other." Strachey did not in the least despise historic truth, but he sought it in the minutiae.

Nothing delighted him more than to make a symbol out of a trifling detail. If he is telling us about Lady Hester Stanhope, the descendant of the great Pitt, he catches hold of the Pitt nose. "The Pitt nose has a curious history. One can watch its transmigrations through three lives. The tremendous hook of old Lord Chatham, under whose curve Empires came to birth, was succeeded by the bleak upward-pointing nose of William Pitt the younger—the rigid symbol of an indomitable *hauteur*. With Lady Hester Stanhope came the final stage. The nose, still with an upward tilt in it, had lost its masculinity; the hard bones of the uncle and the grandfather had disappeared. Lady Hester's was a nose of wild ambitions, of pride grown fantastical, a nose that scorned the earth, shooting off, one fancies, towards some eternally eccentric heaven. It was a nose in fact, altogether in the air." Thus begins the essay on Lady Hester Stanhope; and, as often happens, he reverts to this nose theme at its close, when the heroine is dying:

"The end came in June 1839. Her servants immediately possessed themselves of every moveable object in the house. But Lady Hester cared no longer: she was lying back in her bed—inexplicable, grand, preposterous, with her nose in the air."

Here history seems almost like a symbolist poem. It is enchanting, but it must be admitted that, to obtain this effect, the basic truth has perhaps been sacrificed. This caricature may suggest truth, and even be more truthful than truth itself, but it is not the truth. Yes, those little devils who snigger alongside Clio in her progress and twitch up the good lady's robe are certainly diverting. The best letter-writers and memoir-writers give us keen aesthetic enjoyment. But Fustel de Coulanges is not wrong in distrusting the accuracy of a past thus reconstructed. For the memoir-writer had his partialities; the pamphleteer set down anecdotes which he knew to be false; the letter-writer transmitted baseless gossip. In fact, in certain details which we have been able to scrutinize after him, Strachey was a greater artist than a historian. His portrait of General Gordon is quite unfair. His Disraeli is more ludicrous and less profound than the original. His Queen Victoria is not, during her later years, the vigorous and clear-headed sovereign revealed to us by her published letters. We may say, then, that Strachey, the collector of facts, is wonderful in the wide range of his reading and the conscientiousness of his exploration, but that a tendency to poke fun and an excessive delight

LYTTON STRACHEY

in epigram sometimes make him sacrifice simplicity
and accuracy to sheer light-heartedness.

Reverting, however, to his art of exposition, we
find this admirable in its straightforwardness and re-
jection of eloquence. "Take eloquence and wring its
neck" might well have been a phrase of Strachey's.
He likes the hint, the suggestion. He frequently
praises Stendhal for never insisting. "Perhaps the best
test of a man's intelligence is his capacity for making
a summary. Beyle knew this, and his novels are full
of passages which read like nothing so much as
extraordinarily able summaries of some enormous
original narrative which has been lost." He is pitiless towards the rhetoric of Macaulay and all the
classic historians of England. "From the time of
Cicero downwards, the great disadvantage of oratory
has been that it never lets one off. One must hear
everything, however well one knows it, and however obvious it is. For such writers a dose of Stendhal
is to be recommended. Macaulay, however, would
not have benefited by the prescription, for he was a
hopeless case. The tonic pages of the *Chartreuse de
Parme* would have had no effect on him whatever.
When he wished to state that Schomberg was buried
in Westminster Abbey, he *had* to say that 'the illustrious warrior' was laid in 'that venerable abbey,
hallowed by the dust of many generations of princes,
heroes, and poets.' There is no escaping it; and the
incidental drawback that Schomberg was not buried
at Westminster at all, but in Dublin, is, in comparison

with the platitude of the style, of very small importance."

Next to eloquence, Strachey hates the intervention of morality in history. "Perhaps it is the platitude of such a state of mind that is its most exasperating quality. Surely, one thinks, poor Louis XV might be allowed to die without a sermon from Chelsea. But no! The opportunity must not be missed; the preacher draws a long breath, and expatiates with elaborate emphasis upon all that is most obvious about morality, crowns, and the futility of self-indulgence. . . . There is an imaginative greatness in his conception of Cromwell, for instance, a vigour and a passion in the presentment of it; but all is spoilt by an overmastering desire to turn the strange Protector into a moral hero after Carlyle's own heart, so that, after all, the lines are blurred, the composition is confused, and the picture unconvincing."

He himself is totally exempt from such reproaches. His simplicity of tone is delightful, and reaches a perfected intimacy which makes a truly exquisite blend. Notice his tone in describing the child Victoria: "Warm-hearted, responsive, she loved her dear Lehzen, and she loved her dear Feodora, and her dear Victoire, and her dear Madame de Späth. And her dear Mamma . . . of course, she loved her too; it was her duty; and yet—she could not tell why it was —she was always happier when she was staying with her Uncle Leopold at Claremont."

This intimate suppleness of writing, the style fitting the thought so closely, following its drifting and pauses, is characteristic of many of the best English writers of our time. Strachey himself, who in this was their master, had perhaps inherited it from certain French writers: from Montaigne, from Stendhal in his *Journal*, and from the *Contemporains* of Jules Lemaître, that excellent writer who ought to be more often re-read.

Marcel Proust declared that there could be no greatness of style without imagery, as it was only metaphors which can plunge the mind into reality. And Strachey does not hesitate to heighten the colour of his historical narrative with bold and startling images. Telling of the tragic career of Newman, he says: "He had to force himself to scrape together money, to write articles for the students' Gazette, to make plans for medical laboratories, . . . he was obliged to spend months travelling through the remote regions of Ireland in the company of extraordinary ecclesiastics and barbarous squireens. He was a thoroughbred harnessed to a four-wheeled cab." Again, the meeting of Manning with Newman: "It was the meeting of the eagle and the dove; there was a hovering, a swoop, and then the quick beak and the relentless talons did their work."

He watches the ferocity of Miss Nightingale towards Sidney Herbert: "She took hold of him, taught him, shaped him, absorbed him, dominated him through and through. He did not resist—he did not wish to resist; his natural inclination lay along the same path as hers; only that terrific personality swept him forward at her own fierce pace and with

her own relentless stride. Swept him—where to? Ah!
Why had he ever known Miss Nightingale? If Lord
Panmure was a bison, Sidney Herbert, no doubt, was
a stag—a comely, gallant creature springing through
the forest; but the forest is a dangerous place. One
has the image of those wide eyes fascinated suddenly
by something feline, something strong; there is a
pause; and then the tigress has her claws in the quiver-
ing haunches; and then—!" Or he looks at Queen Elizabeth: "The fierce old hen sat still, brooding over
the English nation, whose pullulating energies were
coming swiftly to ripeness and unity under her wings.
She sat still; but every feather bristled; she was tremendously alive."

And in his desire to make history a work of art
and poetry, Strachey, like Proust once more, will
even strive for effects that are almost musical, the exposition of themes, to be recalled and mingled, of
images introduced, to be elaborated and, at the apt
moment, repeated. The most famous instance of this
is at the close of his Queen Victoria, when the old
Queen, as she lies dying, turns back "to the spring
woods at Osborne, so full of primroses for Lord
Beaconsfield—to Lord Palmerston's queer clothes and
high demeanour, and Albert's face under the green
lamp, and Albert's first stag at Balmoral, and Albert
in his blue and silver uniform, and the Baron coming
in through a doorway, and Lord M. dreaming at
Windsor with the rooks cawing in the elm-trees, and
the Archbishop of Canterbury on his knees in the
dawn, and the old King's turkey-cock ejaculations,

and Uncle Leopold's soft voice at Claremont, and
Lehzen with the globes, and her mother's feathers
sweeping down towards her, and a great old repeater-
watch of her father's in its tortoise-shell case, and a
yellow rug, and some friendly flounces of sprigged
muslin, and the trees and the grass at Kensington."

Is that history? Where are the documents, Fustel
de Coulanges would say, which authorize you to
describe thus what was passing through the dying
Queen's mind? There is no answer. Let us grant that
it is not history: but moving and beautiful it certainly is.

Finally we reach the question of the point of view.
Every historian, Strachey maintains, should have his
point of view. He certainly had his. His detachment
is only in appearance. His hates and loves—his hates
especially—are emphatic. By hiding them under a fine
web of epigram, he increases their strength of attack.
He declared once that he neither imposed nor suggested, but only exposed. But this was only a half-
truth. He suggested because he withheld; he imposed
because he omitted. "Pick the card for yourself," says
the conjurer, handing us his pack: but how careful
he has been in arranging the cards so as to guide our
choice!

What is Strachey's point of view? His originality
lies in the fact that he introduced the ideas and tone
of an eighteenth-century Frenchman into an England which was still very Victorian. The French
translator of *Eminent Victorians*, M. Jacques Heur-

gon, has quoted a significant passage which explains how Lytton Strachey, to many of the younger Englishmen, stood as a guide to their thought. ". . . to-day," he wrote, "the return is once more towards the Latin elements in our culture, the revulsion from the Germanic influences which obsessed our grandfathers, the preference for what is swift, what is well arranged, and what is not too good." In other words, Strachey represented an English reaction against Carlyle, against Gladstone, and therein his function was more than that of a biographer. He extirpated emphasis, both of style and of feeling, from a whole generation.

He might almost be labelled a Voltairean, or perhaps, even more precisely, a disciple of Anatole France. He hated mysticism almost as much as eloquence: "Besides its unreasonableness, there is an even more serious objection to Blake's mysticism—and indeed to all mysticism: its lack of humanity. The mystic's creed . . . comes upon the ordinary man, in the rigidity of its uncompromising elevation, with a shock which is terrible, and almost cruel. The sacrifices which it demands are too vast, in spite of the divinity of what it has to offer. What shall it profit a man, one is tempted to exclaim, if he gain his own soul, and lose the whole world."

So entirely does Strachey feel himself a man of the eighteenth century, that he even reproaches Stendhal for having that admiration for romantic attitudes which, in Frenchmen of the Empire period, consorts so strangely with logic and precision. "It is a quality that Englishmen in particular find it hard to sympathize with. They remain stolidly unmoved when their neighbours are in ecstasies. They are repelled by the 'noble' rhetoric of the French Classical Drama. . . . To judge from M. Barrès, writing dithyrambically of Beyle's 'sentiment d'honneur,' that is his true claim to greatness. The sentiment of honour is all very well, one is inclined to mutter on this side of the Channel; but oh, for a little sentiment of humour too!"

But however much of an eighteenth-century Frenchman Lytton Strachey may have been, he was so in a very English way. It would be a very rough-and-ready approximation to compare him to Voltaire. His mockery is less direct. Voltaire has wit, Strachey has humour. To a puritan people, reserved and passionate, as the English are, humour is a more reassuring form of the comic, because it is more hidden. How can one be angry when nothing hostile has actually been said? Why be indignant over a piece of mimicry? Still less over a quotation? When Strachey wishes to demolish something or somebody, he is often content simply to quote. For instance, he tells us how Cardinal Manning, in his diary, pledged himself to eat no cake during Lent, but added in the margin: "save dry biscuits." Voltaire would have elaborated this with ironic or violent commentary. To Strachey the stinging quotation sufficed to show the weakness of a faith that haggled over self-denial. He is inimitable when he gravely enunciates something which he knows to be absurd, or when he plays with dangerous epigrams. Of Dr Arnold he says: "He believed in toleration, too, within limits; that is to say, in the toleration of those with whom he agreed." Or of Cardinal Manning: "Certainly he was not a man who was likely to forget to look before he leaped, nor one who, if he happened to know that there was a mattress spread to receive him, would leap with less conviction."

English humour is often imbued with sentiment. Strachey has only respect, one might almost say affection, for the faith of a Newman. The affection may be slightly teasing, the fondness of an unbeliever, but sometimes it is moving. Towards Manning he is pitiless, because in his case the demands of faith coincide too precisely with those of worldly ambition. He is cruel towards Monsignor Talbot, the Italian prelate who confused the interests of the Church with private quarrels, and stern towards Gladstone, who sometimes could not distinguish clearly between his hatred and his virtues. But General Gordon, sincere in his madness, Strachey liked.

And in these respects, although French in his style and Voltairean in some of his prejudices, he remains at bottom extremely English. A Cambridge don has remarked that the most important event in the history of English biography was the conquest of Lytton Strachey by Queen Victoria. But the conquest was easy. It counted for something that Strachey sprang from one of the great Whig families. He could depict with true understanding those solid, silent characters, seemingly proof against all enthusiasms, whose sound sense ensures the permanence of England and saves her from all freakish dangers. His famous portrait of Lord Hartington is handled humorously, but with respect. In Queen Elizabeth, an ambiguous and frightening character, he admires those barriers and negations which make her so strongly English. If he retains any kindliness towards a Church, it is towards the Anglican, as bearing all over it the marks of human imperfection. Nearly always, after manhandling some eminent Victorian, he sets him on his feet again. Dare it be said that he himself was, in great measure, an eminent Victorian?

I knew Lytton Strachey. He came one summer to spend a few days at one of the yearly gatherings of intellectuals at the old Abbey of Pontigny. We found him very like his portrait in the Tate Gallery. On the first day we were alarmed by his tall, lanky frame, his long beard, his immobility, his silence; but when he spoke, in his "bleating falsetto," it was in delightful, economical epigrams. He listened to our daily discussions with a politely scornful indulgence. Was he so English that he could be interested only in concrete problems and in definite persons? Was it that his frail, indolent body declined the necessary effort to join in the debate? Or was it perhaps that, being over-fastidious, he considered our ideas so lacking in subtlety that they could not possibly be of interest to him? Looking at him there, we had the impression of an almost infinite disdain, of a wilful abstraction, of a refusal . . . And yet . . . And yet sometimes, for one fleeting instant, a glance would flash behind his spectacles so vividly that we wondered if all this lassitude might not be the mask of a man really amused, and keen, and more Britannic than any Briton.

VII

D. H. LAWRENCE

D. H. Lawrence

THE importance of the part played by a writer in the life of his times is not, and need not be, proportionate to the perfection of his work or the coherence of his doctrine. A flimsy philosophy can easily beguile a whole generation if it is expounded by a great artist, and if it provides an answer, however vague, to questions which, at the moment of the coming of this message, are perplexing men's minds. The writer's character, his gift of eloquence, his personal appeal, all come into play, and he may well have some of the gifts of an apostle without having all the qualities of the novelist.

Such is the case of D. H. Lawrence. Not that he is unworthy of the rôle as a writer. *Sons and Lovers* is a great novel. His fame would be amply accounted for by his essays, his stories (which are often less heavily laden with ideology than his novels), his travel sketches, and his letters. But there is a lot of balderdash in his work. Huxley, for all his admiration, admits that most of his novels are hard to read, and sometimes tiresome. They can hardly be called novels: as Drieu La Rochelle has said, they are rather "autobiographical allegories."

But the man made a profound impression on all

[245]

who came in touch with him. Middleton Murry, who had no reason to pride himself on it, was obsessed by Lawrence. Only someone who loved as Lawrence loved, he concluded, is capable of judging Lawrence. Aldous Huxley, a man of far more comprehensive intelligence than Lawrence, and far more cultured, has made it clear how, in his presence, his weaknesses were instantly forgotten. "To be with Lawrence was a kind of adventure, a voyage of discovery into newness and otherness. For, being himself of a different order, he inhabited a different universe from that of common men—a brighter and intenser world, of which, while he spoke, he would make you free. He looked at things with the eyes, so it seemed, of a man who had been at the brink of death, and to whom, as he emerges from the darkness, the world reveals itself as unfathomably beautiful and mysterious. For Lawrence, existence was one continuous convalescence; it was as though he were newly re-born from a mortal illness every day of his life. . . . A walk with him in the country was a walk through that marvellously rich and significant landscape which is at once the background and the principal personage of all his novels. He seemed to know, by personal experience, what it was like to be a tree or a daisy or a breaking wave or even the mysterious moon itself. He could get inside the skin of an animal and tell you in the most convincing detail how it felt and how, dimly, inhumanly, it thought. . . . One of the great charms of Lawrence as a companion was that he could never be bored and so could never be boring. . . . He could cook, he could sew, he could darn a stocking and milk a cow, he was an efficient wood-cutter and a good hand at embroidery, fires always burned when he had laid them, and a floor, after Lawrence had scrubbed it, was thoroughly clean. Moreover, he possessed what is, for a highly strung and highly intelligent man, an even more remarkable accomplishment: he knew how to do nothing. He could just sit and be perfectly content. And his contentment, while one remained in his company, was infectious."

Mrs Mabel Dodge Luhan, who wrote a curious and life-like book about him, draws a picture which corroborates that of Huxley: "He is one of the most fascinating men I ever met. The first time I ever saw him, he talked for a whole afternoon, almost steadily. He will do this at once and without the slightest self-consciousness if he feels a sympathy in his listener. He talks as brilliantly as he writes, and as frankly. . . . But at the slightest touch of adverse criticism or hostility, Lawrence becomes violent. His vituperation is magnificent. . . . He spares none. He has quarrelled with everyone. He says he has no friends that he has not quarrelled with. . . . Lawrence is a Puritan, really, and his intellectual reaction against it is so violent that he hurls himself against it with all of himself. . . ."

The extraordinary fire of Lawrence's talk, the violence of his anger, his fierce reaction against his own nature, survive in the strength of the written word.

Even when our intelligence resists, we, his readers, are carried away by the torrent, just as those who lived with him. Add to this the fact that the problems which tormented him were those which beset his generation, and it is only natural that his influence was wide and deep.

I

LIFE AND WORKS

HE WAS born in 1885, in a mining district of Nottinghamshire. His father was a collier, a working man. His mother was of gentler stock, and belonged to the lower middle class, speaking the King's English, and not the local dialect of her husband. She had a pleasing handwriting, could write amusing letters, and had read quite "difficult" novels. Married to this attractive and rather feckless miner, she became a working-class wife.

A French biographer of Lawrence, Albert Fabre-Luce, describes his impressions on seeing a family photograph: "The miner's face is glowing with health, with its leonine mane above and the spreading beard beneath. It is a birthday or an anniversary: a heavy watch-chain dangles across his waistcoat, a folded handkerchief emerges from his pocket, a large flower covers the lapel. And beside him is Mrs Lawrence, very small, humbly clasping her hands, al-

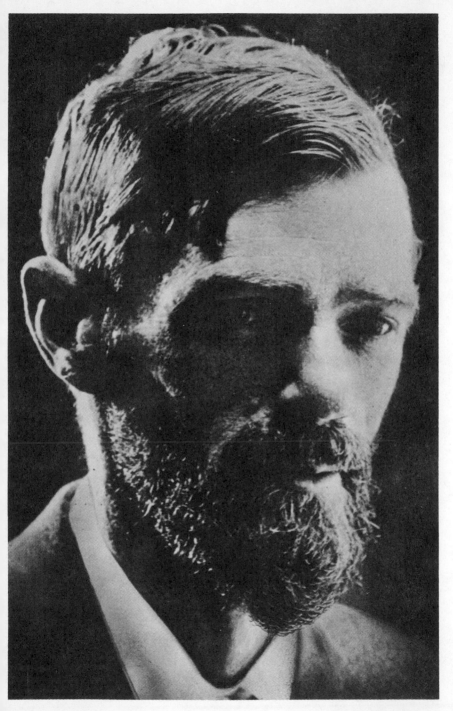

D. H. LAWRENCE

ready looking older than her years. Her small mouth is hardly discernible, and her sad eyes, taking shelter in the depths of their orbits, belie that half-hearted smile. This man and this woman are lost; their union has destroyed them both."

Lawrence's mother was a heroine, a proud woman, respected by everyone. She enjoyed ideas, and philosophic or religious discussions in particular. The father, as he grew older, became a liar, drank too much, and was sometimes brutal. "The wife quite soon came to look down on her husband and to ally herself with the children, especially with the youngest of the family—David Herbert."

He was a sensitive, affectionate boy, with his mother's blue eyes and her earnest intelligence. He soon began to turn away from his father, to whom, nevertheless, he owed much of his nature, all his "coomon" characteristics, the violence of his rages, the strength of his instincts. In *Sons and Lovers* he described the family's anxious life, the homecoming of the father excited by drink, the clattering of the heavy miner's boots on the stone kitchen floor. The children sat up in bed terrified as they heard blows and insults raining on their mother. When the father was injured at work and had to go into hospital, the family enjoyed a blessed spell of peace.

Lawrence, like Proust's hero, loved his mother with an almost unhealthy passion. In later years he was to study the dangers of the excessive fondness which can come into being between parents and children. Several of his novels handle this theme, which he held to be highly important: the drama of the mother who cannot understand that her son's happiness must lie in his perfect relationship with another woman. It is the theme of Mauriac's novel *Genitrix*, and one which Lawrence treated, returned to, and developed throughout his whole work in the form of fiction, and finally in a dogmatic form in *Fantasia of the Unconscious*: "You have done what it is vicious for any parent to do: you have established between your child and yourself the bond of adult love: the love of man for man, woman for woman, or man for woman. All your tenderness, your cherishing will not excuse you. It only deepens your guilt. You have established between your child and yourself the bond of further sympathy. I do not speak of sex. I speak of pure sympathy, sacred love . . . the sympathy of the adult soul. . . . We may be as pure as angels, and yet, being human, this will and must inevitably happen. . . . For in spite of all our intention, all our creed, all our purity, all our desire and all our will, once we arouse the dynamic relation in the upper, higher plane of love, we inevitably wake a dynamic consciousness on the lower, deeper plane of sensual love."

In *Sons and Lovers* Lawrence showed how hard it is for a youth who has found a surfeit of perfection in his mother's love, to form later an equally close bond with another woman. In *Sons and Lovers* the girl Miriam rouses the jealousy of the hero's mother, and is ultimately sacrificed to her: " 'I can't bear it. I could let another woman—but not her. She'd leave me no room, not a bit of room—'

"And immediately he hated Miriam bitterly.

" 'And I've never—you know, Paul—I've never had a husband—not really.'

"He stroked his mother's hair, and his mouth was on her throat.

" 'And she exults so in taking you from me—she's not like ordinary girls.'

" 'Well, I don't love her, mother,' he murmured, bowing his head and hiding his eyes on her shoulder in misery. His mother kissed him a long, fervent kiss."

In real life, as in this novel, there was a Miriam, a very remarkable girl. She was a school-teacher, belonging to a farmer's family not far distant from Lawrence's home. Whenever he could he jumped on his bicycle and went off to see her. She discerned his budding genius and admired his earliest poems. But whereas the Miriam of *Sons and Lovers* becomes the hero's mistress, the real Miriam ("E.T.," who has written her account of all this) describes a Lawrence who was most puritanically afraid of everything connected with sensual experience. Vehemently he thanked God that he had "so far been preserved from that," and he avenged his timidity on the girl: "you have no physical attraction," he would say to her cruelly.

> Body to body I could not
> Love you, although I would.

· · · · ·

You only endured, and it broke
My craftsman's nerve.
No flesh responded to my stroke;
So I failed to give you the last
Fine torture you did deserve.

Moreover, like the heroes in his novels, Lawrence
suffered from his mother's unconcealed jealousy. To
understand him, it must always be remembered that
he began by being an over-affectionate youth, whose
great problem would be to dominate his own power
of affection. Thence no doubt sprang his violence: a
violence of contrast and relief, not at all of strength.
As a man he was always frail. Mrs Mabel Dodge
Luhan describes his excited, nervous quality: "He
simply couldn't bear to have anyone question his
power, his rightness, or even his appearance. I think
his uncertainty about himself, a vague feeling of inferiority, made him touchy."

He won a scholarship to the Nottingham High
School, became a teacher and taught in an elementary
school from the age of seventeen until he was twenty-
one. He was a brilliant pupil, and passed his teaching
examinations with ease. After two years at Nottingham University he taught in a secondary school, and
he was twenty-three when "Miriam," herself a
teacher in a mining village, made copies of some of
his poems, without his knowledge, and sent them to
the *English Review*. Ford Madox Hueffer, then its
editor, invited Lawrence to come and see him. She
launched him on a literary career, he said, as easily
as a princess, by cutting a ribbon, launches a ship.

For several months he had been working on a novel, *The White Peacock*. Hueffer asked for the manuscript, and after reading it he told Lawrence that it had every fault an English novel could have, but that he himself had genius.

In 1910, when Lawrence was twenty-seven, his mother died. Both in *Sons and Lovers* and in his poems he wrote about her death, and it is deeply moving. We can see so clearly this poor old woman with her white hair, treated by her son at once as a mother, as a little girl, as a fiancée. He was full of compassion for her, and had a deep understanding of a soul which had remained virgin because she had never found the man who could bring her into flowering.

> My love looks like a girl to-night,
>   But she is old.
> The plaits that lie along her pillow
>   Are not gold,
> But threaded with filigree silver,
>   And uncanny cold.

In *Sons and Lovers* we see young Paul stricken by his mother's death: "Paul felt crumpled up and lonely. His mother had really supported his life. He had loved her; they two had, in fact, faced the world together. Now she was gone, and for ever behind him was the gap in life, the tear in the veil, through which his life seemed to drift slowly, as if he were drawn towards death. . . . Who could say his mother had lived and did not live? And his soul could not leave her, wherever she was. Now she was gone abroad into the night, and he was with her still. . . . Where was he?—one tiny upright speck of flesh, less than an ear of wheat lost in the field. On every side the immense dark silence seemed pressing him, so tiny a spark, into extinction, and yet, almost nothing, he could not be extinct. Night, in which everything was lost, went reaching out, beyond stars and sun. Stars and sun, a few bright grains, went spinning round for terror, and holding each other in embrace, there in a darkness that outpassed them all, and left them tiny and daunted. . . .

" 'Mother!' he whispered—'mother.'

"She was the only thing that held him up, himself, amid all this. And she was gone, intermingled herself. He wanted her to touch him, have him alongside with her.

"But no, he would not give in. Turning sharply, he walked towards the city's gold phosphorescence. His fists were shut, his mouth set fast. He would not take that direction, to the darkness, to follow her. He walked towards the faintly humming, glowing town, quickly."

A strange young man, this Lawrence, who, at the age of twenty-seven, turned away from that tomb. Sensuous but timid, brutal but sensitive, he calls out for love, yet dreads it. But he was to meet a courageous woman who gave him something that "Miriam" had not been able to bring forth. In the core of his writing, the figure of a wife now takes the place of a mother's. It was in 1912 that Lawrence

D. H. LAWRENCE

found the woman who thenceforward was to share all his life, a German of aristocratic and military family, the wife of an English university professor. "She is ripping—she's the finest woman I've ever met," he wrote to Edward Garnett; "she is the daughter of Baron von Richthofen, of the ancient and famous house of Richthofen—but she's splendid, she is really." She, on her side, was attracted to him with the first words they exchanged.

When Lawrence met Frieda, she was thirty-one and had three children. Her husband provided her with a comfortable and pleasant existence, and her life seemed happy, or at least settled. Lawrence appeared. "From the first he saw through me like glass, . . ." she writes. "'You are quite unaware of your husband.' Suddenly I knew I loved him. . . . After that things happened quickly." He suggested their going away together: "I was frightened. I knew how terrible such a thing would be for my husband, he had always trusted me. But a force stronger than myself made me deal him the blow. I left the next day."

With him she went to Germany. What would the haughty Richthofens think of this obscure lover, so puny and plebeian? Frieda was walking with the most fashionable of her sisters when she saw Lawrence coming towards her in a cloth cap and a mackintosh coat. The sister looked at the foreigner for a moment or two with anxious intensity. "You can trust that man," she said at last. The old Baroness von Richthofen stood out for a few weeks, but she too was

[255]

conquered: it was strange, she said, that an old woman like herself could feel so much affection for a man as she felt for this "Lorenzo."

What was the secret of this power which Lawrence had over women? The art of pleasing? But he was brutal and often offensive. He forced Frieda, accustomed to a life of comfort, to wash clothes, do the kitchen work, carry bedroom pails. In moments of anger he would throw crockery about. Sometimes he struck her, and she struck back. To some of his friends who had difficulty in getting on with their wives, he would advise them to use physical force.

Was it physical attraction? But he was a weakling, and quite soon in his life an invalid. No: underneath the alternating hymns of his female mourners one detects feelings of greater complexity.

These women discerned in Lawrence something primitive, something akin to their own nature. Like them, he had a taste for magic. His wife has said that he alone could teach human beings the art of living. Frail as he was, and so near to death, he had a religious awareness of moments of happiness. Before living with him, she declared, she had not lived at all. Those are the words of a woman whole-heartedly in love. With most men women, poor things, are so bored! How were they ever to replace the man who, alone, knew how to love life?

Above all, he offered them that mixture of strength and weakness which satisfies women more than any other trait, because it rouses at once the maternal and the lover's passion. Lawrence astonished them with his genius, and gave them assurance by his passionate need of them. He declared that he simply could not try to do anything without a woman behind him. He recalled a painter, Böcklin, who could never sit down in a café unless he had his back against the wall, and felt that he could not sit down in the world without a woman at his back. A woman whom he loved seemed to put him somehow into direct touch with the unknown, in which, without her, he felt lost.

Frieda von Richthofen was outstandingly well fitted to give Lawrence this sense of direct communication with the unknown. She was a woman "with no frontiers, a piece of nature." She revealed to the puritan Lawrence the joys of pagan love and liberated instincts. There is a curious and beautiful poem in which he marvels at having discovered, through her, his own body:

She said as well to me: "Why are you ashamed? That little bit of your chest that shows between the gap of your shirt, why cover it up? Why shouldn't your legs and your good strong thighs be rough and hairy?— I'm glad they are like that. You are shy, you silly, you silly shy thing. Men are the shyest creatures, they never will come out of their covers. Like any snake slipping into its bed of dead leaves, you hurry into your clothes." . . .

He quarrelled with Frieda violently. It was not only a lovers' battle, but a class struggle as well. She criticized his manners, and was cruel: "But Frieda is a lady, and I hate her when she talks to the common people. She is not a bit stuck-up . . . but she makes the *de haut en bas* of class distinction felt—even with my sister." But above and beyond these difficulties he was happy with her: "It is astonishing how barbaric one gets with love: one finds oneself in the Hinterland der Seele, and—it's a rum place, I never knew it was like this. What Blasted Fools the English are, fencing off the big wild scope of their natures." Astounded by this new happiness, he set out to try to save others as he himself had been saved. The liberated Puritan, with the customary convert's zeal, would preach an anti-puritan gospel.

Frieda took him away to live in a humble house in the Bavarian Alps: four rooms, a kitchen, a balcony, where Lawrence corrected the proofs of his novel, *Sons and Lovers*, which was then called *Paul Morel*. Occasionally Frieda's mother would descend stormily upon them, waxing furious to find her daughter working in the kitchen, and asking Lawrence who he was that a baroness should black his shoes and empty his slops. He had feelings of triumph. Life now seemed a thing of conquest, not of resignation. A reading of Joseph Conrad infuriated him: "But why this giving in before you start, that pervades all Conrad and such folks—the Writers among the Ruins. I can't forgive Conrad for being so sad and for giving in."

However, here on his Bavarian balcony, he finished *Sons and Lovers*. Sending it to Edward Garnett, he described it: "It follows this idea: a woman of character and refinement goes into the lower class, and has no satisfaction in her own life. She has a passion for her husband, so the children are born of passion, and have heaps of vitality. But as her sons grow up she selects them as lovers—first the eldest, then the second. These sons are *urged* into life by their reciprocal love of their mother—urged on and on. But when they come to manhood they can't love, because their mother is the strongest power in their lives, and holds them. It's rather like Goethe and his mother. . . . As soon as the young men come into contact with women, there's a split. . . . The mother gradually proves stronger, because of the tie of blood. The son decides to leave his soul in his mother's hands, and, like his elder brother, go for passion. He gets passion. Then the split begins to tell again. But, almost unconsciously, the mother realizes what is the matter, and begins to die. The son casts off his mistress, attends to his mother dying. He is left in the end naked of everything, with the drift towards death. It is a great tragedy, and I tell you I have written a great book."

He could justly be proud. *Sons and Lovers* is a great book, and now Lawrence, freed from his past, would try, with novel after novel, to construct his future. In variations on the Frieda theme he was to study the conflict between man and woman, and seek its solution. Initiation into love, thanks to Frieda, but also the battle against Frieda, were to form the subject-matter which he took up again and again in various forms. *The Rainbow* and *Women in Love* were essays in the fulfilment of conjugal life. The "rainbow" is the symbol of the ideal link which ought to unite soul and flesh and achieve a perfected union. Lawrence seeks to show what such a union could be, although in fact both of these novels end with failures.

At last Lawrence and Frieda returned to England. The War came upon Lawrence just when he had married her, a German. What would happen to them? A friend lent them a house in Cornwall, a remote spot where Lawrence for some time had an idea of establishing a colony of writers and friends, who would reject the mechanical and materialist civilization which had engendered this war. "I do like Cornwall. It is still something like King Arthur and Tristan. . . . One can feel free here,—feel the world as it was in that flicker of pre-Christian Celtic civilisation." He found down there an old, aristocratic, magic race of people, ". . . a race which believed in the darkness, in magic, and in the magic transcendency of one man over another, which is fascinating. Also there is left some of the old sensuousness of the darkness, a sort of softness, a sort of flowing together in physical intimacy, something almost negroid, which is fascinating."

He lured Murry and Katherine Mansfield down to Zennor. But there could be no lasting bond between the two couples; Murry depended on the spiritual life, Lawrence sought to depend on the sensual, anxious to alter the world radically, to bring about a new form of love between men and women.

But what form? Not confusing bodily love with
tenderness, and preaching the urgent claims of the
flesh. . . . It was all rather vague, and raised tremendous arguments between the two men. Each
made virtues of his own desires, and attributed those
of the other to weakness.

They occupied neighbouring cottages. Lawrence
crouched in front of the stove, tasting the meat . . .
"*Ist es gut*, Lorenzo?" asked the stout, Teutonic
Frieda; and good it was, for Lawrence was a splendid cook. The Cornish rocks heard endless debates
on Dostoevski, on love and humility, on the War.
Katherine Mansfield hated this countryside, and
doubtless suffered from these abstract furies of the
males. One day Lawrence would be complaining that
Murry was killing him, on the next he would be pro-
posing a ritual ceremony of blood-brothership with
him. Murry hesitated, and talked of mystical love.
"I hate your love!" cried Lawrence. "When you are
like that, I think 'For God's sake, let's get rid of it!'"
A strange friendship, which dragged on for some
years in alternating quarrels and reconciliations, tried
at one moment to become a "stellar friendship," at
a distance, and ended at last in an eternal rupture:
". . . we shall dwell in different Hades" wrote Lawrence. And as it turned out, the cruel ghost of Lawrence was to haunt the hapless Murry from beyond
the tomb.

People's minds were excited and upset by the War,
and when the local folk discovered that Frieda was
a German, the Lawrences were persecuted and treated

as spies. The police carried off letters from the Baroness von Richthofen because they were written in German. If the Lawrences forgot to draw their curtains in the evening, they were supposed to be signalling to submarines. They were harried out of Cornwall and had to take refuge in London. This persecution left a cruel mark on Lawrence, and as soon as possible after the War he sought haven in Italy.

There he wrote *Aaron's Rod*, the story of a thwarted friendship. Lawrence's idea is that man's success on the plane of marriage should be followed by a constructive activity, by the creation of a new society, a task in which he would unite, not now with woman, but with other men. He had an idea for gathering together a group of friends in some new country who would agree to live in accordance with his teaching.

But whilst working in Italy he received a letter which seemed to offer the chance of new experience. It came from someone unknown to him. Mabel Dodge-Stein-Luhan (the three names of her successive husbands), an American by birth, had married an Indian and lived at Taos in New Mexico. In her letter she told Lawrence that she was an admiring reader of his books and himself, and believed that for a man like himself, with a liking for primitive life, life amongst the Mexican Indians would perhaps mean happiness. He accepted, and set off, by way of Ceylon and Australia.

This journey, Huxley remarks, was at once an escape and a search: he was seeking a primitive society where thought had not yet become too conscious and perverted life, and he was escaping from the wretchedness and evils of European civilization. Was it perhaps necessary, he wondered in a letter, for him to try all these places? Was it his destiny to know the world? But he felt that his innermost self remained untouched, more isolated than ever. The wild West and the strange land of Australia were loopholes of escape for himself and from the great problem.

His flight was of no avail: he could not escape from himself. He wrote, in collaboration, a novel about Australia, *Kangaroo*, again the story of a failure, this time of a man with aspirations to leadership. At last he reached Mexico, and we have Mabel Dodge's account of the first contact. Her first impression was of the frailness of Lawrence beside the solid Frieda. He seemed to derive his vitality from her. Frieda seemed to Mabel Dodge a complete but limited being, and Lawrence seemed like a lamb tied to a stake and tugging desperately. She took the Lawrences in an automobile, and they bickered: "'You know I don't know anything about automobiles, Frieda! I *hate* them! Nasty, unintelligent, unreliable things!' 'Oh, you and your hates!' she returned contemptuously.

"'I am a failure. I am a failure as a man in the world of men. . . .'"

Naturally Mabel Dodge soon conceived the notion that Frieda was incapable of inspiring this man of genius with all the works he was capable of producing. It would henceforth be she who would be the "mother" for Lawrence's books. But Frieda put up an energetic fight for her union with him, and in the end wrenched her Lorenzo out of Taos. He brought back two books, *The Plumed Serpent,* in which he tried to show what could be done by mingling the spiritual life of the white man with the instinctive consciousness of the Indian, and another, *Mornings in Mexico.*

The Lawrences returned to Italy. He was stricken by tuberculosis, and was already a very sick man. Living near Florence, he became very friendly with Aldous Huxley, whom he had known since 1915, and who drew him under the figure of Rampion in *Point Counter Point.* It is strange that Lawrence should have protested against this portrait, which strikes us as flattering. "Your Rampion is the most boring character in the book—a gas-bag. Your attempt at intellectual sympathy!—It's all rather disgusting, and I feel like a badger that has its hole on Wimbledon Common and trying not to be caught." But by now he was a dying man, and terribly, overwhelmingly in love with life.

Once again he turned to the subject which had always concerned him so deeply and disturbingly, the sensual life. It is the mingling of a longing for life with a presentiment of the coming end that explains the exasperated sensualism of a book like *Lady Chatterley's Lover.* "I am in a quandary about my novel, *Lady Chatterley's Lover.* It's what the world would call very improper. But you know it's not really improper—I always labour at the same thing, to make the sex relation valid and precious, instead of shameful. And this novel is the furtherest I've gone." In England this novel was prohibited; it was published first in Italy. Then an exhibition of paintings by Lawrence in London was closed by the police, and some of the pictures were confiscated.

For a few months longer, in the South of France, he clung on to life, writing a story which only appeared posthumously, the story of a resurrection, *The Man Who Died*. With an almost voluptuous joy, he lent himself in anticipation a sort of earthy metapsychosis.

I shall blossom like a dark pansy, and be delighted there
    among the dark sun-rays of death.
I can feel myself unfolding in the dark sunshine of
    death
To something flowery and fulfilled, and with a strange
    sweet perfume.

In 1929 he was at Bandol, then went up to Venice, to a sanitorium. "I am rather worse here—such bad nights, and cough, and heart, and pain decidedly worse here—and miserable. Seems to me like *grippe*, but they say not. It's not a good place—shan't stay long—I'm better in a house—I'm miserable." He spent about three weeks in the sanitorium, and then, as he disliked the place he went off on foot one evening to a village some distance away. It was his last flight.

He died a few days after his forty-fifth birthday. He is buried at Venice. Over his grave they carved his emblem, a symbol of resurrection, the Phoenix which he had himself designed.

II

MAN, CIVILIZED AND REAL

IF EVER there was a writer who longed to preach a gospel, to offer men a faith, it was Lawrence. But to define that faith is not easy. "You ask me about the message of the *Rainbow*. I don't know myself what it is: except that the older world is done for, toppling on top of us: and that it's no use the men looking to the women for salvation, nor the women looking to sensuous satisfaction for their fulfilment. There must be a new world."

What must this new world be? According to Lawrence, it should apparently be, first and foremost, a return to an older world. The society which he likes and praises is the Mexican tribe, or the poorest of Italian villages. He had liked Cornwall in so far as it had remained primitive; when he was in Italy he became interested in the Etruscans, and when in Mexico in the Axtec civilizations. He turned always to the oldest, the most aboriginal things he could find. The modern world, he felt, had substituted for the real and natural man, an artificial being, inevitably unhappy and unbalanced because he has denied his instincts.

When Lawrence read Galsworthy he cursed those

heroes, the rich Forsyte bourgeois: ". . . they have lost caste as human beings. While a man remains a man, a true human individual, there is at the core of him a certain innocence or naïveté which defies all analysis, and which you cannot bargain with, you can only deal with it in good faith from your own corresponding innocence or naïveté. . . . Money, of course, with every living man goes a long way. With the alive human being it may go as far as his penultimate feeling. But in the last naked him it does not enter. With the social being it goes right through the centre. . . ."

The social man is no longer in communion with the universe. Indeed, he bisects it: on one side he puts the external world and its laws, and on the other his own person; between himself and the whole world he fancies he discerns a conflict. The natural man, on the contrary, preserves mysterious links of union with the universe. It is whole, undivided. Human groups may be against him. What matter? He is part and parcel of the universe. Every great man, every truly religious being, feels within himself this spark, this kernel of pureness through which he is in communion with the universe. But in society man no longer has this refuge; money is his only salvation; money controls even his feelings. In the Forsyte world every character is determined by bank balances: either he acquires one, or possesses one, or desires one, or lacks one.

It is true that even among the Forsytes, that is to say in Victorian or Edwardian England, there are found certain sentiments which are designated as love or passion: but what love, and what passion? The basest of beings, Lawrence thinks, is the social man trying to play the real man. This produces the sentimentalist, the man devoid of true instincts who manufactures his sentiments by intellectual methods and convinces himself that they are genuine; but these sentiments are recognizably false inasmuch as they do not obliterate the social man. When Forsytes are in love they are constantly worrying about what the other Forsytes are thinking, how the couple will live, what will be their proper social standing, and they are never free from the preoccupation of money.

Murry once wrote to Lawrence saying that he hesitated to marry Katherine Mansfield because she had money and he had none. Lawrence replied with a rare scolding. This, he rightly thought, was the feeling of a social man, a Forsyte sentiment. "When you say you won't take Katherine's money, it means you don't trust her love for you. When you say she needs little luxuries, and you couldn't bear to deprive her of them, it means you don't respect either yourself or her sufficiently to do it. . . . She must say, 'Could I live in a little place in Italy, with Jack, and be lonely, have rather a bare life, but be happy?' If she could, then take her money. If she doesn't want to, don't try. But don't beat about the bush. . . . You must say, 'How can I make myself most healthy, strong, and satisfactory to myself and her?' If by being lazy for six months, then be lazy, and take her money. It doesn't matter if she misses her luxuries: she won't die of it. . . . But, you fool, you squander yourself, and not for *her*, but to provide her with petty luxuries she doesn't really want. You insult her. A woman unsatisfied must have luxuries. But a woman who loves a man would sleep on a board. . . . Make her certain—don't pander to her—stick to *yourself*—do what you *want* to do—don't *consider* her—she hates and loathes being considered. You insult her in saying you wouldn't take her money."

So the social man is the creature in whom instinct is overlaid by money and by what other people think. But what would the natural man be like? Lawrence's model is very different from that of Rousseau or of Tolstoy, "Rousseau's 'noble savage' was a creature who, had he been a race horse, might have been described as by Savoyard Vicar out of Madame de Warens; Tolstoy's, the religious and resigned peasant. . . . While Lawrence's 'noble savage' is a being of whom no conception was possible before the researches of modern anthropologists and sex-psychologists."

Lawrence's natural man lives mainly through the body. The modern sporting youth, the Boy Scout camping out in the open, are nearer to the natural man than were their fathers. The renaissance of the body is perhaps the only feature common to the new civilization which is springing up around us. But the body is not enough. Lawrence wants men to listen also to their hearts. As Drieu La Rochelle has said, "he had an acute sense of the intermediary forces which exist in man, between body and mind." If Murry had listened to his heart, he would not have paused to worry about Katherine Mansfield's private income.

III

IN PRAISE OF DARKNESS

IF WISDOM lies in bringing ourselves nearer to the natural man, how should we live that life of wisdom? How can we join up again with the natural man? By a conscious, analytical process? No approach could be more opposed to Lawrence's ideas. The soul of man is a vast and dark forest, pulsating with untamed life; to analyse that soul is in itself a mistake. Lawrence is the foe of all psychoanalysis and introspection: he was sick to death, he declared, of people turned in on themselves, and strove for a new, impersonal activity, authentic and vital.

This impersonal activity cannot be attained by intellectual processes. Intelligence illuminates a narrow zone, and the intellectual chooses to believe that this luminous band is the sole reality. But the Powers of Darkness take their revenge on the intellectuals, and Lawrence sides always with the Powers of Darkness against the Powers of Light. He has profound respect for night, which is the time of love, for the night in whose propitious shadows the instincts lurk and prowl. He thinks that going to bed late is an error equivalent to that of sleeping too far into the day; sleeping only six hours is better than prolonging sleep when the sun is up. All men and women should be forced out of bed at dawn, especially the highly strung; soon after dawn all human beings should be at work. If they obeyed this rule, nervous diseases would disappear. Lawrence would never echo Goethe (whom of course he hated), and cry "Light! More Light!" On the contrary, his cry would be: "More darkness!"—in the physical as well as in the spiritual sense. "My great religion is a belief in the blood, the flesh, as being wiser than the intellect. We can go wrong in our minds. But what our blood feels and believes and says, is always true. The intellect is only a bit and a bridle. What do I care about knowledge. All I want is to answer to my blood, direct, without fribbling intervention of mind, or moral, or what-not. I conceive a man's body as a kind of flame, like a candle flame, for ever upright and yet flowing: and the intellect is just the light that is shed on to the things around. And I am not so much concerned with the things around—which is really mind—but with the mystery of the flame for ever flowing."

But once again, how are we to come back into contact with this flame if we have been parted from it by the life of society? Abandon yourself, Lawrence advises; stop trying to keep everything under control of your will, don't struggle to dominate your conscious life; let yourself be carried on; and welcome the night, the whole night, which, like winter, strips the trees of all the green and leaves surviving only the dark underground roots. . . . Plunge back into the darkness and non-knowing, for a deep winter must come before the spring.

In the eyes of anyone striving to find true knowledge through surrender to instinct, scientific research and methods stand condemned. Huxley records Lawrence's passionate dislike of science, and how he always expressed himself on this subject in the most unreasonable style. "All scientists are liars!" he would declare; and when Huxley in argument flourished some experimentally proved fact before Lawrence, the latter would cry: "Liars! Liars." "I remember in particular," writes Huxley, "one long and violent argument on evolution, in the reality of which Lawrence always passionately disbelieved. 'But look at the evidence, Lawrence,' I insisted, 'look at all the evidence.' His answer was characteristic. 'But I don't care about evidence. Evidence doesn't mean anything to me. I don't feel it *here*.' And he pressed his two hands on his solar plexus." And indeed it is not at all certain that, in the case of evolution, the solar plexus was not right.

He would be tempted to seek the science of life and of nature amongst savage races, or amongst the Ancients, far sooner than from the scientists. He believed with all his heart, he declared, that the great Pagan world which preceded ours had a science of its own, a vast body of knowledge which from the point of view of life was perhaps perfect. This antique wisdom was taught by Druids, Etruscans, American Indians, and Chinese in symbolic forms, and for that reason the intense potency of symbols consists largely of memories. That is also the reason why the great myths and symbols which dominate life in the beginnings of our history are the same in all countries, for all races, and are all inter-related.

Lawrence, then, believes in ritual, in dances, in communal song. In the past, he thinks, there used to be a sound and sane form of society, that of the primitives. And we are now suffering from being thwarted in that bodily communion which for them was an everyday matter. When Lawrence himself lived amongst the Indians, he described their communal rites with intense admiration. In their dances he saw a meaning which was in itself a discipline, as they had preserved the secret of the animistic dances. They performed them to increase their power over the living forces of the earth, and the dances called for the utmost concentration and great reserves of physical endurance.

Although Lawrence proclaims his scorn of theories, he is obviously in fact one of the theorists of certain modern movements. The passion for collective re-joicing, so elaborately cultivated in post-war years in Russia and Germany, is a very ancient craving, analogous to those which Lawrence wished to see revived. And it is quite true that, for the masses, these desires are natural. But it is open to question whether the deliberate apprenticeship of a cultured man, like Lawrence, to a primitive life may not be even more artificial than the social life elaborated by the Forsytes.

IV

THE SENSUAL LIFE

To the truth of this he would probably have agreed. Primitive ritual and dance, a surrender to communal life, are not available to everybody. But in Western Europe, over-civilized as it is, there remains one means, and only one, of liberation from the excesses of intellect, and that is the sensual life. In regard to this, Lawrence's ideas have been distorted and betrayed; he would have been horrified by many who style themselves his disciples. In *Point Counter Point* Rampion's wife says to him: "You're an absurd old Puritan. . . . " And there is every reason to suppose that this is what Frieda told Lawrence. It is also what we read in Mabel Dodge. The accusation riled Lawrence because he knew it was true. By birth, and more particularly by upbringing, he was a Puritan. Growing up, he had rebelled against these teachings, but in spirit only, not in practice. Theoretically he approved Frieda's aristocratic tolerance of a sort of conduct which he had been taught by his mother to regard as deadly sin. But actually something within him kept protesting.

It was to combat Puritanism, to free instincts which he felt to be natural and healthy, that he strove for a harmony between the spirit and the animal which lives on in us. But although Lawrence protested against repression of the instincts, he is even more ardent in his condemnation of debauchery. He is quite horrified by obscenity. "I tried Casanova, but he smells. One can be immoral if one likes, but one must not be a creeping, itching, fingering, inferior being, led on chiefly by a dirty sniffing kind of curiosity, without pride or clearness of soul." Or, to quote again the Rampion in Huxley's novel: "It's not instinct that makes Casanovas and Byrons . . . it's a prurient imagination artificially tickling up the appetite, tickling up desires that have no natural existence. If Don Juans and Don Juanesses only obeyed their desires, they'd have very few affairs." Nothing of the essential Lawrence can be truly understood except by realizing that it is a religious aspect for the sexual life.

To him, love means a prolonged understanding between the two beings, a patient adaptation of two bodies and of two souls, which in the end create together a jewel of trust, a stone of mutual peace, emerging from the violence and chaos of passion.

And in his view the real love story only begins where, in most cases, the poets leave off. It is his greatest pride to be able to say to the woman of his life, long afterwards: "Look! We have come through!"

Intellectual sensuality, too, he hates as much as libertinism. In *Women in Love* he introduces a woman who is a sort of pedant of sensuality, who is told the truth about herself by a man: " 'Passion and the instincts—you want them hard enough, but through your head, in your consciousness. It all takes place in your head, under that skull of yours. . . . You want to clutch things and have them in your power. And why? Because you haven't got any real body. . . . You have only your will . . . and your lust for power. . . . You want it all in that loathsome little skull of yours, that ought to be cracked like a nut. . . . If one cracked your skull perhaps one might get a spontaneous, passionate woman out of you, with real sensuality.' "

Furthermore, if woman has become thus distorted, it is the fault of man: the real difficulty about women, as Lawrence sees it, is that they must always be trying to adapt themselves to male theories about women. If a woman is completely herself, it means that she is what her type of man wished her to be. If a woman is hysterical, it is because she does not understand what she ought to be, what model she ought to follow, to what picture of a woman as conceived by a man she ought to approximate. . . . Men are prepared to accept women as equals, as males in skirts, as angels or devils, as babies or machines, or instruments, as saints or pairs of legs, as servants, as encyclopaedias, as ideals or obscenities: but the one thing, says Lawrence, as which he will not accept her is a human being, a real human being of the feminine sex.

The spontaneous woman is as admirable in Lawrence's eyes as the artificial one is detestable. Because she remains nearer than the man to the living centres of primitive life, she is an absolutely necessary interpreter between man and the universe. He regards her as indispensable, at the same time, like Kipling, standing in some fear of her. He shows how readily she reverts to savagery. He believes in man's having a mission distinct from woman. "In a way, Frieda is the devouring mother . . . [she] says I am antediluvian in my positive attitude. I do think a woman must yield some sort of precedence to a man, and he must take this precedence. I do think men must go ahead absolutely in front of their women, without turning round to ask for permission or approval from their women. Consequently the women must follow as it were unquestioningly. I can't help it, I believe this. Frieda doesn't. Hence our fights."

In point of fact Frieda does not believe in the supremacy of the man because, with all the spiritual strength of a leader of men, he is a weakling. And this he doubtless understood himself for amongst the characters in his novels, as in Stendhal's, there are always, side by side, the man that Lawrence would have liked to be, and the man that he was. The first is strong, healthy, happy in love, free from shame, in fact the anti-Hamlet. The second shows himself much weaker than the hero, having the same ideal but incapable of achieving it. In fact, if Lawrence had been the real Lawrencean hero, he would never have written the novels of Lawrence.

INSOLUBLE CONFLICTS, VAIN REMEDIES

WE HAVE isolated two characteristics of Lawrence:
the effort to transcend the civilized man and reach
again the natural man and communion of bodies; and
the hope of achieving this through the senses and
thanks to the intercession of woman. A third point
would be a strong awareness of class warfare, not in
the Marxist and economic sense, but in a Lawrencean,
psychological way.

In all his books Lawrence contrasts the aristocrat
with the common people. He realizes the conflict better because it is within himself. He is the son of a
working man, but his culture is that of the favoured
classes. And he was acutely conscious of the clash.
As one of the working class, he declared, he could
feel the middle classes cutting some part of his vitality when he found himself in their company. Charming and well-bred, he admitted that they were. But
they dammed up some part of his being. It left him
wondering why he did not live with his own class;
and he could only answer that their vital vibrations
were restricted in other directions. Working-class
people were deeper and more profoundly emotional
than the others, but they were also narrow-minded,
prejudiced, unintelligent. Here too was a prison, and
he was left stranded between two camps.

Perhaps the solution of this conflict, also, should be sought in sensuality? Lawrence delights to show women of high birth finding happiness, moral and, even more, physical, in the love of a man of the people. His own marriage with Frieda was a symbol of this. But the solution is not perfect. Love and conflict are coexistent. His mother had been a tragic example of this. Even when the aristocrat is willing to become one of the working people, there is a difference of kind which persists. Even if he behaves as a workman behaves, the aristocrat remains the amateur.

And what of equality? Where is there equality in nature? There everything is at war, and the most vital have to win their place in the sun at the expense of the less vital. Consider the striking *Reflections on the Death of a Porcupine*. Lawrence tells how in Mexico, in the depths of a forest, he comes across a porcupine, as big as a small boar, a strange, rather beautiful creature. A few days later the dogs come home from the woods, injured by the porcupine. What is to be done? The porcupine must be killed. And Lawrence, who has never taken life, takes a gun and, with repugnance, destroys this form of life. Then he thinks it all over. Nobody can start a ranch in New Mexico unless he is resolved to kill the porcupine. No porcupine can live unless it resists the dogs, and the dogs in their turn destroy and are destroyed. Even so with men and with peoples. The leader is the man who is strong enough to be leader.

There is an element of despair in this; but how

could Lawrence feel other than despairing once he began to reason consciously? Foe to intellect though he is, he is too intelligent not to discern the futility of some of his precepts. To become natural, to become spontaneous? But man is never spontaneous in the sense that the vulture and the sparrow are spontaneous. Man cannot live by instinct alone, because he has a mind. The most savage of men has his ideas. He has devoured the apple, the fruit of the Tree of Knowledge. What can he do? He must accept the fact that man is an animal possessing ideas; he must recognize that in spite of his ideas man remains an animal often rather lower than the ape, and that despite his animal nature he can act only in accordance with certain abstract ideas. But again, what must be done in the face of this conflict which is rending every man?

First and foremost, replies Lawrence, do not seek a solution. Be simpler, far simpler; do not worry about the whole universe; never wonder to what end the world has been created. There is no such end. Life and love are life and love; a bunch of violets is a bunch of violets, and to push an idea of finality with it is utterly destructive. Live and let live. Love and let love. Follow the natural curve of blossoming and fading. . . .

Such is the gist. And hence comes his doctrine of heedlessness. He expounds it one day in Italy on his balcony, watching men at work in the sunshine, when he is questioned by his neighbour, a little, old, blue-eyed Englishwoman, about politics, about Fascism, about the future of the world. And why, why, he thought in his exasperation, were modern people so ignorant of what they had at their hands? This little blue-eyed lady had come all the way from England to find mountains and lakes and cherry-trees: why was she resolutely blind to all these things now that she had them? Why did she look from afar at Mussolini, who was not there for her, and at Fascism, which in any case was invisible. Why wasn't she content with just being where she was? Why couldn't she be happy with what she had?

Wisdom lies in flight from the blue-eyed lady's thoughts, in losing oneself in contemplation of man wielding the sickle, of animals and plants. Nothing is so genuine in Lawrence as this mute communion with nature. He knows animals like brothers, loving to spy upon their lives, their lovemaking, their footprints in the snow. He imagines the sensations of the strangest among them, and has written moving poems about a couple of tortoises, an essay on the death of a porcupine. A fine black stallion symbolizes for him all the male forces, and in the story entitled *St Mawr*, man and horse live on the same plane and are jealous of each other. We may picture Lawrence crouching in the forest grass, with his faun's beard, patiently watching the movements of a squirrel, a rabbit, a stag-animal himself, a creature "without frontiers, a piece of nature." For a moment, in the quietude of intuition, all conflicts then stand resolved. The poet has brought to birth again a virgin world.

VI

CONCLUSION

A YOUTH of genius suffered from painful conflicts.
Despising his father, he was torn between his mother
and his first love, between puritanism and desire.
These agonies, mastered and transcended, bore fruit
in a masterpiece, *Sons and Lovers*. Then he passed
through the difficult ordeal of a change of class. He
watched the upper classes with an unspoilt eye, and
he found people who no longer knew how to live.
Having himself found in a marriage of the senses, if
not peace, at least self-respect, he longed to preach a
gospel of sensualism to all and sundry. Life, he declared, was only tolerable if mind and body were in
harmony, with a natural balance between them, and
if each respected the other. The doctrine was more of
a novelty, perhaps, to Anglo-Saxon Puritans than
to "Mediterranean" races, but to all it is important.
In an age when men were drunk with words and
concepts and systems, Lawrence taught them to respect their instincts and their bodies. To save us,
ideas, like gods, must become incarnate. Lawrence
strove to make his doctrine visible in works of art.
In his poems and in his stories he succeeded, but not
always in his novels. By an odd paradox, the advocate
of the unconscious was a too conscious novelist. Too
weak to submit to laws, he believed he was freeing

himself by denying the conventions: whence *Lady Chatterley's Lover*, and, on the social plane, the flights to Italy and Australia and Mexico. If Lawrence had been a whole and full man, the true Lawrencean hero, he would have accepted society and the conventions as the complete poet (like Baudelaire or Valéry) accepts rhyme and fixed metre. But the partial failure of a prophet does not refute his prophecy, nor does the martyrdom of Lawrence belie his faith.

VIII

ALDOUS HUXLEY

Aldous Huxley

I

LIFE AND WORKS

IT IS tempting to translate the heredity of Aldous Huxley into French terms. Let a Frenchman imagine a young man whose paternal grandfather was Marcelin Berthelot, whose father was Alfred Croisset, whose maternal great-grandfather was Guizot, whose maternal grand-uncle was Sainte-Beuve or Joubert, and whose aunt was Madame de Staël: he will then behold a French equivalent of the genealogical tree of Aldous Huxley. In actual fact, he is the grandson of Thomas Huxley, one of the greatest scientists and sturdiest minds that England has produced. Thomas Huxley's son, Leonard, taught Greek at Charterhouse, and later at the University of St Andrews. He married a granddaughter of Dr Thomas Arnold, the famous headmaster of Rugby, who strove to make its boys grow into Christian gentlemen.

Leonard Huxley and Julia Arnold had two sons: Julian, a biologist and writer of unusual talents, and Aldous Huxley, our immediate concern. Aldous Huxley, therefore, has lived from childhood amongst people of fine and amazingly varied culture. In most cases, it would be too ingenuous to try to explain all the features of a man's mind by hereditary characteristics. But in the case of Huxley, it must be borne in mind that the originality of his talent consists of the combination of a poetic nature with a scientific culture. He appreciates (as does Paul Valéry in France) the language of science, even more than the practice of experiment. Like his grandfather, Professor Huxley, he has a wide French culture, the place held sixty years ago by Renan being for him held by Anatole France, André Gide, and Valéry.

Huxley replied once to an American interviewer that, in regard to himself, he could tolerate only reticence. Here, therefore, we have no autobiographies *à la* Wells, no confessions *à la* Lawrence. What we know of his life is straightforward. He was educated at Eton and Balliol, and amplified his studies by much travelling, in Italy, in France, and in Belgium, where he married. At the age of seventeen he lost his mother, and after this bereavement was regarded as a son by his aunt on the Arnold side, Mrs Humphrey Ward, the famous liberal novelist. He wrote from his adolescent days, and began, like most youths, with poetry, showing remarkable gifts from the very first.

His first novels were of a type familiar to French readers. In the setting of an English country-house, the characters, men of learning, sensualists or pleasantly ridiculous, controlled from far above by the author, exchange conversation worthy of a Jérôme Coignard or a Bergeret—but a Bergeret who is more of a physicist than a philologist, who professes science rather than the humanities. In qualities of imagination, craftsmanship and grace, if not in profundity, *Crome Yellow* and *Limbo* (a collection of stories) constituted a very remarkable opening. The succeeding novels, *Antic Hay* and *Those Barren Leaves* (especially the first part of the latter) were much less dominated by the convention of dialogue *à la* France. But it was with *Point Counter Point* that Aldous Huxley entered a higher zone.

Point Counter Point is not in the accepted form of the novel—a continuous narrative of the life of one character or of several. It is rather a cross-section of contemporary intellectuals. Writers, scientists, painters, men and women of fashion, all the elements included in the section are described, and through them are made visible the beliefs, the emotional reactions, the comic aspects of a certain English *intelligentsia* about the year 1926. A foreign reader will find the revelation of an England quite unknown to him: cynical, anarchic, brilliant. It was only a small group, and already it is dispersed. But the aesthetes of the nineties, likewise, were only a minute group, and their influence has been considerable.

Since this novel, Huxley has written books of travel, notably *Jesting Pilate*; volumes of essays, *Music at Night*, and *Do What You Will*, which include an extremely interesting essay on Pascal, which approaches the severity of Valéry towards its subject; some short stories, *Two or Three Graces*; and an excellent novel of the future, *Brave New World*. Few writers, in any country, are more widely read and appreciated by the young. He is, of course, young himself, having been born in 1894, and he may be expected to produce a total of books so numerous that the present criticism is even now called for, because Aldous Huxley, more than any other writer, represents an attitude towards life which is that of one part of his generation, both in France and in England.

II

THE ENCYCLOPAEDIST

INTELLECTUALLY, he is admirably equipped. Anatole France may have had a perfect classical culture, but he knew nothing of the scientific theories of his time beyond what had been popularized in his younger days by Renan and Berthelot, and possibly Claude Bernard. But whatever subject he is handling, Huxley speaks as an expert. If he is analysing French verse, he does so as Paul Valéry might. If he is comparing the Taj Mahal and St Paul's Cathedral, his point of view is that of an architect. If he is describing, as in *Point Counter Point*, the experiments of an elderly nobleman who has been grafting a tadpole's tail where a leg should be, he does so like a trained biologist: "'Tail becomes leg,' he said meditatively. 'What's the mechanism? Chemical peculiarities in the neighbouring . . . ? It can't obviously be the blood, or do you suppose it has something to do with the

ALDOUS HUXLEY, BY VANESSA BELL

electric tension? It does vary, of course, in different parts of the body. Though why we don't all just vaguely proliferate like cancers. . . . Growing in a definite shape is very unlikely, when you come to think of it. Very mysterious end. . . .' "

If he has incidentally to mention in an article the Oxford India-paper editions, he is quick to inform us that this kind of paper is impregnated with mineral constituents which render it opaque. And it is not surprising, a few lines further on, to find him confessing that the Encyclopaedia Britannica is his favourite reading, and that turning over its pages, with their vast stores of variegated facts grouped according to the chances of alphabetical order, is his mental vice.

A mental vice! We are sometimes tempted in reading Huxley to agree with his self-criticism, for in his novels the encyclopaedic knowledge will sometimes inundate a scene where it has no right to be. Just when we are beginning to feel moved by one of the women characters in *Point Counter Point*, who is pregnant and about to lose her lover, it is disconcerting to read suddenly: "Six months from now her baby would be born. Something that had been a single cell, a cluster of cells, a little sac of tissue, a kind of worm, a potential fish with gills, stirred in her womb and would one day become a man—a grown man, suffering and enjoying, loving and hating, thinking, remembering, imagining. And what had been a blob of jelly within her body would invent a god and worship. . . ."

Such thoughts and the facts which they reflect are intrinsically interesting, and the passage might be viewed as having a sort of Baudelairean beauty. But we are fully aware that Huxley has deliberately checked our emotion, and switched us over to a different subject. Was he right to do so? Would Turgenev or Tchekov have done it? At that moment in our reading it was not those physiological details that we wished to learn about: it was about Marjorie's feelings, not about the processes within her body. And if Marjorie at that moment thought of her child, she certainly did not do so in these terms. Huxley says as much himself in the sentence that follows. These shifts from one plane to another, these shifts of key, are disturbing and disappointing; they paralyze the emotion which the opening of the book had already started in us.

It might possibly be a fine problem in acoustic science to study the vibrations set up in the air of the auditorium by the voice of Berma declaiming Phèdre, but we are grateful to Proust for not choosing this aspect of that famous scene to describe. Huxley, for his part, cannot resist the temptation of giving us a little lecture about physics and physiology in connection with a concert: "The shaking air rattled Lord Edward's *membrana tympani*; the interlocked *malleus, incus* and stirrup bones were set in motion so as to agitate the membrane of the oval window and raise an infinitesimal storm in the fluid of the labyrinth. The hairy endings of the auditory nerve shuddered like weeds in a rough sea; a vast number of

obscure miracles were performed in the brain, and
Lord Edward ecstatically whispered 'Bach.'"

The device is obvious, and seems comparatively
easy. Huxley sees the danger of it himself when he
depicts the novelist Philip Quarles, who has to mention a cook in one of his books and starts off with
the sentence: " 'From the time when Shakespeare
was a boy till now, ten generations of cooks have
employed infra-red radiations to break up the pro-
tein molecules of spitted ducklings; . . .' one sentence, and I am already involved in history, art and
all the sciences. The whole story of the universe is
implicit in any part of it. The meditative eye can
look through any single object and see, as through
a window, the entire cosmos."

This is true. But it is no less true that art depends
on selection, so that to a mind like Huxley's the problem of the novel should be set in approximately these
terms: "Can I imbue my narrative with this sense
of universal symphony which overwhelms me when
I contemplate the most trifling spectacle, and do so
without being pedantic, and also without writing
books dragged out of infinity?"

III

HUXLEY often answers this question in the most
satisfactory way, attaining a genuine poetry, ironic
and painful, by alternating the cosmic with the hu-

man themes. There are passages in *Point Counter Point* which remind us that he has in him the elements of a great poet, and that he might well write the *De Rerum Natura* of our day. Excepting Proust, nobody has so clearly conceived the universe as a whole, wherein actions and reactions perpetually cross each other and join each other, where life is simply a universal and concerted music, with harmony and modulations, in which man takes up, on a different octave and in a different tone, the songs of love and hate which the animals also sing.

"I have quite decided that my novelist must be an amateur zoologist. Or, better still, a professional zoologist who is writing a novel in his spare time. His approach will be strictly biological. He will be constantly passing from the termitary to drawing-room and the factory, and back again. He will illustrate human vices by those of the ants, which neglect their young for the sake of the intoxicating liquor exuded by the parasites that invade their nests. His hero and heroine will spend their honeymoon by a lake, where the grebes and ducks illustrate all the aspects of courtship and matrimony." In Aldous Huxley, as in Philip Quarles, we can see an uncommon and really new blending of science and poetry.

And in Huxley, we are aware, this combination is conscious and intended. He has devoted one whole essay to the examination of what technical advantages a writer can derive from his scientific knowledge. He believes that the juxtaposition of two aspects of the same human event, one described in scientific, the other in emotional, terms, will produce a new and possibly beautiful dissonance. "Juxtapose, for example, physiology and mysticism (Mme. Guyon's ecstasies were most frequent and most spiritually significant in the fourth month of her pregnancies); . . . juxtapose chemistry and the soul (the ductless glands secrete among other things our moods, our aspirations, our philosophy of life)."

With the spatial symphony there is blended, in Huxley's novels, a symphony in time. He is no less sensitive to the poetry of historic unity than to that of cosmic unity, and he discovers curious subtle links between simple facts which apparently are quite unrelated. In an essay on comfort he shows how central heating was incompatible with feudalism, which required the great lord to declare his power by living as a giant might, in rooms that were a hundred feet long and thirty feet high, and that the modern armchair is incompatible with absolute monarchy, which insisted that only the king could be comfortably seated.

When Huxley travels he is continually drawing comparisons, and any spectacle enables him at once to build up a system. Attending a festival in India, and observing that the ceremonies were slackly performed because, to an Oriental, the thing symbolized is of much greater import than the symbol, he instantly derives a defence of the West and of materialism. The theory is disputable, but plausible and well argued, with a definite terminology and a dialectical strictness which are all the more astonishing because Huxley's work contains scores of other theories which, although often contradictory, are all expounded with equal talent.

A tithe of all this writing, perhaps even less, would have made the reputation of an eighteenth-century celebrity. Arnold Bennett noted in his diary that Huxley's favourite words seemed to be *incredible*, *inconceivable*, and *fantastic*, but added that the erudition of his visitor was incredible, inconceivable, and fantastic. Rarely could one point to a mind so active and alertly adaptable. One's only doubt is whether the extent of the canvas does not sometimes prevent us from taking in the whole picture.

IV

HUMOUR AND ART

IN HUXLEY's early books his passion for general ideas was tempered, or side-tracked, by humour. In *Crome Yellow* the method was that of Anatole France: comical themes developed in a professorial tone. France nearly always built up a conversation on two opposite themes: one serious and the other frivolous, or one outrageous and the other sensuous. If Dr Trublet, in the *Histoire Comique*, recounts one of Plato's myths, the actress Nanteuil interrupts with a dresser's advice. If the *Dies Irae* rolls thunderously through a church before a catafalque, its stanzas are interrupted by crude or silly conversations. Similarly, at the beginning of *Antic Hay*, Gombauld's reverie swamps the hymns and sermon with a meditation on the hardness of church benches and the need for pneumatic cushions.

Quite soon Huxley freed himself from the Anatole France influence, and showed a more vigorous sense of the comic which, in his portraiture at best, recalls Dickens. There are good examples in *Two or Three Graces*, which provides excellent satire in the picture of Hubert, the bore. Another example, more cruel and somewhat painful, is that of Burlap in *Point Counter Point*.

Somewhere Huxley praises Chesterton for his artistry in words. He deserves the same tribute. The desire for scientific precision, which is one of his most consistent mental traits, makes him hate the ill-defined word. He gives a sound drubbing to Professor Whitehead and Dean Inge for talking about the "real essence" of religion. Not only does he write well, but he constructs his books well, not in the sense of the Flaubertian novel (he would be quite capable of achieving a book of that kind if he so desired), but in a musical sense. What he attempted in *Point Counter Point* was the orchestration of several themes: "The musicalization of fiction. Not in the symbolist way, by subordinating sense to sound. . . . But on a large scale, in the construction. Meditate on Beethoven. The changes of moods, the abrupt transitions. (Majesty alternating with a joke, for example, in the first movement of the B flat major quartet.) More interesting still the modulations, not merely from one key to another, but from mood to mood. A theme is stated, then developed, pushed out of shape, imperceptibly deformed, until, though still recognizably the same, it has become quite different. . . . Get this into a novel. How? The abrupt transitions are easy enough. All you need is a sufficiency of characters and parallel, contrapuntal points. While Jones is murdering a wife, Smith is wheeling the perambulator in the park. You alternate the themes. More interesting, the modulations and variations are also more difficult. A novelist modulates by reduplicating situations and characters. He shows several people falling in love, or dying, or praying in different ways—dissimilars solving the same problem."

Finally, novels may well be excellently constructed and written, yet not be deeply interesting to our own time. But Huxley, like D. H. Lawrence, had the fortune, and the skill, to deal with just those problems which interest the most intelligent of our contemporaries, and to treat them in the exact tone which they wanted: without romantic or sentimental verbiage; the strict simplicity of a biologist's language; no timidity before ideas; an interest in sexual questions which recalls that of the seventeenth century in religion; a quiet cynicism which belongs as definitely to the nineteen-twenties as Wilde's epigrams did to the eighteen-nineties.

Of this modernity, Huxley is fully aware. One of his characters, Lucy Tantamount, attacks the older generation:

"'You speak of the old as though they are Kaffirs or Eskimos.' 'Well, isn't that just about what they are? . . . And wonderfully intelligent—in their way and all things considered. But they don't happen to belong to our civilization. They're aliens. I shall always remember the time I went to tea with some Arab ladies in Tunis. So kind they were, so hospitable. But they would make me eat such uneatable cakes, and they talked French so badly, and there was nothing whatever to say to them, and they were so horrified by my short skirts and my lack of children. Old people always remind me of an Arab tea-party. Do you suppose we shall be an Arab tea-party when we're old?'" And on another occasion the same Lucy Tantamount, scolding her lover, says to him: "'You think in such an absurdly unmodern way about everything. You might as well walk about in a stock and a swallow-tail coat. Try to be a little more up to date.' 'I prefer to be human.'—'Living modernly's living quickly,' she went on. 'You can't cart a waggon-load of ideals and romanticisms about with you these days. When you travel by aeroplane, you must leave your heavy baggage behind. The good old-fashioned soul was all right when people lived slowly. But it's ponderous nowadays. There's no room for it in the aeroplane.'—'Not even for a heart?' asked Walter. . . . Lucy shook her head. 'Perhaps it's a pity,' she admitted. 'If you like speed, if you want to cover the ground, you can't have luggage. . . .'"

In Aldous Huxley at the time of *Antic Hay*, there

was still something of Lucy Tantamount. But it goes
on diminishing.

V

INTELLIGENCE AND SENTIMENT

HERE, then, is an almost miraculous combination: a
writer of the highest intelligence and the widest
knowledge, very amusing when he chooses to be,
an artist in words and phrase, an ingenious innovator
in the construction of the novel, a critic of fine
(perhaps over-fine) taste, a paradoxical and brilliant
essayist of unfailing accuracy in his information. We
admire him, we feel the liveliest pleasure in reading
him, we feel certain that he will never utter a platitude or make a blunder, and that if by some chance
we think he has gone astray, he will himself correct
his bearings in the next paragraph. We enjoy this
sense of certainty. He satisfies us, enchants us, lavishes
his gifts on us. And yet, Strachey would say. . . .

And yet, even in all this perfection there is something that disappoints. The reader feels it. In *Point
Counter Point* he is brought into the company of
people who all converse most remarkably, and hears
sparkling discussion of the most important subjects;
but none of these people ever stops talking brilliantly, in order to live, to be like ourselves, to suffer. Mallarmé once asked to be given the notes which
had been taken during one of his discourses, in order,

[300]

he said, "to put a little obscurity into it." Sometimes we are left wishing that Huxley would add a little silence, and a good deal of sensitiveness. Only one figure is missing from his books: the ordinary man, whom Chesterton would declare the only important man. Not the only one, let us grant, but the man without whom life is inconceivable.

"In a recent essay," Edmond Jaloux has written, "Aldous Huxley refers with some scorn to the vulgarity of a great many novelists, and in particular of Dickens. In reading Mr Huxley, I sometimes wondered why, with all his extraordinary gifts, he had such difficulty in attaining the pitch of vital intensity which is indispensable to a novelist, and in reading these recent pages of his, I understand this difficulty. . . . A great novelist has a duty to be vulgar, because life is vulgar and men are vulgar, and the claim of the novelist is to reproduce life. It is just this vulgarity which Mrs Virginia Woolf lacks, or M. Jean Giraudoux in France, but in Balzac and Dickens and Dostoevski it is the fundamental quality."

If Huxley does not share adequately in the sentiments and passions of common men, it is because, by a tendency natural in a man of scientific culture, he is constantly tempted to isolate in the human or racial passions such measurable causes as will enable him to classify them amongst phenomena already familiar. Think, for instance, of the terror which a Pascal feels in contemplating "the eternal silence of the spaces of infinity." This shocks Huxley, as it angers Valéry. Why, they both ask, such weakness in a mind which otherwise is so vigorous? Huxley proceeds at once to a physiological explanation: it is because Pascal was a sick man. Why does he want to prevent men from taking pleasure in enjoyments? Because his own sickness prevented him from doing so. The sick body of Pascal, he says, was *naturaliter Christianum*.

Why, again, does Baudelaire feel "the dark despotic anguish, the black flag upon his bowed skull"? Because this is the common state of the waking debauchee. Our ancestors used physiological terms, such as "spleen" or "black bile," for these disordered states, and although they may have been mistaken about the precise organ to be blamed, they were right in fixing upon some organ or other.

Indeed, it is a fact that physiological states influence the spiritual state; but it is not proved that they entirely determine it. Millions of men have been fevered without being Pascals, debauched without being Baudelaires. The interactions of mind and body are not well understood. Can it even be said that psychology and sociology are sciences? Certainly not in the sense in which physics and astronomy are sciences. But such is Huxley's natural liking for scientific culture that he shows more intellectual tolerance towards a shaky theory with a vaguely scientific air about it, than towards a mystic at prayer or a woman in tears. (For instance, he takes quite seriously J. W. Dunne's *Experiment with Time*, an amusing book, but no more "scientific" than the agonies of Pascal.)

[302]

Furthermore, it is not only the sentiments of others that he dissects thus objectively, indeed too objectively. He is as ruthless towards himself as towards Pascal. A fondness for generalization overcomes even his own emotions. His political inclinations would be democratic, but democracy is not scientific, and so stands condemned. Chesterton, a democrat, is a great writer, and is admired by Huxley; but in Huxley's opinion Chesterton argues wrongly. According to Chesterton, the ordinary man should be left to do the important things by himself, and it is as absurd to offer to make his laws for him as to blow his nose for him. But Chesterton overlooks the fact that the ordinary man has no desire to make laws. Statistics prove that in fact a large number of electors never vote. Huxley quotes figures showing that, in an English bye-election 53 per cent of the electorate voted, and asks how many of those who did vote really take an intelligent interest in politics in the interval between elections. Compare the number of voters enrolled in the different political parties with the total figures of the electorate, and some indication will be given of the proportion between those who are interested in politics and those who don't care. The latter, he declares, are in an enormous majority.

Thus, although Huxley is at heart drawn towards democrats and revolutionaries rather than towards conservatives, the scientist in him realizes that the modern view of human nature is much closer to the traditional Catholic conception than to that of Helvetius, or Babeuf, or Shelley. The scientist examines the figures, and bows. Only 53 per cent vote. Very well: let us be objective and drop democracy.

Is he not right? Should not theories be built upon facts? Would it be right for him to follow the lead of his passions when his reason proves their folly? No. But it might nevertheless be desirable for him sometimes to have less trust in the validity of pseudo-scientific theory, and to show a fitting contempt for statistics, and to have a warmer sense of the reality of the passions: for that too is fact.

VI

THE "BOVARYSME" OF HUXLEY

BUT so complex and complete is Huxley that he has set forth these objections himself, as skilfully as could be desired. It is trite to remark that Huxley is too intelligent. But he is also too intelligent to be too intelligent. Sometimes the reader thinks he has caught him red-handed in an act of shameless rationalism. He accuses himself of finding the rôle of rationalist one which is all too easy to play. But within a few pages he is shrewdly condemning the excesses of rationalism, and he realizes how Pascal was led to Catholicism by the very stupidity of rationalists.

"What! Will he deny his own reason?" protests the scientist. Not at all. He regards reason as a tool, which, like any other, can be used well or ill. But as regards life in general, it is impossible to have exact data to start from, and consequently reasoning is impossible.

It is a character in *Point Counter Point*, the wife of Philip Quarles, who gives expression, better than any critic of Huxley, to the uneasiness which we feel before this perfect thinking-machine. She does not know how to talk to her husband, whom she feels to be enclosed in his concepts, with no human contacts, in fact a stranger in the world of men: "It is difficult to know what to say to someone who does not say anything in return, who answers the personal word with the impersonal, the particular and feeling word with an intellectual generalization."

How stern and objective Huxley can be is quite clear, even when the question touches matters which must touch him deeply. "I perceive," he says, "that the real charm of the intellectual life—the life devoted to erudition, to scientific research, to philosophy, to aesthetics, to criticism—is its easiness. It's the substitution of simple intellectual schemata for the complexities of reality; of still and formal death for the bewildering movements of life. It's incomparably easier to know a lot, say, about the history of art and to have profound ideas about metaphysics and sociology, than to know personally and intuitively a lot about one's fellows and to have satisfactory relations with one's friends and lovers, one's wife and children."

We may say, then, that Huxley's distrust of intellectualism is intellectual, and grant that for an intellectual there is no other way of distrusting it. The

man who lives too much by intelligence is forced
to invent instinct afresh, by a supreme effort of the
intelligence. It is a strange method; and a close examination will show that it was also through the intelligence that Pascal and D. H. Lawrence achieved
surrender, in the one case to faith, in the other to
instinct. The intellectual who knowingly follows this
process is more of a realist than one who remains enclosed within a pure system without ever resuming
contact with the earth. An intellectual is not necessarily an ideologue. If he pursues his search to the
end, he will discover at last that even the relativist
portion is not final, that a moment comes when intelligence touches the bedrock of instinct, and in the
end, as Chesterton showed so well, that, despite the
divergencies of the blind, the elephant is the elephant.

VII

CONCEPTION OF THE WORLD

OF THE nature of the elephant, that is to say the universe, what can we know? What conception of the
world does Huxley put forward? If, as Auguste
Comte teaches, all civilizations pass in succession
through periods of fetishism, metaphysics, and posi-
tivism, Bernard Shaw still belongs to England's metaphysical period, and Huxley represents the positivist
age. His work can show no Life Force, no Superman, no Powers of Darkness. On experiments he

builds up hypotheses. He is always ready to abandon
the hypothesis if it is belied by a new experiment.

Where will this method lead us? It will certainly
enable man to acquire a greater power over the universe. We shall more easily produce a greater abundance of wealth; we shall have more leisure; we shall
get rid of much physical suffering. From this moment a glimpse can be caught of the dawn of the
Best of Worlds. But whereas in the Utopias of H. G.
Wells, after the samurai triumph over stupidity, human happiness becomes paradisiacal, the Huxleyan
Utopia is a pessimistic one. So little real happiness
will come from the conquests of science that, in many
cases, men will renounce using them.

"Technically, it would be perfectly simple to reduce all lower-caste working hours to three or four
a day. But would they be any the happier for that?
No, they wouldn't. The experiment was tried, more
than a century and a half ago. The whole of Ireland
was put on to the four-hour day. What was the result?
Unrest and a large increase in the consumption of
soma; that was all. Those three and a half hours of
extra leisure were so far from being a source of happiness, that people felt constrained to take a holiday
from them. The Inventions Office is stuffed with
plans for labour-saving processes. Thousands of them.
. . . And why don't we put them into execution?
For the sake of the labourers; it would be sheer
cruelty to afflict them with excessive leisure."

The denizens of the *Brave New World* escape
from passion and suffering by taking *soma*, which is

a harmless and potent opium. They die painlessly looking at pictures, but their happiness is negative, and the most sensitive among them have a nostalgic yearning for the time when passions were real and sufferings more faithful.

Huxley avows his preference for feeling sober over feeling the most delicious intoxication. He rejects those illusions in which all men indulge, more or less consciously. He regards human nature, with its mixture of animalism and reason, as fated to wretchedness. This is another form of the doctrine of original sin, and it is not surprising that he believes Catholicism to be in closer contact with the real man than was the optimism of the eighteenth century.

Where is the remedy for this deplorable state of mankind to be found? In religion? Possibly: but if we are going to play the theological game, says Huxley, we must remember that it is a game. Perhaps the acceptance of certain religious conventions is necessary if life is to be tolerable. Every art has its conventions, and the most exacting of all arts is life. . . . Yes, but a religion tolerated in this spirit is no longer religion. . . . Then where is the remedy? In reason? But it cannot be said that the pragmatic value of pure rationalism is necessarily superior to that of non-rationalized beliefs. Besides, the great mass of men is not interested in reason and is not content with the teachings of reason.

There is a courage in this strict honesty, and perhaps also a sort of self-indulgent masochism. Through certain phases of Huxley one detects the mental

states of Baudelaire, and Baudelaire is one of the poets
from whom he quotes most frequently. All the
Baudelairean elements show themselves, under control, in Huxley—the intelligence, the weariness, the
attempt to escape weariness and thought by the highly
intellectual desire of cruel sensuality. If he remains
what he has been, he will have reflected with extraordinary brilliance the period of lucid and lofty despair
which followed the war of 1914-1918. But already
he seems to have been evolving. D. H. Lawrence
said of him: "There's more than one self to everybody, and the Aldous that writes those novels is only
one little Aldous amongst others—probably much
nicer—that don't write novels—I mean it's only one
of his little selves that writes the books . . . it's not
all himself. No, I don't like his books: even if I admire a sort of desperate courage of repulsion and re-
pudiation in them. But again, I feel only half a man
writes the books—a sort of precocious adolescent.
There is surely much more of a man in the actual
Aldous."

The "actual Aldous," like so many civilized men,
achieves real life, with its instincts and passions,
through the arts, and particularly through poetry and
music. Both of these arts he speaks of with feeling
and comprehension. The life of a period, he says, can
be synthesized only by the poets: the encyclopaedias
cannot do it because they are concerned only with
man's intellectual surface, and do not even touch the
lower layers, the kernel of his being. And in an essay
entitled *The Rest Is Silence*, he writes: "From pure

sensation to the intuition of beauty, from pleasure
and pain to love and the mystical ecstasy and death
—all the things that are fundamental, all the things
that, to the human spirit, are most profoundly significant, can only be experienced, not expressed. The
rest is always and everywhere silence. After silence
that which comes nearest to expressing the inexpressible is music. (And, significantly, silence is an in-
tegral part of all good music.)"

Whenever Huxley wishes to express the harmonies
of life he makes use of musical images: amongst the
melodies which are interwoven to make up the human counterpoint he finds songs of love and anacre-
ontic songs, marches and savage dances, songs of
hate and noisy songs of the comic. In our study
of Katherine Mansfield we note that her mystical
awareness of the universe and human life was attained by the simultaneous apprehension of the tragic
and the ludicrous, the exceptional and the everyday.
It is only when we accept the idea of the world
being neither simple nor entirely intelligible that we
begin to understand it. The true philosophy is religion—or it is art, which is a religion in its own way.

VIII

AN AMERICAN essayist, Thomas Beer, once called the
eighteen-nineties the "mauve decade." It is tempting
to describe the years between 1920 and 1930 in Eng-

ALDOUS HUXLEY

land as a steel-blue decade, a militant, clean-cut
decade. Its generation wrung the neck of eloquence,
as its master Strachey would have wished. It hated
false sentiment, pushing sincerity to cynicism and
cynicism to cruelty. Take as an example of the post-
Huxleyan novel, Evelyn Waugh's *A Handful of
Dust.* Here, underneath the casing of quite a frivolous narrative, is a more tragic and naked vision of
the folly of men and women than the harshest pages
of Swift, and no doubt it represents an inevitable
reaction after an orgy of sentimentality culminating
in massacre.

Betrayed by its leaders, growing up in a painful
period of transition, unhappy and therefore distrust-
ful, a young generation which has too often seen glittering words serve to mask ignorance and selfishness
demands a precise style and an unbending honesty.
Huxley is one of the first novelists whose culture has
been truly modern, who can manipulate without effort those concepts, old and new, which at this stage
of the twentieth century form the general system
of an intelligent man. Every period of swift change
produces its encyclopaedists: in England today they
are H. G. Wells, Aldous and Julian Huxley, Bertrand
Russell, and J. B. S. Haldane.

The danger, for Huxley as for most of us, might
have been to become the slave of a prodigious instrument, and to attempt the application of scientific
recipes, effective in the external world, to the ruling
of the internal world. That would be an ingenuous
and perilous mistake. Abstract reasoning, applied to

the conduct of political and economic affairs, leads
to disaster. But if the intelligence can raise and widen
itself to the point even of ruling intelligence itself,
nobody is more capable of doing so than Huxley.
"Stupidity is not my strong point," he might say
with Monsieur Teste, in Valéry's book. Like that
character, Huxley understands, demonstrates, re-
fashions, and distrusts every system; but like the creator of Monsieur Teste, he is saved by the poetry of
the systems and of disdain.

IX

KATHERINE MANSFIELD

Katherine Mansfield

A CH, Tchekov! why are you dead? Why can't I talk to you, in a big darkish room, at late evening. . . ." The voice is Katherine Mansfield's, conjuring up in her journal those impossible, longed-for encounters with people whom we shall never know and who were born to become our friends. It is like the Abbé Mugnier saying that his great regret was not to have been the chaplain on St Helena or the confessor of Stendhal. And we too, as we read her journal, constantly regret that we could not have sat with her on some terrace in Provence or Tuscany, talking about the art of writing, which she understood as Tchekov did, and about the life which she loved with such ardour and despair.

She died young, leaving behind only a few stories, longer and shorter; but she is a great writer, one of those who added deep truths to English literature of the present day, because she knew that spontaneity and sincerity are of far greater import than verbal brilliance, strangeness of feeling, or novelty of ideas.

I

SHE was born Kathleen Beauchamp, in New Zealand, in 1888. Through some of her stories we catch glimpses of her family, colonial, but still very English, with her efficient, highly practical grandmother, her mother, frail and delicate, who nevertheless lived her life more richly than anyone, her very "male" father, with his masculine activity and lack of subtlety, her aunt, still quite young, pretty and watching the dawn of love, the elder sisters, with a younger brother and sister as well.

Now that we can read in her biography, by Ruth Mantz and Middleton Murry, about the real Beauchamp family, we can see that Katherine, in some of these stories, scarcely altered anything. But it took her a long time to acquire, with regard to New Zealand and her childhood, the detachment which enabled her to love them, to understand their beauty, to paint them. Katherine Mansfield was neither a happy nor a tranquil little girl. Her father had chosen to leave a large town in New Zealand in favour of a settlers' village, and there, with the baker's and laundry-woman's children, she was educated at the village school. Her family thought her slow and lazy; she was blamed for not being quick-witted, like her sisters; and yet, even then, she was trying to write.

At a very early age she wrote a novel, *Juliet*, in which she depicted her anger and sorrows. "Juliet

[316]

was the odd moment of the family—the ugly duck-
ling. She had lived in a world of her own—created her
own people—read anything and everything which
came to hand—was possessed with a violent temper,
and completely lacked placidity. She was dominated
by her moods which swept through her and in number were legion. She had been, as yet, utterly idle at
school, drifted through her classes, picked up a quan-
tity of heterogeneous knowledge and all the plead-
ings and protestations of her teachers could not in-
duce her to learn that which did not appeal to her.
She . . . wrapped herself in a fierce white reserve.
'I have four passions,' she wrote in an old diary—
'Nature, people, mystery, and, the fourth no man
can number.' Of late she had quarrelled frequently
with the entire family through lack of anything definite to occupy her thoughts. She felt compelled to
vent her energy upon somebody, and that somebody
was her family." That is a remarkable passage to come
from a child.

The bonds of Empire are sentimental rather than
political. Certain colonial families, like the Beauchamps, keep in close touch with England, which remains the sole centre of their civilization. Mr Beauchamp considered it essential that Kathleen, at the
age of thirteen, should be sent to complete her education in London, where she entered Queen's College, in Harley Street. There, as in her own home,
she was a solitary and a dreamer. Sometimes she
wrote. Her journal and letters are striking, in their
seriousness and their acute sense of the beauty of the

world: "I have just returned from a midnight service. It was very, very beautiful and solemn. The air outside was cold and bracing, and the Night was a beautiful thing. The Church looked truly very fit for God's house tonight. It looked so strong, so hospitable, so invincible. It was only during the silent prayer that I made up my mind to write this. I mean this year to try and be a different person, and I wait at the end of this Year to see how I have kept all the vows that I have made tonight. So much happens in a year. One may mean so well and do so little. . . . Tomorrow is the first of January. What a wonderful and what a lovely world this is. I thank God tonight that I *am*."

But these high resolves soon faded, and Kathleen did little sustained work. Later she was to regret it. "I was thinking yesterday of my *wasted, wasted* early girlhood. My college life, which is such a vivid and detailed memory in one way, might never have contained a book or a lecture. I lived in the girls, the professor, the big, lovely building, the leaping fires in winter and the abundant flowers in summer. The views out of the windows, all the pattern that was weaving. My mind was just like a squirrel. I gathered and gathered and hid away, for that long 'winter' when I should rediscover all this treasure—and if anybody came close I scuttled up the tallest, darkest tree and hid in the branches."

She edited the school magazine, and wrote a good deal of verse which has been preserved, fluent and graceful. In one form or another, music or poetry or story-telling, she was impelled to give expression to the peculiar note which life sounded for her, and which, in Katherine Mansfield's belief, did not sound just thus for anyone else: by now she was believing in herself. But the time came when her father came over to bring her back to New Zealand. She felt that now she really needed London; and, in so many words, she set down her intention of making herself so intolerable that they would be forced to send her back!

She returned to Wellington. The Beauchamps had returned to the city, and occupied a large house. Her father had become a man of mark in commerce, banking, or public activities: soon he would be Sir Harold Beauchamp. He quite realized that his daughter wished to write; he was fond of her, and thought her gentle and delicate, but weak, rather unreal, aloof from the world and life. Here in the Antipodes she would think only of London, imagining the crowds coming out of the theatres, longing for the company of people with whom she could talk about poetry and books and feelings. In Wellington life was dull and drab, with no pictures, no books. Was there a soul she knew who had even heard of Rossetti? Her thoughts kept turning to her friends at Queen's College.

"A year ago we sat by the fire, she and I, hand in hand, cheek to cheek, speaking but little, and then whispering, because the room was so dark, the fire so low, and the rain outside so loud and bitter.

"She, a thin little figure in a long, soft black frock, and a string of amethysts around her white throat.

"Eventually it grew so cold that I dragged the

blanket from the bed, and we wrapped ourselves up in it, smiling a little and saying, 'We feel like children on a desert island.' With one hand she held the rough, gaily-striped thing up to her chin; the other hand lay in mine. We talked of fame, how we both longed for it, how hard the struggle was, what we both meant to do. I found a piece of paper, and together we wrote a declaration vowing that in the space of one year we should both have become famous. And we signed the paper and sealed it; then, dedicating it to the gods, dropped it into the fire. For a moment a bright light, and then a handful of ashes. By and by she fell asleep, and I gave her my share of the blanket, and arranged a soft pillow in her low chair. The long night dragged coldly through, while I watched her, and thought, and longed, but could not sleep. Today, at the other end of the world, I have suffered, and she, doubtless, has bought herself a new hat at the February sales. *Sic transit gloria mundi.*"

Writing? Yes, she felt born for that. But how should she write, and what? She filled countless notebooks: "I am full of ideas tonight. And they must at all costs germinate. I should like to write something so beautiful, and yet modern, and yet student-like and full of summer. . . . Here is silence and peace and splendour. . . . Far away I hear builders at work upon a house—and the tram sends me half crazy. Let it be a poem. . . ." But nothing that she wrote satisfied her. "I can write nothing at all. I have many ideas but no grip of any subject. I want

KATHERINE MANSFIELD, FROM THE PAINTING BY MISS ANNE ESTELLE RICE

to write verses—but they won't come. . . . I should like to write something just a trifle mysterious—but really very beautiful and original." It is deeply moving, this vague presentiment which a great artist has of what her art will be, at a time when it is still asleep in the limbo of real feeling.

What she wrote fell quite easily into the form of very short stories, which she called "vignettes." It was her father who first secured her the joy of seeing herself in print, in a Melbourne magazine. When the editor asked her for an account of her life, she wrote, rather as Byron once did: "You ask for some details as to myself. I am poor—obscure—just eighteen years of age—with a voracious appetite for everything—and principles as light as my prose—" In those days she was noting in her journal, with admiration, Oscar Wilde's remark: "I do not want to earn a living; I want to live."

Well, living meant returning to London. "In London. To write the word makes me feel that I could burst into tears. Isn't it terrible to love anything so much? I do not care at all for men, but *London*—it is Life. . . ." And the exasperations of family life made her all the more eager to be off. "Even when I am alone in my room, they come outside and call to each other, discuss the butcher's orders or the soiled linen and—I feel—wreck my life. It is so humiliating. And this morning I do not wish to write, but to read Marie Bashkirtseff. But if they enter the room and find me merely with a book, their tragic, complaining looks upset me altogether."

Sustained by her resolve to become an artist, Katherine Mansfield had an inner strength which enabled her to preserve her balance, and a power of persuasion which enabled her to convince her father and obtain an allowance from him. In July 1908 he allowed her to leave New Zealand, and she left never to return.

She settled in London. She had made Wilde her master, and, with the naïveté of methodical youth, she extracted from reading him a dangerous doctrine concerning the artist's duty of experience. She wanted to sacrifice her person to enrich her art. The day was to come when she regretted it: "but it hadn't *all* been experience. There is waste—destruction too."

In this way she lived an absurd romance. It was her belief that she would marry a man with no prejudices, who would not only protect her but respect her right to live as an untrammelled artist. She found a music teacher who apparently accepted this strange agreement, married him, found him absurd, and left him after a few days. A period of extreme loneliness and depression followed: "I felt rather like a frightened child lost in a funeral procession." Her health was poor; she had no real home, and sought vainly for a possible refuge. Her mother came to London to see her, but they did not understand each other. She was now expecting a child, not her husband's, and she had to go abroad to hide her condition and the coming birth. She was sent to a village in Germany, where she wrote a whole series of short stories and sketches, which made up her first book, *In a German Pension.*

They were realistic, rather biting, alternating natural humour with cynicism and bitterness. With highly Anglo-Saxon strokes she painted a caricatured, unpleasant Germany, a mixture of sentimentality and guzzling, pride and poverty. She described how, in the pension, there was a Baron who sat at a table by himself, revered at a distance by the other guests for his noble rank, and who explained to the young Englishwoman that he ate alone and in silence so as to have time to eat twice as much. Frau Fischer, owner of a candle factory, had violent sensual desires, and gravely told everybody so. Fräulein Sonia, the "modern soul," fainted in the arms of the Herr Professor. . . . It was all very queer, and sometimes tragic. The book was cleverly written, but Katherine Mansfield soon began to dislike it. She regretted the smug superiority of its "foreigner's" point of view. Doubtless she had faithfully described what she had seen, and Germany, in part, was like that; but certainly Germany was not only that. Later she forbade the reissue of the book, although she was in dire need of money at the time.

But when she wrote these stories, she was delighted to have them printed in a weekly paper, the *New Age*. She returned to London, lived alone, and worked. One day she received a letter from a young writer, John Middleton Murry, asking her to contribute to a small literary review published at Oxford. She met him, and found an enthusiastic and fluent young undergraduate. They met frequently, and before long were planning to publish a new review, to be called *Rhythm*. She said that she was not quite in sympathy with the *New Age*: "They have a conviction that I can only write satire. And I'm not a very satirical person—really. . . . I believe in something. . . . Let's call it truth. It's a very big thing. . . . We have to discover it. That's what the artist is for—to become true by discovering truth. . . . Truth is so important that when you discover a tiny bit of it, you forget all about everything else—and all about yourself."

She suggested that Murry should rent a room in the small flat where she was living. He agreed, and for a long time they carried on separate lives, though living thus side by side. In the end he married her. He hesitated before doing so, because he was poor, while she received a little money from her family. Neither of them earned anything appreciable. *Rhythm* died, as nearly all young reviews die. Katherine Mansfield had published some of her stories there, and did not know where she could place her work. Editors did not seem to understand the interest of the manuscripts she submitted, and perhaps they were not altogether wrong. What she wrote at this time was good, but a little too good; it lacked just that ring of truth which she longed above all things to capture. She had not yet discovered, or rather rediscovered, the fountainhead of her strongest impressions, which lay in her New Zealand childhood. But it was still near enough for her to be able to free herself from them and recreate them in her writings.

The War broke out. Katherine Mansfield's young

brother arrived from New Zealand to enlist. He was certainly the one person she loved above all others. He brought back all their childhood memories. Thanks to her journal, we catch glimpses of them walking in a London garden . . . a pear fell from an old tree. . . .

" 'Do you remember the enormous number of pears there used to be on that old tree?'

'Down by the violet bed.'

'And how after there'd been a Southerly Buster we used to go out with clothes baskets to pick them up?'

'And how while we stooped they went on falling, bouncing on our backs and heads?' . . .

'Do you know that I've never seen pears like them since?'

'They were so bright, canary yellow—and small. And the peel was so thin and the pips jet—jet black. . . .'

'The pips were delicious.'

'Do you remember sitting on the pink garden seat?' "

And so the dead past rose again, gleaming and alive, suddenly now as lovable as it had been hateful in the days when it was the present. Her brother had told her he was sure of coming home from the war. In him, it seems, this war was a mysterious but absolute certainty. " 'It's so curious—my absolute confidence that I'll come back. I feel it's as certain as this pear. I couldn't not come back.' " He went, and was immediately killed.

This was the great agony of his sister's life. She left the real world for good, and gave herself over entirely to the refashioning of that tiny world of the past which, in memory, and blending with the image of her brother, became a place of enchantment.

"I think I have known for a long time that life was over for me, but I never realized it or acknowledged it until my brother died. I am just as much dead as he is. The present and the future mean nothing to me. I am no longer 'curious' about people; I do not wish to go anywhere; and the only possible value that anything can have for me is that it should put me in mind of something that happened or was when he was alive.

" 'Do you remember, Katie?' I hear his voice in the trees and the flowers, in scents and light and shadow. Have people, apart from these far-away people, ever existed for me? . . .

"Now—now I want to write recollections of my own country. Yes, I want to write about my own country till I simply exhaust my store. Not only because it is 'a sacred debt' that I pay to my country because my brother and I were born there, but also because in my thoughts I range with him over all the remembered places.

"Then I want to write poetry. The almond tree, the birds, the little wood where you are, the flowers you do not see, the open window out of which I lean and dream that you are against my shoulder, and the times that your photograph 'looks sad.' But especially I want to write a kind of long elegy to you

. . . perhaps not in poetry. Nor perhaps in prose. Almost certainly in a kind of *special prose*."

She was now beginning to suffer from the illness that in the end killed her, tuberculosis of the lungs, and she left England for Bandol, in the South of France. Her husband accompanied her, but had soon to return to England; in any case, she wanted solitude for the sake of the work which was to occupy her last year, work of similar quality and kind as that of Proust, the capture of memory, the search for time past. The finest works of art, it may be, require this total detachment, this death before death.

When Katherine Mansfield published the first of her new stories, very few critics discerned the unique character of what lay before them. Like so many people in the post-war years, they confused strangeness with beauty. They preferred Dostoevski to Tchekov, and Katherine Mansfield seemed to them too simple. Fortunately she had admirers of taste and influence, such as D. H. Lawrence, Sydney Schiff (that excellent novelist "Stephen Hudson" and a friend of Proust), the young novelist William Gerhardi, and Lady Ottoline Morrell. Still better, the public, which is generally receptive to a quality of naturalness, discovered her with delight. Her first collections of stories, *Bliss* and *The Garden Party*, began to show signs of real "selling" success.

But she grew more and more ill, wandering from the terraces of Provence to the Italian hills. She had an idea that the weakness which prevented her from writing was not merely physical. She became convinced that she could attain the supreme objectivity which was her literary ideal only by a sort of abstraction, a purging of all egoism from her nature. It was essential that this purification should be accomplished before she could advance, before she could feel worthy of expressing the complete truth.

In this spirit she entered a "spiritual brotherhood" at Fontainebleau, founded there by certain Russians, where she believed she could achieve a complete regeneration. After three months there she sent for Middleton Murry to join her. He arrived on January 9, 1923. "I have never seen," he wrote, "nor shall I ever see, anyone so beautiful as she was on that day; it was as though the exquisite perfection which was always hers had taken possession of her completely. To use her own words, the last grain of 'sediment,' the last 'traces of earthly degradation,' were departed for ever. But she had lost her life to save it. As she came up the stairs to her room at 10 P.M. she was seized by a fit of coughing which culminated in a violent haemorrhage. At 10.30 she was dead."

II

HER THEMES

BEFORE attempting the difficult task of analysing Katherine Mansfield's talent, we should bear in mind, in outline at least, some of the subjects she chose to handle: her choice is in itself the beginning of a definition. Take for instance *The Garden Party*.

The Sheridans are giving a garden party. The weather is ideal, warm and windless, and the sky is cloudless. Everything is almost too perfect, and, just as sometimes one hears music that is too lovely and feels afraid of life, so one feels, in reading the opening of this story, that this too happy family is swaying on the brink of tragedy. Some women are sketched in a few strokes: the mother, an Englishwoman of good family, conversing competently about her garden and vegetables, quite youthful still in spite of her grey hair. "My darling child," she says to her daughter, "you wouldn't like a logical mother, would you?" Laura is one of the daughters, intelligent and sensitive. She is listening to the talk of the workmen as they pitch a marquee in the garden for the party. She finds them delightful, these four men in shirt sleeves! And she reflects on class distinctions and the folly of such things, not as a man might, by reasoned theory and coherent argument, but like a woman, in snatches of feeling and unfinished sentences. She goes indoors, where her mother is busy with little flags for the sandwiches. Suddenly disaster. . . . The pastrycook's man, delivering the cakes, announces that a workman has just been killed by a traction engine, one of the men living in those little houses on the road at the foot of the grounds. He was quite young, and he has left a wife and children. Laura is terrified, and wants the whole party to be cancelled.

" 'Stop the garden party? My dear Laura, don't be so absurd.' 'But we can't possibly have a garden party with a man dead just outside the front gate.' That really was extravagant, for the little cottages were in a lane to themselves at the very bottom of a steep rise that led up to the house. A broad road ran between. 'But my dear child, use your common sense.' "

So the garden party goes on, and is a great success. Oh, how delightful it is to talk with happy people, and shake hands, and smile. . . . "My word, Laura! You do look stunning. . . . What an absolutely topping hat!" And slowly the perfect afternoon blossoms to fullness, and fades, and closes its petals. In the evening, as there are some sandwiches left over, Laura's mother suggests that she might take them down to the children of the dead man.—"But, mother, do you really think it's a good idea?"—But once again nobody sees it as she does. It seems that it is a very good idea. It will be dreadful, she thinks, to go into a dead man's house carrying sandwiches. . . . No, it isn't even dreadful. . . . The sister-in-law receives her there.—"You'd like to look at 'im, wouldn't you?"—and before she can say no, Laura finds herself in the presence of death, for the first time in her life. "There lay a young man, fast asleep —sleeping so soundly, so deeply. . . . What did garden parties and baskets and lace frocks matter to him? . . . All is well, said that sleeping face. This is just as it should be." She goes home, thinking that life is— what, fundamentally? Painful? Wonderful? You can't tell: life is like that. And the reader may think of Turgenev's remark: "the terrible thing is that there is nothing terrible."

Prelude, another long story, begins with a very close description of a removal of the Beauchamp family, here styled the Burnells. The carriage goes off and the children are left for a last trip; they will be coming on later, with the vans. . . . A journey in the dark for the little girls, Kezia, who is Katherine Mansfield, and Lottie, who is Katherine's sister. And here is the new house, so far as the sleepy children can see it, in a green garden. Linda Burnell, the mother, has a weak heart and takes no part in the work. Stanley, her husband, is full of male selfishness, and in the upheaval of the move insists on his dinner and his slippers: a drone, useless and in the way. The grandmother and servants do all the work. Aunt Beryl, helping, is in a bad temper and jostles the children. She is quite young and very pretty. At night, as she undresses, she looks out for the unknown young man who will give her a house of her own. But does he exist?

There follow some scenes of admirable comedy. Stanley Burnell, having rented the house himself, refuses to see any faults in it. The children discover the aloes in the garden, the poultry-yard, and a whole world of wonders, where Aunt Beryl, exiled by a brother-in-law's power far from town, where young men abound, can see little that is not hateful. Alice, the housemaid, hates Miss Beryl, who after all isn't her mistress but orders her about. Linda Burnell loves her husband because he is simple and genuine, but is afraid of him because he is too strong and is killing her with child-births. Yes, it is true: she loves him, yet she hates him. How absurd life is, how laughable. . . . The grandmother looks at the fruit trees and thinks of the jam. She is really bringing up Kezia and Lottie by herself, and the old lady has an illusion of finding again her own two daughters, in the days when *they* were small and obedient. Beryl, up in her room, in the moonlight, is writing a letter. It is packed with grievances and woes. She knows that what she has written is not accurate, and that she is exaggerating the situation. But she goes on with the letter in the same tone: it is a different Beryl who is writing. She looks at herself in the mirror. . . . Who is this creature? She remembers a few rare moments when she has really been herself. Then she reflects: "Life is rich and mysterious and good. . . ." But Kezia comes in: "Aunt Beryl, mother says will you please come down?" Beryl smiles, and goes down. That is all.

At the Bay shows us the same characters, in a house at the seaside: the story of one day in one family. Two major themes are interwoven: that of the passing hours, and that of the two sexes. The morning mists are lifting, and disclose the placid sea; the sheep go past, the family awakes; the male, before going off to work infuriates the females—wife, sister-in-law, children. They all heave a sigh of relief when at last he disappears. Then the female race goes down to the beach. Beryl bathes with the dangerous Mrs Harry Kimber, whose bathing dress scandalizes the beach. Her husband, Harry Kimber, keeps prowling round the girl Beryl, and in the evening he comes to her window and calls her. . . . . She goes down, against her own will, and then, terrified by the man's desire, takes to flight. "'You are vile, vile,'" said she. "'Then why in God's name did you come?'" stammered Harry Kimber. Nobody answered him. A cloud, small, serene, floated across the moon. In that moment of darkness the sea sounded deep, troubled. Then the cloud sailed away, and the sound of the sea was a vague murmur. . . . All was still."

The subjects of the shorter stories are equally simple. One evening Bertha Young is coming home. What are you to do, when you're thirty, and when you turn the corner of your own street and feel yourself suddenly overwhelmed by a sense of beatitude . . . ? How lovely life is! She loves her husband, Harry; she has an adorable baby; charming friends are coming to dine. Through the drawing-room windows she can see a pear-tree in blossom, tall and slender, not one petal faded. The whole evening is perfect, divine. At last the guests are leaving. Miss Fulton, a pretty young woman, rather odd, is the last to go. Harry goes out to see her into the taxi, and in a mirror Bertha sees her husband leaning over the other woman, kissing her with obvious familiarity. In a flash her happiness crumbles away, but the pear-tree is as lovely as ever, as heavy with blossom, as tranquil.

Another story. The old colonel is dead. His daughters are going through his clothes, a little frightened of touching things which, only yesterday, were sacred. "Father would never forgive them. . . ." How did he come to allow death to touch him? And yet these things simply must be disposed of. . . . Who is to get his top hat? How are they to get rid of the nurse who has been looking after him, and shows no sign of going? The two daughters flounder amongst the endless little problems set by death. What have they known of life itself, amongst these old Anglo-Indian friends of their father? Their whole existence has been taken up with looking after him, distracting him, being afraid of him. But now what are they going to do? Here they are, free at last. A vague hope rises, and the setting sun lights up Josephine's face. . . .

III

INTIMATE IMPRESSIONISM

THE method is becoming apparent. It is not that of those English novelists who take up a story at the moment of the hero's birth and slowly conduct it through a consecutive series of incidents towards a final catastrophe or into the luminous deltas of contentment. What Katherine Mansfield does is to select a family, a setting, and there make a deep cut into time, describing the impressions of the people during the brief chosen moment, and telling us nothing about them except through their own thoughts and remarks at that moment. From the opening lines, she makes them speak, and mentions them by name, without making any effort to instruct us about them. We come to know her heroes rather as we know our fellow-passengers in a railway carriage, or our neighbours in a restaurant: that is to say, by building them up from their conversation.

Nor is Katherine Mansfield's method that of the French novelists, such as that of François Mauriac in *Genitrix* or *La Fin de La Nuit*, which likewise make an incision in time. The French novelists, like the French tragedians, choose for such a process a moment of crisis, whereas one particular feature of Katherine Mansfield's art is that, for the theme of her composition she chooses an ordinary day, a day marked only by some small family event—the Burnells' removal, a garden party, a child's journey with her grandmother, an episode after a bereavement. It is precisely the intensity of this commonplace day which quickens our emotion or our sense of wonder, just as is done by those artists who can convey a sense of all the beauty of the world by painting a plate of fruit and a white table-cloth.

Crisis it may be, for everything is a crisis in life, but a crisis in miniature. That a painting need not be large to be great has been proved by Chardin, Vuillard, and many others. That a short story can contain and suggest as much truth about the world as a long novel, had been shown by Tchekov and Mérimée, whom Katherine Mansfield held in passionate admiration. But it is doubtful whether

Tchekov himself would have dared to build up anything on a foundation so fragile as that of *Prelude*. Amongst his stories, *An Ordinary Story* is a crisis in the sense of the French tragedies; *Three Years* is a short novel, and Tchekov says more than once how he regrets it cannot be longer. But here Katherine Mansfield parts company with her master. "Tchekov made a mistake," she says, "in thinking that if he had had more time he would have written more fully, described the rain, and the midwife and the doctor having tea. The truth is one can only get *so much* into a story; there is always a sacrifice. One has to leave out what one knows and longs to use. Why? I haven't any idea, but there it is. It's always a kind of race to get in as much as one can before it *disappears*."

The more skilled her artistry becomes, the more she is freed from the superstition of subject-matter. Some of her early stories, those preceding what may be called her "mystical" period, which begins in 1915, with the death of her brother, are as carefully contrived as the stories of Maupassant. Others are reminiscent of Villiers de l'Isle-Adam. But these stories are far from being her best. It is only when Katherine Mansfield is no longer herself that she is saved. She is right in believing that her very brevity helps her. A story of hers will often remind one of those mutilated sculptures, which become all the more beautiful in our eyes as it is our own genius which roused and quickened by that of the artist, reconstructs its missing head or limbs.

IV

A FEMININE UNIVERSE

So IT is an impressionist art. But this would be quite an inadequate definition. We should add first, a *feminine* impressionism. The name of Tchekov has frequently been mentioned in these last few pages; and Katherine Mansfield herself often refers to him, to say that he was one of the few men whom she would have understood and admired. But we should not seek more exact resemblances between these two. The world of Tchekov is a male world: the thoughts and the conversations of its inhabitants are filled with ideas and activities. The world of Katherine Mansfield is primarily a feminine world. The house, clothes, children, women's cares—and more exactly, those of well-to-do women—are the things that matter. With the household cares she likes to mingle the feelings of women, their judgements of people, their musings. The men in Katherine Mansfield's pictures scarcely seem to have any work to do: that does not interest her. What is Stanley Burnell's job in life? Does she tell us? I have forgotten. What we do know, is what his wife thinks of him.

In the universe of women, the truth about people is discovered slowly, through the accidents of long talks. In *New Dresses*, Mrs Carsfield and her mother are finishing off certain green cashmere dresses with apple-green belts. The husband has gone out and the two women are talking about children. Through their remarks, which are inextricably connected with their womanly occupations, the characters of the children and all the relationships of the family are revealed to us: "Mrs Carsfield worked the machine, slowly, for she feared the green thread would give out, and had a sort of tired hope that it might last longer if she was careful to use a little at a time; the old woman sat in a rocking chair, her skirt turned back, and her felt-slippered feet on a hassock, tying the machine threads and stitching some narrow lace on the necks and cuffs. The gas jet flickered. Now and again the old woman glanced up at the jet and said, 'There's water in the pipe, Anne, that's what's the matter,' then was silent to say again a moment later, 'There must be water in that pipe, Anne,' and again, with quite a burst of energy, '*Now*, there is— I'm *certain* of it.' Anne frowned at the sewing machine. 'The way mother *harps* on things—it gets frightfully on my nerves,' she thought. 'And always when there's no earthly opportunity to better a thing. . . . I suppose it's old age—but most aggravating." Aloud she said: 'Mother, I'm having a really substantial hem in this dress of Rose's—the child has got so leggy, lately. And don't put any lace on Helen's cuffs; it will make a distinction, and besides she's so careless about rubbing her hands on anything grubby.'

" 'Oh there's plenty,' said the old woman. 'I'll put it a little higher up.' And she wondered why Anne had such a down on Helen—Henry was just the same. They seemed to want to hurt Helen's feelings."

Already we know that mother and daughter disagree about the children, that the grandmother's favourite is Helen, the more unruly of the two, whilst the mother's is Rose, the careful one. But we know these things as women know them, without having it clearly stated, without any logical structure being built up.

Women and their moods, their secret alliances against the male, that particular voice in which they talk together in the evening, the long conversations of a mother and daughter, their mysterious bonds of union with certain objects. . . . About all such things nobody has ever spoken better. Virginia Woolf also has told about them very well, and *Mrs Dalloway* is perhaps the only novel which Katherine Mansfield might possibly have written. But Virginia Woolf is a lover of ideas; she can beat men on their own ground; she is one of the best English critics of the day. Perhaps she does not give us so close a contact with the feminine soul. In France, Colette often comes very close to what Katherine Mansfield was seeking, and this she herself recognized. "I've re-read *L'Entrave*," she wrote. "I suppose Colette is the only woman in France who does just this. I don't care a fig at present for anyone I know except her. But the book to be written is still unwritten."

That last remark means, presumably, that Colette's

world is not yet simple enough, not sufficiently devoid of adventure for Katherine Mansfield's taste.
The fact remains that Colette, a woman of genius,
was practically the first woman who dared to be entirely feminine in a book. Before her, admittedly,
there were excellent women writers—a Madame de
Sévigné, a Madame de La Fayette; but they were
playing men's parts, imitating male styles, writing
masculine novels which yet lacked the compact solidity of books really written by men. The novels of
Madame de Staël, or George Eliot, or George Sand,
are interesting; but they are hybrid books, half male,
half female. When Emily Brontë's masterpiece
reached its publishers, they believed it to be the
work of a man. But who could read a passage from
Colette or Katherine Mansfield and mistake them
for men? It is a peculiar and fortunate feature of our
age that women have accepted their womanhood.
The emancipation of women has perhaps cured an
inferiority complex; in receiving the rights of man,
have they also been given the courage to be women?

V

HER MYSTICISM

CROSS-SECTIONS of the feminine universe, very finely
cut—this might serve as a first definition of the work
we are examining; but it is one which still lacks the
essential. The virtue of Katherine Mansfield's stories

lies not merely in their truthfulness, but in their poetry. The characters are plunged in a real world, where their actions are controlled by the great natural rhythms—the hours of the day, the seasons, the tides, the courses of the stars. "I feel always trembling on the brink of poetry," she wrote.

The idea, in her work, is never explicitly stated. There are no formal metaphors, but they are suggested. One of the characters in *Prelude* lets drop the remark that the aloe flowers only once in a hundred years, and Linda Burnell fancies that it is flowering on that day. The symbol is not explained, but need it be? The blossoming pear-tree is linked up with the happiness of Bertha Young. A tiny lamp in a doll's house, a fly killed by a banker—these small things become centres for stories. It is a property of the greatest art to give the concrete support of an object in this way to an undefined emotion. This is why the titles of certain stories of Mérimée are so felicitous: the Etruscan vase was only an insignificant accessory in the story to which it gave a title, but it is right that the story itself should be associated with the memory of this object. Incarnations of this kind bring about a mystical communion between man and nature.

As a method of diagnosing a writer's philosophy, it would not be altogether useless to discover what words he uses most frequently. In the case of Katherine Mansfield one would find *beautiful . . . delightful . . . exquisitely . . .* It is the beauty of the world that impresses her more than anything else. From early childhood she kept her enchanted dream of a summer morning in New Zealand. "All is harmonious and peaceful and delicious. We camp in a pine forest—beautiful. We are like children here with happiness. We drive through the sunset—then supper at the hotel. And the night is utterly perfect. We go to the mineral baths. The walk there down the hill is divine. Then we go home—tired—hot—happy—blissfully happy. We sleep in the tent . . . wake early. . . . The birds are magical." And it is not only the New Zealand of her childhood which is bathed in this magical illumination. In her letters and journals she is constantly expressing the ecstasy of her mystical communion with a landscape, English or French. "And yet one has had these 'glimpses,' before which all that one has ever written . . . that one has ever read, pales. . . . The waves, as I drove home this afternoon, and the high foam, how it is suspended in the air before it fell. . . . What is it that happens in that moment of suspension? It is timeless. In that moment . . . the whole life of the soul is contained."

Shelley had moments like these, and Rupert Brooke likewise. It is characteristically Anglo-Saxon, this perfect joy given by nature; and the strange thing is how often this instinctive happiness is mingled with a theoretic pessimism. To Katherine Mansfield's heroines the world is harsh and frightening. Nearly all her stories are of moments of beauty suddenly broken by contact with ugliness, cruelty, or death. But things must be accepted thus. Life is just this mixture, as Laura divines so clearly at the end of *The Garden Party*.

The diversity, and the way in which we try to crowd everything into it, even death itself, is exactly what is so disturbing to a girl of Laura's age. She feels that things should be different, but life is like that, and we did not make it so. In life the garden party and the death of the workman happen on the same day, at the same time of day. Laura may protest that things like that *ought* not to happen at the same time, but Life answers: "Why not? In what way do they differ?" They happen, and it is inevitable. But there is beauty in the inevitability.

In 1920 Katherine Mansfield wrote to her husband: "And then suffering, bodily suffering . . . has changed forever everything; even the *appearance* of the world is not the same—there is something added. *Everything has its shadow.* Is it right to resist such suffering? Do you know I feel it has been an immense privilege. Yes, in spite of all. How blind we little creatures are! It's only the fairy-tales we *really* live by. And if someone rebels and says, life isn't good enough on those terms, one can only say: 'It is!' We resist, we are terribly frightened. The little boat enters the dark fearful gulf and our only cry is to escape— 'put me on land again.' But it's useless. Nobody listens. The shadowy figure rows on. One ought to sit still and uncover one's eyes. I believe the greatest failing of all is *to be frightened*. Perfect Love casteth out Fear."

And what is the rôle of the artist confronted by the wonderful and terrible spectacle of life? First of all, to depict the spectacle with perfect accuracy and complete sincerity. Why should he tell a lie? Why should he seek "effects"? He must write something worthy of that rising moon, that pale light, and be simple as one would be simple before God. Above all, he must not sneer, as she did once, in the days of *In a German Pension*; for, say what she may, Katherine Mansfield had a satiric mind. But she refuses to be a satirist: "What will happen to Anatole France and his charming smile? Doesn't it disguise a lack of feeling? Life should be like a steady, visible light. . . . To be wildly enthusiastic, or deadly serious— both are wrong. Both pass. One must keep ever present a sense of humour. It depends entirely on yourself how much you see or hear or understand. But the sense of humour I have found of use in every single occasion of my life." But this sense of humour must at the same time be held in check, and recognized as only a preparation, a means of clearing away little things to leave room for the big things, and for this beauty of the world which fills the soul. To make oneself worthy of being a writer, one has to become purified and detached. And in the closing pages of her journals we feel that she has attained this purification: "But now that I have wrestled with it, it's no longer so. I feel happy—deep down. *All is well.*"

KATHERINE MANSFIELD

And "all is well," we might echo, whenever we finish one of Katherine Mansfield's finest stories. All is well, or more precisely, all is exactly thus. Before the greatest art, which is also the simplest, silence is the only expression of delight.

THE END

X

VIRGINIA WOOLF

Virginia Woolf

TIME is the only critic whose authority is beyond dispute. In time's crucible, the most solidly established reputation may turn to ashes, while a seemingly precarious one emerges intact. A quarter of a century after her death, Virginia Woolf retains her position in the history of literature, and also her readers. Her complete works are in every library in England. But her influence is acknowledged far beyond the frontiers of her own country. I remember when her *Mrs Dalloway*, for which I had written a preface, first appeared in France. The French reading public was amazed and delighted. Here, it felt, was an Englishwoman who had understood the lesson of Proust, a highly cultivated woman more concerned with poetry than with erudition, a writer with Colette's genius for penetrating the world of the feminine, yet vitally interested in technique. Indeed, this concern with the technical aspects of writing was to make her one of the forerunners of the modern French novel. What will remain of her works? Some novels, certainly, such as *Mrs Dalloway*, *To the Lighthouse*, *The Waves*, or the haunting *Orlando;* her literary criticism (*The Common Reader*); and those inimitable essays, effortless in their grace yet of consummate

[349]

artistry, and so totally English, *A Room of One's Own* and *The Death of the Moth*. She was both a master of traditional English prose and the creator of a new style.

I

SHE was born in 1882, the daughter of Sir Leslie Stephen, that "Phoebus Apollo turned Benedictine" whom Meredith portrayed with a mixture of admiration and irony in *The Egoist*. It was a challenge indeed, at once arduous and exalted, to be Sir Leslie's daughter. The family had for generations held high administrative office. Sir Leslie himself, after taking orders, had renounced them to become the leader of an agnostic and liberal school and one of the pillars of Cambridge University. His first wife was a daughter of the illustrious Thackeray. He was well known both as a sportsman (he was president of the Alpine Club) and as the editor of the monumental *Dictionary of National Biography* and of a number of reviews. His children grew up surrounded by eminent men: Thomas Hardy, Henry James, Edmund Gosse and others. Because Virginia suffered from poor health, he undertook to educate her himself. He gave her access to his library, where she found Plato and Sophocles, Spinoza, Hume and John Stuart Mill. Sir Leslie, at once a rationalist and a moralist, unbearable and delightful, tended to equate morals with good manners. The manners in that circle were impeccable, as was the intellectual honesty. Sir Leslie did not seek to impose his ideas or display his erudition. Virginia read whatever she chose, in other words, everything; she thought as she chose too, and made up her mind to write. The old gentleman died of cancer in 1904, leaving his children a comfortable competency, a keen sense of honour and a taste for understatement.

Virginia, her sister Vanessa, and her two brothers lived in London in the house in Bloomsbury which was to become the very synonym of a refined, unpedantic culture, associated with immense talent and somewhat contemptuous of anything outside its own sphere. I knew that "Bloomsbury set" very well in the mid-twenties. It was at once dazzling, exclusive and pleasant. Vanessa had married Clive Bell, the art critic. Then, in 1912, Virginia married Leonard Woolf, a "Cambridge intellectual" and political essayist. In 1917, they founded a publishing house, the Hogarth Press. Lytton Strachey, famous for his biography of Queen Victoria, was one of the luminaries of a group that included many, and of the highest order: Roger Fry, for instance, one of the first to introduce the post-impressionist French painters to the English public, and who revealed to Virginia in the medium of painting what she was to attempt in literature; Desmond McCarthy, the foremost literary critic of his time; Lewes Dickinson; J. M. Keynes, the economist; and, on the fringes of the group, E. M. Forster, T. S. Eliot and the youthful David Garnett. They formed a splendid constellation of first-rate minds with a disinterested love of beauty, a sophisticated immorality and the certitude that a man is civilised only to the extent that he loves art and literature. Like all powerful coteries, this one had its enemies. Violent writers—D. H. Lawrence, for example—decried these rich aesthetes as snobs. The charge was unfair. A snob pretends to admire what he does not admire; the Bloomsbury set admired only what it regarded as genuinely admirable, and its taste was exquisite.

Virginia Woolf began with literary criticism, devoting essays to classical writers such as Montaigne, Sterne, Jane Austen and George Eliot and to contemporaries such as Joyce, Bennett and Fry. Then came her novels, from *The Voyage Out* (1915) to *Between the Acts* (1941). Her readers, both English and French, considered her, together with Joyce and Proust, as one of the originators of the modern novel. Nevertheless, she was not moved solely by aesthetic considerations. Both in her essays and in her novels she waged a spirited campaign in favour of the moral emancipation of women. The writer's social function was the subject of her "Leaning Tower" essays. Here she showed that, before 1914, the best English writers (with the exception of Dickens and D. H. Lawrence) had issued, like herself, from the wealthier classes, and had been educated at public school and university. These writers had not despised the other classes; they had simply not known them. They had lived in a stucco and gold tower, with no desire to descend from it, but rather to make it accessible to all. After 1914, the tower had become a leaning tower. And

VIRGINIA WOOLF

when you survey the landscape at an angle, you realise
that you are living at an unnatural altitude. Young
writers were therefore becoming conscious of their
class, their wealth, their education. They felt ill at
ease, angry with the builder of the tower, that is, with
society. To assuage their guilty conscience, they
would satirise that society in the person of some
retired admiral or armaments merchant. It was another
way of saying, like a schoolboy, "It wasn't I, Sir,
it was the other fellow!" But the excuse was not
valid. In 1930, the writer could no longer ignore what
was going on in Russia or in Spain. He saw that his
tower was built on injustice. Yet he could not jettison
his education, nor even his wealth, for one must live.
Did D. H. Lawrence, a miner's son, live like a miner?
Living as they were in this false position, how could
modern novelists create genuine, vital characters as
had the nineteenth-century novelists? The modern
writer's essential self was paralysed because his superficial self reasoned too much. Satire is a poor coun-
sellor. At least the writer of "The Leaning Tower"
had the courage to speak the truth about herself.

She hoped, in 1939, that a classless society would
emerge out of the war, a society in which everyone
would have access to culture. The two groups excluded from the active life of the nation—women and
the poor—would, she hoped, be reintegrated in it. Such
was the democratic feeling of one reared essentially
as an intellectual aristocrat. But she was not to have
time to proclaim her newly found faith. She had long

been subject to nervous depressions so severe that she feared for her reason. At the time I knew her, I thought her very beautiful, with her long, gentle and intelligent face, her fine eyes, her air of honesty. Marguerite Yourcenar, who saw her towards the end of her life, describes her as worn with thought, her face ravaged, her expression desolate. She had had a number of spells of vertigo, and hallucinations, and she lived in terror of their recurrence. On finishing a book she would have such attacks of melancholia that she would seek refuge in a nursing home. She had often thought of suicide, and the war intensified this obsession. Both the Woolfs' house and the Hogarth Press were destroyed by bombs, and even in their cottage in the country they could not escape the bombing. Virginia was not afraid, but she was exhausted. John Lehmann, who was managing the Hogarth Press at the time, saw her shortly before her death to discuss her latest novel, *Between the Acts*. He found her terribly shaken and incapable, according to her own admission, of revising her MS. All her life she had been obsessed—like Shelley—by water. In April 1941 she decided to drown herself. Her walking stick, her hat, and a note for her husband were found on the river bank. The note read: "I have the feeling that I shall go mad. I hear voices and cannot concentrate on my work. I have fought against it, but cannot fight any longer. I owe all my happiness in life to you. You have been so perfectly good. I cannot go on and spoil your life."

After his wife's death, Leonard Woolf dedicated

himself to her memory and published some valuable works including *A Writer's Diary* (1915-1940) and two collections of essays (*The Death of the Moth* and *The Moment*), as well as an autobiography containing considerable material for a biography of the wife he had so cherished and admired.

II

BEFORE going on to the novels which constitute the essence of her work, we have to touch on a very personal aspect of Virginia Woolf, namely, her championship of women's rights.

The substance of her case for woman is contained in a delightful little book, *A Room of One's Own*, based on two papers which she had read before two women's colleges on the subject of women and fiction. She concentrates on what appears to be a minor point —that a woman must have a room of her own if she is to be able to write fiction. She begins with a description of a visit to "Oxbridge"—a composite name for Oxford and Cambridge—where, because she is a woman, she is forbidden to walk on the grass reserved for Fellows. And why do men, at Oxbridge, drink wine, while women have to drink water? Why is one of the sexes so prosperous and the other so poor? She goes to the British Museum to see what has been written on women. It is terrifying. Men have written hundreds of volumes on women. And why not women on men? Professors, sociologists, novelists, journalists—all have written about women and all have defended contrary opinions. Napoleon believed women to be incapable of education; Dr Johnson thought the contrary. Goethe revered them; Mussolini despised them.

In point of fact, she explains, women have eternally served as mirrors possessing the magical and delightful power of reflecting man's features twice life size. Napoleon and Mussolini insisted on woman's inferiority because, were she not inferior to man, she would not aggrandize him. And that is why a woman arouses much more anger than a man when she criticizes a book, an attitude or a person. If woman begins to tell the truth, the figure in the mirror will shrink. How can man continue to make laws, to preside over banquets, if he cannot see himself in woman's eyes twice the size he really is?

But this situation naturally engenders bitterness in women. Before 1918, how could a woman of Virginia Woolf's class earn her living? By making artificial flowers, reading to old ladies, teaching kindergarten .... And why not by writing? Take the Elizabethan age, the age of Shakespeare. Not a single woman contributed to the impressive and brilliant body of plays and sonnets produced in that great period. Yet woman was the heroine of the plays, the subject of the poems. In the sphere of the imagination, then, she was of the highest importance, but in practise of very little. Suppose Shakespeare had had a sister as marvellously gifted as he. She would have written nothing; she would have been betrothed at the age of seventeen to a draper's son. And if she had said, "I

VIRGINIA WOOLF

hate the idea of marriage," her father would have beaten her. What opportunity would she have had to prove her genius?

Even for a man, of course, it is not easy to be a great writer. Material circumstances are hostile. Dogs bark, people bother you, your health breaks down. Keats, Flaubert, Carlyle—they all complained. But for a woman the difficulties are far greater. For a very long time, there was no question of her having a room of her own. Even in the nineteenth century, Jane Austen would hide her MS when she heard a visitor approaching, Charlotte Brontë, for all her genius, remained poor and unhappy, and George Eliot was forced to withdraw from society because she was living with a married man, while at the very same time young Tolstoy was free to live with any woman he chose, gipsy and titled lady alike. Moreover, the values which the critics take seriously are masculine values—those of Kipling's officers or Galsworthy's businessmen. Yet feminine values are needed too for a masterpiece. Shakespeare was androgynous; so were Proust and Tolstoy. Give women as much intellectual freedom as men, and you will see what poetry they will produce. Shakespeare's sister will have her chance. Indeed, after 1918, she did have her chance, and a room of her own, and some freedom. Whence that magnificent crop of women writers —Margaret Kennedy, Rosamund Lehmann, Rebecca West, Victoria Sackville-West, Katherine Mansfield, Ivy Compton-Burnett and so on. Whence also Virginia Woolf's great works.

WHAT kind of novels would she write? And first of all, which novelists did she admire and which did she not like? While acknowledging H. G. Wells' intelligence and Arnold Bennett's technical skill, and feeling some gratitude to Galsworthy, she accused these solid and competent writers of being material- ists. What did their characters live for? They spent their time in well-upholstered first-class railway car- riages, and the destiny towards which they travelled so luxuriously was eternal bliss in the very best hotel in Brighton. In short, according to Virginia Woolf, these novelists employed their talent, their immense craftsmanship, to write of things of no consequence, and to make the trivial and transitory appear true and enduring.

Was life really as they saw it, she wondered? Must novels be like that? "Look within and life, it seems, is very far from being 'like this.' Examine for a moment an ordinary mind on an ordinary day. The mind receives a myriad impressions—trivial, fantastic, eva- nescent, or engraved with the sharpness of steel. From all sides they come, an incessant shower of innumer- able atoms; and as they fall, as they shape themselves into the life of Monday or Tuesday, the accent falls differently from of old; the moment of importance came not here but there; so that if a writer were a free man and not a slave, if he could write what he chose, not what he must, if he could base his work upon his own feeling and not upon convention, there would be no plot, no comedy, no tragedy, no love interest or catastrophe in the accepted style, and perhaps not a single button sewn on as the Bond Street tailors would have it. Life is not a series of gig lamps symmetrically arranged; but a luminous halo, a semi-transparent envelope surrounding us from the beginning of consciousness to the end."

That is what the writer should portray, this flickering of life, these thoughts which flit back and forth like fish swimming in a lighted aquarium. As Proust put it, a moment is not just itself; it is a vessel filled with memories, odours, images. Has anyone ever caught this living multiplicity? Virginia Woolf admired the English classics—authors like Defoe, Jane Austen, George Eliot. But they did not have what she was looking for. Her admiration for Thomas Hardy was wholehearted, but he was an epic poet rather than a novelist. She followed Joyce's experimentation with interest, but his books left her with a sense of constraint, of being hemmed in, rather than of being uplifted and liberated. Why was this? Perhaps because of his excessive concern with technique; perhaps also because of his emphasis on the indecent. Joyce, she felt, was probably closer to the reality of life than Galsworthy, but you realised, as you read *Ulysses*, how much of life it excluded; and it sufficed to reread *Tristram Shandy* or *Pendennis* to realise that what was most important in life was missing in Joyce.

Of course, there were the great Russians. There

we find a feeling for man, an understanding not only of the mind but also of the heart. In Tolstoy, in Tchekov, in Dostoevsky, there is compassion for human suffering, a straining towards a goal worthy of every effort, a goal which is really holiness. And yet . . . . And yet she discerned in this admirable art something which remained wholly alien to English taste. The soul is the principal character of the Russian novel. But an Englishman does not like to talk about his soul; he finds the word uncongenial. The soul has little sense of humour, no sense of comedy. Dostoevsky's novels are "seething whirlpools, gyrating sandstorms, water-spouts which hiss and boil and suck us in. . . . We open the door and find ourselves in a room full of Russian generals, the tutors of Russian generals, their step-daughters and cousins and crowds of miscellaneous people who are all talking at the tops of their voices about their most private affairs." And she concludes: "Dashed to the crest of the waves, bumped and battered on the stones at the bottom, it is difficult for an English reader to feel at ease." Even with Tchekov the English reader is bewildered, for all his admiration of the writer's craft, by the choice of subjects, by all these stories and plays without endings. With Tolstoy, he is on more solid ground again. Here is an aristocrat who has known life in all its forms. His senses, his intellect are acute, powerful. Nothing escapes him, neither the beauty of women, nor that of horses. Whatever he portrays is astonishingly true. Yet always a kind of fear urges us to escape his implacable gaze. Always, at the centre of his books, there is some Pierre, some Levin, who asks—even as he enjoys it—what is the meaning of life, so that the world turns to dust and ashes before our feet.

Where, then, was Virginia Woolf to find what she sought? As a matter of fact, in the French writers. In Montaigne first of all, with his suppleness, his flexibility, of whom she wrote with great intelligence, and particularly in Proust. Here, thoughts move in chains of memories, grasping the here and now. At the heart of each being Proust divines an infinite reservoir of memories, and a scent, a fragrance, suddenly revives a whole slice of the past that one had thought dead. Yes, Proust came fairly close to the form of novel of which she dreamed, yet a gap remained. First, because she was so essentially English, an Englishwoman of Bloomsbury with her own world, which she wanted to portray; and secondly because she was a woman and wanted to give substance to a woman's world. But that, it might be objected, had been done before, by writers like Jane Austen, George Eliot or the Brontës. No, George Eliot had been a masculine author; the Brontës had not been conscious enough of their femininity. In a word, there was only one way for Virginia Woolf to find the novel as she conceived it, and that was to write it.

IV

WHAT, precisely, was her aim? First of all, to produce a modern novel, one which could belong to no other period than her own. What, then, was characteristic of the period around 1920? In painting, impressionism and post-impressionism. Could the novelist, like the painter, escape from a false realism? Could he juxtapose impressions, paint nuances of nuances? Could he say, "This is how a thing appears to the character at a particular moment by contrast with another moment"? Would not the reader retort, "I want a story, characters . . . I don't follow you"? Possibly, but the attempt must be made. The modern writer, Virginia Woolf felt, was fettered by the convention of chronology. The convention had been acceptable in the days of Dickens or Balzac, when novels had appeared in fascicles or as serialisations, "to be continued in our next." Indeed, had the chronological order not been followed, readers would have cancelled their subscriptions to the publications concerned. But such exact chronology, Virginia Woolf maintained, did not correspond to reality. For, in our minds, past, present and future are all fused. Time is not homogeneous. There are moments of ecstasy which seem infinite and long sandy stretches which leave scarcely a trace in the memory.

Was all this new? Had it not always been so? Were there any grounds for thinking, in the years around the First World War, that the time had come to write a different novel, a modern novel? Virginia Woolf believed that there were. Not that one literary school had succeeded another as day succeeds night, but that the mores had changed very fast. The war had emancipated women. Bergson and Freud had

transformed philosophy. Tools which had faithfully
served one generation were inadequate to the needs
of the next. New ground must be broken; in particular, people must be made to concede that a novel
does not need a theme, only a pretext. Her great
novels were to be without plots. Clarissa Dalloway is
to give a party in the evening. She spends her day
preparing for it. The whole novel is simply this one
day in Mrs Dalloway's life. Mrs Ramsay's children
want to take a boat to the lighthouse which they can
see from their house. Mr Ramsay says that the
weather will not permit it. The trip does not take
place until many years later, after Mrs Ramsay is dead.
That is all, and it is masterly.

Nor should a novel, according to Virginia Woolf,
be "social." Although very sensitive to injustice, she
believed, with Tchekov, that moralising spoils a
work of art, and that a novel must in fact be a work
of art like *War and Peace* or *Remembrance of Things
Past*. But in every work of art there is an order. However close the modern novelist wishes to come to
reality, he must not return to original chaos. Proust
had built his novel in the manner of a cathedral. What
would Virginia Woolf do, for whom experience was
a torrent, a floodtide of images? For those most
characteristic functions of the novel, namely, to
record innumerable impressions, to show how lives
intertwine, seem incompatible with an order, with
an art form. Art shows us life at a distance; the novel
must stay very close to life. "The most complete
novelist must be the novelist who can balance the two

powers so that one enhances the other." A quality which Proust—and she herself—illustrated admirably.

The landscape which she portrayed was a very limited one. What did she know really well? Cambridge intellectuals, Bloomsbury writers, politicians, women with fine houses and well-trained servants. She has been accused of being Mrs Dalloway herself, that is, an upper-middle-class lady. What if she was? Proust said rightly that what was necessary was not that the writer should know every social circle but that he should "take off" in his own little 'plane and fly over his own particular circle. However limited that circle, if he can see it from above like a landscape to be portrayed, the work will be good. What if Virginia Woolf describes a woman of the upper middle class? A queen's manners, writes Proust again, can be as interesting as those of a seamstress. Virginia Woolf writes about D. H. Lawrence that he "is not a member like Proust of a settled and civilised society. He is anxious to leave his own class and to enter another. . . . The fact that he was a miner's son and that he disliked his condition gave him a different approach to writing from those who have a settled station and enjoy circumstances which allow them to forget what those circumstances are." I am not so sure that she forgot her own circumstances herself; she delighted in her sense of belonging to Cambridge and Bloomsbury. Yet her deep compassion and understanding made up for that trait.

So both the social novel and the problem novel were ruled out. There were to be no characters such

as could be encountered in the street, like Rastignac
or Goriot. Virginia Woolf's characters are formed
of the shower of impressions which rains down upon
them, gradually transforming their approach. How
far we have come from the Victorian and Edwardian
novelists! If the ancestor of this type of novel was
Proust, its descendants are Robbe-Grillet and especially Nathalie Sarraute. Towards the end of her life,
in *The Waves*, Virginia Woolf attempted a novel
which was simply a poetic and lyrical meditation.
Marguerite Yourcenar has defined these novels, "biographies of Being." The French literary critic, Max
Fouchet, has proposed subtitles for Virginia Woolf's
novels: for *To the Lighthouse*, "What Is Life?"; for
The Waves, "Solitude." Each of these books, he says,
resumes one and the same pursuit. "Here are characters traversed by time as starfish by the waters of
a current; here are books with horizons as indetermi-
nate as those of water and sky. The weary waves of
the work beat softly, break and die on the same
shores, adorning the elusive sands with shells in which
you hear the sound of the inner sea."

But let us see all this in her writings.

v

"Mrs Dalloway said she would buy the flowers herself." For Mrs Dalloway and her faithful Lucy have
to get everything ready for the party tonight. So she
goes out. What a crisp morning! Like the kiss of a
wave! On just such a morning, at Bourton, she

plunged into the open air. Bourton, the house where she was brought up, reminds her of Peter Walsh, who loved her then. He was a bit mad, and he left for India when she agreed to marry Richard Dalloway, so much more decorous, now a respected member of Parliament and who will one day be in the Cabinet. Hadn't Peter Walsh told her that she would marry a Prime Minister and that she would be a perfect hostess? She had cried about it at the time. Now she tells herself, as she crosses the Park, that she had been right, that Richard Dalloway leaves her free, whereas with Peter she would have had to say everything, share everything.

She walks towards Piccadilly and Bond Street, looking at the shop windows and daydreaming, wondering how her life would be could she live it all over again. She loves Bond Street in the early morning with its flags flying, its shops—no splash, no glitter, a roll of tweed in a tailor's window, a few pearls. She goes into the florist's. A car passes, mysterious, the blinds drawn, setting off eddies of rumour. Is it the Prime Minister? The Queen? The Prince of Wales? Septimus Smith, suffering from shell-shock, looks too, terrified. A thousand thoughts shatter against that closed car. Aeroplanes pass overhead, writing smoke letters. Septimus tells himself that this is a signal for him from the celestial powers, and his eyes fill with tears.

What is astonishing here is that everything is present at once; we follow Clarissa as she goes home, the mysterious car proceeding to Buckingham Palace, the 'planes, the unfortunate young man who is losing his reason.

"Mrs Dalloway will see me," says an elderly man in the hall. What a surprise! It is Peter Walsh, just back from India; he is in love with a married woman out there and has come to England to arrange for a divorce. "How heavenly it is to see you again!" exclaims Clarissa. She invites him to her party. Peter Walsh starts carping again, as he always used to. So she gives parties! She is surprised that he should be so little changed, finding fault, growling, playing with his pocket knife. He seizes her by the shoulders. "Tell me, are you happy, Clarissa? Does Richard . . . ." The door opens and Mrs Dalloway's daughter comes in. Peter Walsh greets her, says, "Goodbye, Clarissa," and leaves the house quickly, as Big Ben sounds the half-hour. Remembering the terrible day when the youthful Clarissa refused him, he reassures himself; no, no, she is not dead, and he is not old! He gives himself over to daydreaming about Clarissa. She loves life. She is a sceptic. Possibly she tells herself, since we are a doomed race, chained to a sinking ship, and since life is a bad joke, let's try to mitigate the sufferings of our fellow prisoners and decorate the dungeon with flowers . . . .

Septimus Smith and his fantasies form a counterpoint. Virginia Woolf's diary shows us that she found it an ordeal to write these pages describing a mental turmoil which she sometimes experienced herself. Septimus' little Italian wife, Rezia, consults a psychiatrist, Dr Holmes. Health, Dr Holmes tells her, depends largely on ourselves. They go to a specialist, Sir William Bradshaw. "Try to think as little about yourself as possible," Sir William tells Septimus. What splendid advice! The young couple feel deserted. Sir William is too prosperous to understand the afflicted.

Counterpoint: Richard Dalloway lunching without his wife at Lady Bruton's, who likes politics but not politicians' wives. But Richard Dalloway is eager to see Clarissa again. On his way home, he buys her flowers. What a miracle that he should have married her! There he is, young still, walking in the sunshine to his Westminster house to tell Clarissa that he loves her. That, he thinks, is happiness. "But how lovely," says Clarissa, taking the flowers. Her husband cannot bring himself to say that he loves her. It isn't done. But she understands. His Clarissa always understands without his having to speak. Then he sets off for the House of Commons, where there is to be a debate on the Armenians. Clarissa is far more interested in her roses than in the Armenians. Richard will hold it against her; so will Peter. She and her parties, Peter will exclaim! But they are both wrong to think her worldly. She loves life, that's all. Since morning, she has been in a kind of ecstasy. The walk, Peter, these roses. How is it possible that at the end of all this there is death, and that no one in the world will know how much she has loved every moment? Counterpoint: Septimus Smith throws himself out of the window. He is not killed instantly but hideously mangled. The ambulance carrying him away passes

Peter Walsh, its bell clanging. One of the triumphs of civilisation, Peter thinks.

It is the evening of the party. The Prime Minister is coming, Lucy tells the cook. To the cook, busied over her saucepans, it matters little indeed whether there is one Prime Minister more or less. The guests begin to arrive. "How delightful to see you," says Mrs Dalloway to each of them. The Prime Minister makes his appearance. Escorted by Mr and Mrs Dalloway, he tries to act the part, and really he does it very well. Nobody looks at him. But they all feel to the marrow of their bones that the majesty of the nation is passing. Only they would not show it. What snobs, thinks Peter Walsh. Someone mentions the young man who has killed himself, Septimus Smith. Why talk about death at a party? thinks Clarissa. Peter watches her. What is this terror,, this ecstasy? he wonders. It is Clarissa. For there she is.

The story is thin enough. Actually, there is no story at all. Peter Walsh's return, Clarissa's party, Septimus Smith's death do not make a story. What is admirable is the shimmering of all these myriads of impressions, the noise of the street, the thundering of the 'planes, the delicacy of the flowers, the shower of memories mingling, intersecting, interweaving, so that we pass without quite knowing how from Clarissa's girlhood friendships to the Prime Minister in her drawing room; in counterpoint, there is the tragedy of Septimus Smith and his charming young wife. The action is the more moving if we remember that there was much of Clarissa Dalloway in Virginia

Woolf and a little of Septimus Smith, much dignity and a little madness.

VI

CLARISSA, cold and beautiful, retains in marriage a virginity which clings to her like a shroud; Mrs Ramsay, of *To the Lighthouse*, is essentially the wife and mother, having countless friends staying in her house by the sea and taking the entire opposite sex under her protection for reasons which she cannot explain, except perhaps that men negotiate treaties, rule India, control finance. Her children respect her extreme courtesy, her strange severity. As for Mr Ramsay, a philosopher by profession but not by nature, he loves to disillusion his six-year-old son, James, who hopes to go out to the lighthouse next day. "If it's fine," his mother says. "But it won't be fine," announces his father. James could kill him, standing there, "lean as a knife, narrow as the blade of one, grinning sarcastically, not only with the pleasure of disillusioning his son and casting ridicule upon his wife, who was ten thousand times better in every way than he was (James thought), but also with some secret conceit at his own accuracy of judgment." For Mr Ramsay is never wrong, never forgets a disagreeable fact and loves to make his children realise that life is hard. (Those who knew the family tell us that Mr and Mrs Ramsay are portraits of Sir Leslie and Lady Stephen, which gives us some insight into Virginia Woolf's childhood.)

[370]

"It won't be fine," Mr Ramsay states, and his wife accepts his verdict. Only in that case she will not have to make sandwiches. That's all. It is natural for her to think along these lines, because she is a woman busied all day with this and that; a sponge saturated with other people's emotions. Her husband says, "it will rain," or "it will not rain," and a paradise of security opens up before her. There is no man she respects more. She is not worthy, she feels, to tie his shoelaces. And what of him? What are his thoughts? Does he hope to leave a name for posterity? But how long will such fame last? Who will speak of the dying hero two thousand years hence? And what are two thousand years anyway? Nothing, if you survey them from a peak across the immense desert of the ages. The pebble we kick will last longer than Shakespeare. Upon which, putting his pipe in his pocket, Mr Ramsay salutes the beauty of the world. Then he looks at his wife. She knows what he is thinking: "You are lovelier than ever." She looks back at him, smiling. He knows, even though she has not said a word, that she loves him. (Just like Richard Dalloway.) Yes, you were right, she thinks; it will rain tomorrow. She does not say it, but he knows that she thinks it. And she looks at him smiling because she realises that she has just triumphed. Such are men and women; alone yet together; not enemies, but strangers.

The years pass. Mrs Ramsay is dead. James is sixteen, Cam seventeen, and they are finally going to the lighthouse with their father. The wind swells the sails of the little craft. Mr Ramsay quotes poets on the sea. James continues to regard his father as a tyrant (go to the lighthouse! don't go! do this! fetch me that!). Now James, for the first time in his life, is quite close to the lighthouse. It is a bare, sheer tower, set on a rock, so different from the lighthouse of his childhood, silvery, shrouded in the distant mist, with a yellow eye that opened softly in the evening. So the lighthouse was not like that! You could see the windows and a tuft of green grass on the rock. A man comes out of the tower and looks at the boat through his fieldglasses. Mr Ramsay is engrossed in a book; he turns the pages with a gesture that irritates his son. Suddenly snapping the book closed, he states that they are nearly there. He is hungry and opens the package of sandwiches. But it was not Mrs Ramsay who had made them. Mr Ramsay stands at the bow, tall and erect, as one who says, "there is no God." Then he jumps lightly onto the rock, like a young man. At the same moment, a woman painter on the shore is trying to recapture Mrs Ramsay's features for a portrait. She watches the boat drawing up alongside the lighthouse. Suddenly she turns back to her canvas; she has seen what was missing, and with urgent intensity adds it. Mrs Ramsay appears alive. Through art, time has been foiled. After so many years, James has been to the lighthouse. What did he find? Nothing. A picture of life.

In *The Waves*, the novel becomes a poem. Six characters speak in alternating verses broken by lyrical meditations. A poem? An oratorio, rather, in which six soloists sing in turn their conceptions of time and death in stylised monologues. The six are divided into three pairs: Louis and Rhoda, enamoured of solitude, disgusted with the flesh; Jinny and Neville, closer to the world of the senses; Bernard and Susan, "impregnable territory." The bond among the six is Percival, the friend of each of them, loved by all of them, whom we never meet and who leaves for India with his regiment and dies there. To each of his friends Percival is a different man, embodying each one's secret desire. "For one," writes Monique Nathan, "he is a pagan god, for another, a barbarian chief, for a third, a luminous furrow, for a fourth, love. All long to be united to this substantial hero, with his calm, rock-like face. He alone can unify the disparate and confer existence upon them. And there he is, dying far away, preventing them from closing the blue steel chain which links them, leaving them alone, hovering between life and death."

There is great beauty in *The Waves*, but it is the beauty of the prose poem rather than of the novel. The author had set herself the difficult task of symbolizing in short lyrical poems, interpolated in the text, the passage from childhood to maturity, from dawn to sunset, reflected in the green-blue waves which sweep the sands clean. These lyrical passages are marvellously written, too well written, and the analogies are too clearly sought by the author. They interrupt the narrative and destroy its credibility. The reader forgets the characters and can think only of the author's ingenuity, and this destroys the romantic illusion. Bernard's last monologue, spoken when he is old and alone, sounds the death knell: "Lord, how unutterably disgusting life is! . . . Let me be alone! Let me cast and throw away this veil of being, this cloud that changes with the least breath, night and day, and all night and all day. . . . What enemy do we now perceive advancing against us? . . . It is death. Death is the enemy. It is death against whom I ride with my spear couched and my hair flying back like a young man's, like Percival's, when he galloped in India. I strike spurs into my horse. Against you I will fling myself, unvanquished and unyielding, O Death!"

Virginia Woolf's last novel, *Between the Acts*, following the lyricism of *The Waves*, marks a return to the romantic technique, not the traditional romanticism but her own particular brand. The entire action takes place within a twenty-four-hour span, as in *Mrs Dalloway*. A pageant is to take place, as it does every year, on the Olivers' terrace. "Between the acts" of the show, the human comedy reasserts itself. In the centre, a young couple: the Olivers' son, Giles, and his wife, Isa. Around them, relatives, friends, actors, the village—an excellent frame for a satire of English society and also of the historical past. Moreover, the action takes place in 1939, between the two great acts of the century, the two world wars. Neighbours, beginning with the beautiful and wealthy Mrs Manresa, come to attend the pageant. Mrs Manresa is fascinated by the virile beauty of young Oliver;

Giles' wife, Isa, is attracted by a gentleman farmer. The play, narrating the history of England from the Middle Ages to the age of Queen Victoria, is interspersed with comments from the audience. This creates a past-present counterpoint, while there is a love-hate counterpoint between Giles and Isa Oliver. Finally the guests leave and Isa and Giles remain alone. They will fight a little, like the fox and its vixen before they mate, and then embrace. The book's poetry lies in the rhythm of the scenes and the contrast between the infinite shadow of the historical past and the brief flash of our own existences.

On the subject of this novel, Virginia Woolf wrote in her diary: "But to amuse myself, let me note: . . . a centre: all literature discussed in connection with . . . incongruous living humour: and anything that comes into my head; but 'I' rejected: 'We' substituted: to whom at the end there shall be an invocation? 'We'. . . the composed of many different things . . . we all life, all art, all waifs and strays— a rambling, capricious but somehow unified whole— the present state of my mind? And English country; and a scenic old house—and a terrace where nursemaids walk—and people passing—and a perpetual variety and change from intensity to prose—and facts—and notes; and—but eno'!" That was what she hoped to write and that, really, is what she achieved. As she put it herself, she felt quite triumphant about the book, and felt it was an interesting experiment with a new method. It was more quintessential, she felt, than the others. Once again, women are central to the novel. Once again, the conflicts do not break out. Giles gives up Mrs Manresa, Isa the gentleman farmer. Why? Because human beings are solitary and cannot meet. In an earlier version of *The Waves*, Bernard's last words were not "O Death!" but "O Solitude!"

Only in one case do the masculine and feminine personalities really unite; that is when they belong to the same human being. I have said before that, in Virginia Woolf's opinion, the greatest minds had been androgynous. She herself, one day, took delicious pleasure in creating a fantastic character, Orlando, who changes sex from one century to the next. At once Faublas and Mademoiselle de Maupin, Casanova and Cagliostro, Orlando, like Shakespeare, has a hundred different lives. In whatever form he appears, however, he constantly resembles the lovely Vita Sackville-West, heiress to a great name and to one of the most splendid castles of England, Knole. After three centuries, Orlando aspires to a mystical communion with nature, the only love which does not deceive. But just as she (she is a woman now) lies stretched on the moor, breathing the perfume of the plants and surrendering herself to the cold embraces of the grass, a horseman arrives at a gallop. He will marry her, and that will solve nothing. And how should it solve anything? By joining opposites in Orlando, Virginia Woolf had hoped to amalgamate them. But all that emerged, once more, was a divided being—parts, fragments. This pageant of the androgynous being was no more than an escapade for Virginia Woolf, but what fun it had been to write!

VII

I HAVE not said anything about *Night and Day*, or *Jacob's Room*, or *The Years*, because to understand Virginia Woolf it suffices to read the two or three novels which I have analysed, some fine essays, her literary criticism and *A Writer's Diary*, published posthumously by her husband, Leonard Woolf, and which is of great assistance in following the writer's inner development. What we have to do here is not to draw up a well-known list of works, but to recall clearly what Virginia Woolf sought to do and the influence she exerted.

She undoubtedly wanted to discover a new technique for the novelist which would make it possible to portray the inner reality very truthfully; she wanted to show, moreover, that this reality could be only an inner one. Unlike Sartre, Virginia Woolf, in her maturity, did not judge; unlike Lawrence, she did not preach. She was concerned simply to offer the reader a fresher and newer view of life, to open his eyes, to enable him to discover, under surface events, the barely perceptible movements of thoughts and emotions.

Like Proust, she experimented at length with the dislocation of time. I do not know whether Nathalie Sarraute or Robbe-Grillet have read her much, but she had sought earlier than they to give objects their true value and to reveal the power and the riches of silence. Like Proust, again, she believed in the mystical value of the rare moments when the writer, or one of his characters, suddenly loses his individuality in the contemplation of nature. Like him, she found eternity in the moment; like him, she relegated the great abstract movements to the confines of her work and concentrated her attention, her tenderness, her despair, on the individual instead.

It was a very courageous position, and one which is basically very useful to mankind at a time when systems, ideological struggles and confusion reverberate around us constantly through "committed" writers, through the radio, through television. Virginia Woolf was very little concerned with these sounds of the world. She was interested in the truth which is made up of two truths, that of reason (masculine) and that of imagination (feminine). The union of these two truths, she felt, would make a reality. But such union is impossible of achievement. Neither Richard and Clarissa Dalloway nor Mr and Mrs Ramsay are really united. The men who direct the affairs of this world have their partisan solutions, which are unreal. The role of woman, according to Virginia Woolf, is to reintegrate man in reality, in nature. I think she was right.

Human beings all need to find themselves, to break out of the armour of conventions, false duties, false beliefs, in which most of us remain encased. They need this "solitude for two" produced by the fusion of masculine and feminine. But is such a fusion possible? One feels that Virginia Woolf doubted it. Hence her finest novels convey a sense not so much of bitterness as of melancholy, explaining or leading up to the river and her own death. It remains that she succeeded better than anyone else in depicting her own particular reality, and that her books, like Proust's, are as wide in scope as their subjects are slender. In the apocalyptic times in which we have been living since her death, she has lost none of her greatness. To quote Bernard Blackstone: "Virginia Woolf's world will survive as the crystal survives under the crushing rock masses." What was once so true does not die.

XI

GRAHAM GREENE

Graham Greene

IT IS not easy nowadays for a novelist to get people to read his books. Since Proust, Joyce, Virginia Woolf, Kafka, what was once new has become conventional. Violence and eroticism could at one time shock the reader, but writers have pushed audacity so far in these areas that it would seem difficult to go any farther. What literary criticism has dubbed "the new novel" achieves its effects by sudden departures from chronology; by deliberate elimination of plot, biographical incident, characters; by stress on "things"; by intentional incoherence of language; by paradoxical emphasis on banalities and silences. But if such artifices interest the literary, they disconcert the common run of readers. Graham Greene has had the rare and fully deserved good fortune both to capture a large segment of the reading public and to win the respect of serious critics. The reason, as we shall see, is that he can sustain a plot as skilfully as any detective-story writer while constructing it round an eternal theme, that of Good and Evil. He is a metaphysical novelist and at the same time a sensual one; a swift and brilliant story-teller; a formidable satirist. He wins on all fronts. And that has been his aim. A "Catholic" literature, he once said in an interview, would no longer be literature; indeed, the term was an implied criticism, and he felt, on the contrary, that the writer should never be afraid to follow his thought to the bitter end. He had always, he said, wanted to write novels of adventure and had not intended, at first, to express his religious convictions in his writings; doubtless he had done so unconsciously. And that is why he has succeeded on both levels.

I

HE WAS born in 1904 at Berkhamsted, where his father was headmaster of a public school. Most artists have been strongly marked by their childhood. Greene's seems to have been a troubled one. On the one hand there was heaven—the family home with its bookshelves laden with books; on the other hell—school, promiscuity, toilets without locks, regimented walks along suburban roads, schoolboy cruelty, the conformity imposed at the time by English mores and which he describes in *England Made Me*. On the far side of heaven and hell there was escape through books, the strange books he loved —stories of pirates or of sorcerers, and especially *King Solomon's Mines*, which gave him for all time a fixation about Africa and adventure. Others, during their student years, have heard the first strokes of destiny in the Greek tragedies. For Graham Greene, destiny entered upon the scene with a novel by Marjorie Bowen, *The Viper of Milan*. Reading it, the young man became aware of his vocation and formed an image of the world in which Evil triumphs and tragedy dogs every success and every joy, because the swinging of the pendulum cannot be stopped. The books he had read left Graham Greene with a zest for danger, a nostalgia for the cheerless tropics, and a predilection for the metaphysical novel. Just as only a doorway separated hell from heaven in the young Greene's mind, as he went from school to home, so his writings were to be situated on the frontier between Grace and Sin.

He completed his studies at Oxford, in that most highbrow of colleges, Balliol. It is perhaps the unusual juxtaposition of Oxford and Balliol on the one hand, and vagabondage and exoticism on the other, that lends his writing its inimitable dissonance. He started his career as a journalist, an excellent apprenticeship for a novelist. You see, you investigate, you describe. That was how Charles Dickens had started too. In 1926, Greene became a Catholic. It was an intellectual rather than an emotional conversion. Catholicism seemed to him to provide a truer image of life, the solace of confession and absolution, grace. From 1926 to 1929 he was an assistant editor of *The Times* and published a novel, *The Man Within*, in which a smuggler, after betraying his associates, awaits their vengeance and can find only in death a refuge from the "man within" who accuses him. We may note here that refuge in death was to be the favourite solution of Greene's heroes.

But the longing for the exotic was becoming

unendurable. He set off for the Republic of Liberia, where he made a protracted stay; then he undertook an inquiry in Mexico. In the tropical regions of Africa and America he found the weary, feverish, vulnerable heroes he sought. He brought back travel books: *Journey Without Maps* and *The Lawless Roads*, and especially characters for future novels.

The first of the series which might be called "Grace and Sin" appeared in 1938 with *Brighton Rock*. It is not Greene's best book. I prefer *The Heart of the Matter, The Power and the Glory* and *The End of the Affair* as more human, more plausible novels. Yet there is much truth, too, in this portrayal of the slums of Brighton, in the type of the successful gangster who lives in the best hotel in Brighton and has got himself accepted, even by the police, as a respectable member of the middle class, and especially in the pathetic pair of youngsters, Pinkie and Rose. Pinkie is a seventeen-year-old boy with the pride of Lucifer, whose insane ambition it is to be a gang leader, but whose weapons are the weapons of schoolboys—a compass, a razor blade, vitriol. Rose is an artless little maidservant who understands nothing of the tragic adventure in which she is involved. Both are Catholics, but Pinkie, the rebellious angel (*Credo in unum Satanum*), ends by choosing damnation and commits suicide. The grace of God seeks vainly to penetrate this closed heart imprisoned in its habitual hatred. He resists grace with all the bitterness implanted in him by school benches, the cement schoolyard, the spectacle of foul lechery. Rose accepts

Pinkie's crime; she is sorry not to have taken her own life with him, and yet she will be saved because with all her heart she has loved the odious boy.

Thus the concept of redemptive love, which was to be the main theme of Greene's finest book, appears for the first time at the centre of *Brighton Rock*. The two youthful outcasts are as moving as the best characters in Dickens, and in Pinkie's cruelty there is something of Jean Cocteau's Dargelos. This is great praise. Yet the reason why I do not rank this book as one of Greene's very best is that the detective story—the investigations of Ida Arnold, the coarse but warmhearted woman who turns amateur detective to track down a murderer—holds a disproportionate place in it. But in 1940, a truly magnificent novel, *The Power and the Glory*, was to place Graham Greene, alongside François Mauriac for whom he feels a fraternal admiration, among the great Catholic novelists and, more generally, among the great novelists of our day.

During the Second World War, the Foreign Office sent him to West Africa, first to Lagos, in Nigeria, then to Freetown, in Liberia. Here was a new opportunity for understanding curious and troubled individuals. Since the war he has published a number of books, some of which he calls "novels," because he considers them serious, and others "entertainments," because he considers them light. Yet metaphysics sometimes enters into the entertainment too. The finest of his novels are: *The Heart of the Matter*, *The End of the Affair*, *The Power and the Glory*, *The*

Quiet American and, more recently, *The Comedians*.
Among the entertainments the author includes *Our
Man in Havana*, which is indeed extremely entertaining but is also a merciless satire of secret service activities, and *Stamboul Train*, which is much more than
"entertainment."

To this prolific literary production we must add
some essays (Graham Greene is an excellent critic),
plays (*The Living-Room, The Potting Shed*), short
stories and a film—*The Third Man*—which enjoyed
a well-deserved success and remains famous for its
haunting and monotonous refrain. Graham Greene
has also assumed the literary management of various
publishing houses, most recently of The Bodley Head.
He is presently living in the south of France, at
Antibes, but is ready to rush to any place where
there is fighting, where men share suffering and sin.
That is how he came to be in Malaysia, then in
Indochina, to see the guerilla warfare and corruption
at close quarters. Greene, whose Catholicism is somewhat akin to Balzac's, has extended his Human
Comedy to all the continents. As he sees it, the bond
between men is less the nation than temptation, crime
and pardon.

II

"AFTER the death of Henry James, a disaster overtook
the English novel. . . . For with the death of James,
the religious sense was lost . . . and with the religious sense went the sense of the importance of the

GRAHAM GREENE

human act. It was as if the world of fiction had lost a dimension; the characters of such distinguished writers as Virginia Woolf and E. M. Forster wandered through a world that was paper-thin." This severe and probably unfair comment on the English novel comes at the beginning of an article on François Mauriac. Greene greatly commends the French novelist for creating characters who have the solidity and stature of men with souls to save or lose, and whose individual acts are less important than the power—God or the devil—which prompts them.

Such commendation is not surprising at all, for Mauriac, in Graham Greene's estimation, has achieved in his writings precisely what he aims at himself: to restore to the novel a dimension—the religious sense —which it had lost, and to human actions their significance. For however these actions may sometimes appear, they remain terribly serious in another world. We shall see that Graham Greene is often concerned to portray base, corrupt individuals. Why? Because the self-satisfied pharisee does not think of turning to God. The outcast, on the other hand, needs that Love; he is nostalgic for "that which was lost." Replying to a woman journalist who had asked him for the keynote to his writing, Greene quoted the scriptural "God so loved the world . . ." and added that what he sought to do was to portray a world that was very hard to love, a world that only God could love. Significantly, as an epigraph to one of his novels, Greene cites these words of Léon Bloy: "There are places in man's poor heart which do not yet exist and into which suffering enters so that they may exist."

In *The End of the Affair*, Sarah, the sinner, is torn between her love for her lover and her love for God. God wins the day: "I believe there's a God—I believe the whole bag of tricks; there's nothing I don't believe; they could subdivide the Trinity into a dozen parts and I'd believe. They could dig up records that proved Christ had been invented by Pilate to get himself promoted, and I'd believe just the same. I've caught belief like a disease. I've fallen into belief like I fell in love." But she is terrified of having to choose between a sin which she cherishes and a faith which for her is a certitude. "I pray to God He won't keep me alive like this." And her prayer is granted. Once again, death is the only solution.

Many Catholic readers find in these novels rather too much delectation in the flesh and in violence. Adultery, prostitution are described not merely realistically, but with enjoyment. Phuong, the Vietnamese girl in *The Quiet American*, for whom it is perfectly natural to sleep with everyone, is not condemned. Quite the contrary. She appears as a charming and irresponsible little animal. Believers go to confession and receive absolution knowing full well that they have no firm purpose of amendment and that they will return to their sins as the dog returns to its vomit. They are to be pitied and pardoned. Life is like that. We live in a period of eroticism and violence, and Graham Greene accepts the fact. God's mercy is infinite; he will recognise his own.

GRAHAM GREENE

Non-religious readers, for their part, have sometimes objected to the constant recurrence of the
religious theme, to the unexplained and unexplain-
able miracles, to the stubbornness with which individuals who will eventually be saved seem determined
to work their own damnation. They have said: "Graham Greene is more Catholic than a cradle Catholic
because he is a convert; he is a Catholic with greater
insistence than a French Catholic because, as an
Englishman, he belongs to a community in which
Catholics are a minority and therefore aggressive."
There is some truth in this observation. I had noted
the same trait in Maurice Baring, another English
convert, and I am not disturbed by this constant
concern to reaffirm a belief. Maurice Baring and
Graham Greene both came to Catholicism at a time
of uncertainty and desolation in their lives. Suddenly
they had the feeling of encountering love, understanding, pardon. Can they be blamed for trying to communicate this good news and this great hope to all their
readers? But while Baring accepted, and even loved
the hierarchical society in which he had been brought
up, Graham Greene's sympathies lie with the unfortunate, with those who are unable to adapt themselves
to a world in which they feel hunted and in which
violence and fear hold sway, a world which Baring
never knew. His writings are a protest against a
pharisaical society which continues to preach the
bourgeois virtues, but has ceased to practise them.
He feels that civilisation has regressed since the Middle Ages. Criminal profiteers appear in our day as

respectable citizens. Abstract concepts have taken the place of the sacraments. The reason why Graham Greene has often criticised the Americans (sometimes bitterly, as in *The Quiet American*, sometimes with amused sympathy, as in *The Comedians*) is that they seem to him to possess that clear conscience linked to a few sonorous words such as "freedom" and "democracy" which effectively blinds them to the frightful reality.

Young Pyle, the "quiet American," is not a bad man—far from it. He has come to Indochina, in the days when the French are fighting under de Lattre, inspired by a genuine anticolonialism and 'an ardent anticommunism. Pyle believes that the Vietnamese are with him against the Communists; he tries to help them by preparing plastic charges for them.

To an English journalist who more or less represents Greene himself, Pyle says: "You should be against the French. Their colonialism."

To which the journalist replies: "Isms and ocracies. Give me facts. . . . Anyway, the French are dying every day—that's not a mental concept. They aren't leading these people on with half-lies like your politicians—and ours. I've been in India, Pyle, and I know the harm liberals do."

Young Pyle supports a Vietnamese general, Thé, whom the Americans like, heaven knows why.

"If he came to power with our help, we could rely on him," says Pyle.

"How many people have to die before you realise. . . ."

"Realise what?"

"That there's no such thing as gratitude in politics."

"At least they won't hate us like they hate the French."

"Are you sure?"

In the light of what has happened since, we see that the harsh realism propounded by Greene—or by his mouthpiece—is in fact less harmful than the naive liberalism of this quiet American who is finally killed after having done a great deal of harm, with the best possible intentions. *Corruptio optimi pessima.*

This attitude, hostile to drawing-room liberals, to doctrinaires, to hawkers of fine phrases, is in some ways reminiscent of Kipling's. Despite himself, perhaps even unconsciously, Graham Greene retains something of the religion of his childhood, which was Protestant. His God, like Kipling's, is often the Eternal, the Lord of Hosts, of the Old Testament. His idea of predestination has overtones both of Jansenism and Calvinism. Evil forms a part of human nature. An agnostic pharisee like Pyle believes himself to be outside the province of evil, but his good intentions generate only disaster and murder. Severity, corrected by grace, is more humane.

III

In *The Heart of the Matter*, one of Greene's finest novels, the hero's goodness leads both to his temporal ruin and to his eternal damnation. The action takes place somewhere in West Africa. An English official,

Scobie, is there as deputy police commissioner. He is an honest man who carries out a thankless task to the best of his ability, in the sticky heat of an airless town, during the Second World War. His two worst worries are the Vichy French in a neighbouring colony and the Syrian traders who try to smuggle industrial diamonds to Germany on neutral vessels. He finds little consolation at home. His wife, Louise, an Emma Bovary type, reads poets whom her husband does not appreciate. Their only bond is that they are both Catholics, convinced and practising, she by birth, he a convert. "Poor Louise, he thought, it is terrible not to be liked." And no one, in fact, in the little British colony, likes this woman who is different from everyone else and reads books that no one else reads. As for Scobie himself, does he love Louise? He is sorry for her; he feels bound to her because she is so pathetically unattractive. She is unhappy in this physical and moral atmosphere, and begs her husband to send her to South Africa. He can join her there later. He would like to give her this satisfaction, but he would need £200 for the journey and installation expenses, and he does not have them. The bank will not make the loan. Yusef, one of the Syrian traders whom he has to watch, knows that Scobie is short and offers to lend him the money. But is it ethical for a policeman to borrow money from the man he is watching? Scobie knows that it would be wrong. At the same time, Louise is unhappy and, out of compassion, he takes the risk, telling himself that after all it is only a 4 per cent

loan, that he will pay the interest and that Yusef is
asking nothing in return. A grave surrender of principle; the first step towards dishonour.

Louise leaves; Scobie remains. "Why do I love
this place so much? Is it because here human nature
hasn't had time to disguise itself? Nobody here could
ever talk about a heaven on earth. . . . Here you
could love human beings nearly as God loved them,
knowing the worst." Through over-kindliness, he
has placed himself at Yusef's mercy and also at the
mercy of a young official, Wilson, who is engaged
in espionage in the colony for the benefit of the
British secret service under the cloak of some vague
activity. Louise, before going away, has read poetry
with Wilson, and the latter, stranded in this intellectual desert, has become attached to this Bovary and
come to hate Scobie. After a couple of incidents, the
rumour spreads that Scobie has been bought by Yusef.
Every one of these Englishmen has a native "boy,"
and all these "boys" tattle, so there can be no secrets.

Once more, Scobie proceeds to err through kindliness. The survivors of a shipwreck are tossed upon
this African shore, among them a young widow,
Helen, only twenty years old and not even pretty.
But Scobie, as we know, is drawn to the friendless.
"He had no sense of responsibility towards the beautiful and the graceful and the intelligent. They could
find their own way. It was the face for which nobody
would go out of his way, the face that would never
catch the covert look, the face which would soon
be used to rebuffs and indifference that demanded

his allegiance." Helen becomes Scobie's mistress. Out of pity, he swears he will never desert her. Out of pity, he writes to her. A "boy" steals the letter and hands it over to those who are hunting Scobie. The noose tightens.

So here he is at the heart of a new tragedy. When he married Louise, he promised to protect her happiness (and he believes in the holiness of marriage). He has told Helen, "I'll always be here if you need me as long as I am alive." And that, too, is a sacred vow. What should he do? He tries to pray. The Lord's Prayer? But it is not daily bread that he needs. "He wanted happiness for others and solitude and peace for himself."

Louise returns; Helen complains; Scobie is anguished: "I can't bear to see suffering, and I cause it all the time. I want to get out, get out!"

But where? He knows very well where he would like to go: to his death. But he is a Catholic. He realises that suicide is the ultimate sin, for which there is no more pardon. And yet he cannot continue living. His actions follow him, torment him. He has lost the confidence of other people; he knows that he has lost grace. Death remains the sole solution. Scobie plans his suicide methodically. He wants it to look like a natural death. He complains to the doctor of symptoms resembling those of *angina pectoris*, gets a prescription for sleeping pills, puts aside a dose sufficient to kill him, then makes it appear that he has died suddenly as he is writing his diary, in which he deliberately leaves a sentence unfinished. But he can-

GRAHAM GREENE

not deceive God, nor his personal enemy, Wilson, who tells Louise Scobie that her husband committed suicide.

She goes to consult a priest, Father Rank. She says, "He must have known that he was damning himself."

"Yes, he knew that all right. He never had any trust in mercy—except for other people," Father Rank replies.

"It's no good even praying," she says.

Father Rank claps the cover of the diary to and says, furiously, "For goodness sake, Mrs. Scobie, don't imagine you—or I—know a thing about God's mercy."

That would also seem to be the author's last word on the hero of this novel. Graham Greene certainly does not think that we have any right to classify men as saints and sinners. What, after all, do we know of the secret lives of the saints? There may be saints in our very midst. Scobie, tender, generous, was not so far from being one of them. The ways of Providence, we read, are so impenetrable that we may wonder whether our sins are not stages in every man's slow progress towards perfection. But in Greene's novels there always comes a moment beyond which we know nothing: God alone, we read again, will recognise his own. No man can guarantee that he will love always, and yet each one of us swears to do so, as Scobie does twice. He is a good man, torn between pity and pity; even as he kills himself, he tries not to hurt anyone. But life is such that it is impossible not to hurt anyone. Scobie's last words are: "Dear God, I love. . . ." He has loved his neighbour; he has loved God; and he dies in despair.

Fundamentally, Scobie's error is not to have trusted enough in divine mercy and to have tried to do himself what God would have done so well without him. He has undertaken to protect Louise and Helen. To justify his suicide, he tells himself that Christ too, really, deliberately killed himself. For no one could have killed God had God not willed his own death. These are prideful thoughts, and I think Greene's secret lesson here is one of humility. And yet . . . and yet it would be too easy to abandon those we love by telling ourselves that God will provide. . . . To tell the truth, it is never possible to reach the heart of the matter. And that, precisely, *is* the heart of the matter.

It is a magnificent novel, with its theme of fate relentlessly closing in upon Scobie, trapping him in an iron circle from which he can no longer escape, and with its technical perfection. The sobriety of tone and economy of means are admirable. The narrative moves swiftly, in vivid scenes. The conspirators (Yusef, the "boys") are drawn with as much care as the protagonists. The tropical heat permeates every sentence. The atmosphere of a British colony in wartime is as true as the atmosphere in one of Kipling's Indian short stories. And indeed, the familiarity with this administrative and colonial environment which Greene acquired during his sojourns in Africa enabled

GRAHAM GREENE

him to achieve a high degree of verisimilitude, while the metaphysical character of the "problem" saves the book from any over-naturalistic realism.

IV

IN *The Power and the Glory*, too, the dynamic quality of a cops-and-robbers story is allied to the metaphysical depth of a Catholic novel. But here the drama is more complete than in *The Heart of the Matter* because the hero ends by accepting his fate, and also because this "saint" is a human wreck, a culpable individual, and not, like Scobie, the victim of his virtues. "*In manus tuas, Domine.* . . ."

The action takes place in Mexico at the time of the violent anticlerical revolution when priests were proscribed, hunted down and, if they continued to exercise their ministry, shot. The central figure, therefore, is a priest, the last in Mexico, the others having taken refuge in neighbouring countries, or perished, or apostatised. This last priest remains anonymous. He is "the priest." The villagers know him well and protect him as best they can, help him to hide, even at the risk of their lives, for a harsh young police lieutenant has sworn to shoot the priest or, in his stead, hostages. Greene's superb stratagem is to make his hero an unworthy priest, not merely a hunted tramp, but a sensual man and a drunkard. He has had a mistress, Maria, and a daughter, Brigida. He is always looking for whisky. ("Oh God, I'd like a drink. *Ora pro nobis.*") His breath reeks of alcohol.

Perhaps he is guilty, too, of the sin of pride; he takes pride in being the only priest still to say Mass secretly, at night, in a barn.

He knows his unworthiness and even helplessness. What can he do? What use is he? To get the poor people who hide him shot? But he cannot give up. Once a priest, always a priest. He has received the sacrament of orders; he owes it to himself, he owes it to God to carry the Mass to those who need it, to baptise, to hear confessions, to absolve, to restore peace to troubled hearts. This duty survives all his frailties. And his ministry is obviously useful. The proof is the respect, the eager faith with which he is welcomed by poor creatures who are perfectly aware of his shortcomings, who know the risk they take in harbouring him, but who need him because he is *the* priest, the only priest who can listen to the recital of their sins and absolve them.

As Graham Greene always has to introduce a touch of the ridiculous to bring the sublime down to everyday level, the chief of police has toothache and his one thought is to get to his dentist, Mr. Tench. This police chief, a fat man with a red face, wearing white flannels and pressing a handkerchief to his mouth to still the pain, might be, if not merciful, then at least forgetful, but his deputy is the young lieutenant, one of those uncompromising, abstract, ruthless individuals who turn up in every revolution. Looking at a photograph of the priest taken at a time when the latter was young and happy, "a natural hatred as between dog and dog stirred in the lieutenant's bowels

. . . . He said: 'We will catch him. It is only a question of time.' "

Actually they would not be able to catch him were not the priest obliged, by his sacred ministry, to forego any opportunities he might have of leaving the country. He could have taken a boat, once, under a false name and wearing a disguise, but a dying woman had needed extreme unction, so he had stayed. Tracked down to a village, with the police almost upon him, he should flee, but an old man says: "It would be a pity if the soldiers came before we had time . . . such a burden on poor souls, Father." The priest listens to this confession covering five years. "Make a good act of contrition," he says. His eyes close, his lips and tongue stumble over the absolution, fail to finish. . . . He springs awake again.

"Can I bring the women," the old man is saying, "it is five years. . . ."

"Oh, let them come. Let them all come!" cries the priest angrily. "I am your servant."

So he goes, sinner and saint, from village to village. The little children do not so much as remember a church, with music and lights and prayers. Finally, still carrying his dangerous little suitcase containing a portable altar, Mass wine and hosts, he comes to the village where his former mistress lives. "How's Brigida?" he asks her. Brigida is his daughter and he does not know her. The child knows her catechism, Maria tells him, but will not say it.

"Why not? Why won't you say it?" asks the priest.

"Why should I?" returns the child.

"God wishes it."

"How do you know?"

He is aware of his immense responsibility, of the child's hostility. Maria herself calls him "Father" and seems to have forgotten that they used to be lovers. But she hides him and asks him to say Mass. During Mass, the report circulates that the police are approaching. Despite the mortal danger, the unworthy priest continues to the end and even preaches. "Pray that you will suffer more and more and more. Never get tired of suffering. The police watching you, the soldiers gathering taxes . . . smallpox and fever, hunger—that is all part of heaven—the preparation." The consecration takes place in silence.

The police arrive. Once again, the priest is not recognised because Maria swears that she is his wife and even Brigida, when the lieutenant asks her, "Who's your father?" answers, looking at the priest, "That's him. There."

In the end, the lieutenant triumphs. The priest is captured.

"I suppose," the lieutenant says, "you're hoping for a miracle."

"No."

"You believe in them, don't you?"

"Yes, but not for me. I'm no more good to anyone, so why should God keep me alive?"

Finally the lieutenant says grudgingly, "You aren't a bad fellow. If there's anything I can do for you. . . ."

"If you would give permission for me to confess. . . ."

"But there's no priest."

"Padre José." Padre José is a bad priest who has married and thus saved his skin.

"Oh, Padre José," says the lieutenant contemptuously, "he's no good to you."

"He's good enough for me." Always the same idea; once a man has been ordained a priest he remains a priest, whatever he does.

"All right. You can have him."

The lieutenant tries to keep his word, but Padre José's wife protests against any attempt to have him break the law.

"You aren't a priest any more," she says, "you're my husband."

"My dear . . . I *am* a priest." The woman goes off into a peal of laughter. Padre José makes a despairing gesture. "I don't think it's possible," he tells the lieutenant.

The priest waits in his cell in vain. The lieutenant returns and tells him that Padre José will not come. It is the eternal dialogue between the conscientious judge and the innocent victim, of Javert and of Jean Valjean.

"You had better know everything. You've been tried and found guilty."

"Couldn't I have been present at my own trial?"

"It wouldn't have made any difference."

"No." Indeed, neither the priest nor Graham

Greene believes in the justice of men. "And when, if I may ask?"

"Tomorrow."

The lieutenant leaves, the priest squats on the floor, drinks his brandy, thinks of his sins. "Tears poured down his face; he was not at the moment afraid of damnation—even the fear of pain was in the background. He felt only an immense disappointment because he had to go to God empty-handed, with nothing done at all. It seemed to him at that moment that it would have been quite easy to have been a saint. It would only have needed a little self-restraint and a little courage."

No great loss, this poor man? Who knows? He had done a hard job which he alone had been capable of undertaking. And despite his death, nothing is lost. Luis, a little Catholic boy who has seen the firing squad and the priest's death, hears a knock at the door. He opens and sees a stranger, carrying a small suitcase.

"I have only just landed," says the stranger. "If you would let me come in. . . ." and lowering his voice he adds, "I am a priest."

"You?" exclaims the boy.

"Yes, my name is Father. . . ." But the boy has opened the door and put his hand to his lips before the other can give his name.

So it will all start all over again: power and glory, weakness and strength, suffering and grace. The martyrdom of the anonymous priest has not been in vain, since an anonymous priest takes over from him.

The setting for *A Burnt-Out Case* is a leproserie

GRAHAM GREENE

in the Belgian Congo. Graham Greene has painted this dismal back-cloth with his customary talent, but the story itself is built around the central character, Querry, a man who has enjoyed every kind of success and has now reached a state of total indifference. A voluptuary who no longer cares about pleasure, an artist who no longer believes in his art, Querry, like some lepers, is "a burnt-out case."

The Comedians (1966) is Green's latest book. Is it an "entertainment" or a novel? Both, it seems to me. The hideous and at the same time ludicrous description of "Papa" Duvalier's régime in Haiti, the portrayals of Jones, the imposter, and of the Smiths (an American couple, vegetarians, generous, absurd) belong rather to the sphere of entertainment. But the idea that we are all comedians, or actors, carrying out more or less satisfactorily the bizarre rôles which fate assigns us, would seem to place the book in the series of metaphysical novels. To tell the truth, even when Graham Greene is diverting himself, he cannot help thinking on a grand scale.

v

GRAHAM GREENE's technical skill is on a par with that of the most illustrious novelists. To put down one of his novels after opening it seems almost impossible. Yet he usually begins with a scene of no apparent importance. In *The Power and the Glory*, a dentist's office in Mexico; in *The Heart of the Matter*, the banal encounter of two colonial civil servants. Balzac's novels begin with a general picture of the period or of the group concerned, or with the spotlight, from the very first pages, on the character who is to be central to the action. Graham Greene blurs his preliminaries in a haze of unrelated incidents. Here he is reminiscent of Dickens and most of the English novelists, who love to envelope the outlines of a subject in the mists of the Thames. The French novelist prefers clearer outlines and is less concerned to hide his game. But out of Greene's haze there swiftly emerges a suspense story which, after the first third of the book, opens onto the real conflict, which is both religious and romantic.

It has been said that Graham Greene has gained acceptance for the detective novel as serious fiction. That is true, although Simenon is often entitled to the same tribute. Why has Greene chosen this form to tackle the deep and serious problems which exercise him? Mauriac, too, in *Thérèse Desqueyroux*, makes a crime central to the plot, but no doubt subsists as to the perpetrator. The reader is not kept in suspense by the uncertainties of the chase. Greene appeals to primitive instincts. The hunted man and his pursuers are standard figures in human history. Curiosity, uncertainty are powerful aids to the novelist in holding the reader's attention so that he can then direct the reader to the real, as yet concealed, subject of the book. Greene loves to strew his stories with mysteries which will never be cleared up. Who kills Hale, in *Brighton Rock*, and how, and why? The point is never elucidated. Why, in *The Ministry of Fear*, are

GRAHAM GREENE

the organisers of the bazaar so anxious to retrieve
the cake? We shall never know. It is a good idea to
leave some enigmas; they stimulate lazy minds.

Like all great novelists, Graham Greene has his
favourite little group of types which he uses repeat-
edly, not, like Balzac, under the same names, but
each time as new individuals. There is the Catholic
priest, now culpable and tortured by his demons, now
barely glimpsed, very rapidly giving absolution and
severely silencing anyone who doubts of the divine
mercy. There is the naive woman, simply unaware of
any moral law, lavish with her body and capable of
heroic goodness (Coral, the little dancer in *Stamboul
Train*; Rose, in *Brighton Rock*). And there is, in
particular, the author himself, who creates a self-
portrait in a number of characters, innocent or guilty,
always anguished. There is also the woman who
cannot help committing adultery but who is constantly repenting. Sarah, in *The End of the Affair*,
keeps a diary which shows that she loves someone
more than anyone in the world; she never names this
lover, but we know that it is God.

The minor characters are as carefully constructed
as the major ones. Graham Greene is very concerned
to give them idiosyncrasies, absurdities, memories,
which will make them come to life. Hale, the victim
in *Brighton Rock*, appears only in the first chapters,
but he remains unforgettable. In *Stamboul Train*,
many individuals are travelling in the Orient Express
to unknown destinies, and they are linked to one
another by the most tenuous threads of circumstance,

yet each stands out in clear relief. In *The Power and the Glory*, we barely glimpse the dentist, Maria, Brigida, Padre José, but we remember them as we remember Balzac's Madame Vauquier or Roguin, the notary. Parkis, the detective in *The End of the Affair*, and his little boy, or the Smiths, in *The Comedians*, might have stepped straight out of a Dickens novel.

One objection that might be voiced in connection with this consummate artistry is the author's predilection for vileness, for wretchedness, for the seedy and the neurotic. When Greene presents a morally balanced character, he rarely fails to portray him in a contemptible light. In Balzac and Dickens too we find keen concern with human woe, yet a part of their writings is bathed in sunlight; upright characters are not at a premium in their books, and love is often depicted in the most delicious hues. Graham Greene prefers to emphasise the sordid aspects of life; he returns almost with nostalgia to indigestions, vomitings, savage brutalities, to the base and dreary aspects of sexual adventures. In addition, the physical climate of his novels is usually stifling, the sticky heat devitalising.

Be that as it may, we have to bear two important points in mind. In the first place, it is not true to say that there are no likable characters in his books. Coral, Phuong, Rose are charmingly portrayed. Two of them, of course, are little prostitutes, and the third is very undistinguished, but they are nonetheless likable. Scobie, too, deserves the reader's affection and receives it. There again, of course, he has acted wrongly. Yet how should it be otherwise? And here we come to the second point: Greene's profoundly pessimistic view of human nature unassisted by grace. And who has the right to challenge that view?